ADVANCE PRAISE

"Nate Andres brings the concepts of resilience and authenticity to life with sound, practical advice that empowers the reader to make their sense of purpose an unlock for greater well-being."
—DAVID P. BOYNTON, CHIEF EXECUTIVE AT THE BODY SHOP INTERNATIONAL LTD.

"The REAL model framework has had an impact on me by bringing the words 'authentic resilience' to life. I am further inspired to share this language and these tools with my team as we continue to grow our business."
—SARAH SMITH, CHIEF VISION OFFICER & CO-FOUNDER AT THE DYRT

"Navigating the bumps of life is never easy but learning the tools that help us become more resilient, true to ourselves, and connected to our purpose—and making meaning in our lives—is necessary. Nathan Andres shares how."
—TODD CORLEY, SENIOR VICE PRESIDENT OF INCLUSION, SUSTAINABILITY, AND COMMUNITY AT CARHARTT

"This book is transformational and will have a positive impact on many people. There's something very powerful about sharing your own story and using it to help others. Nathan Andres delivers."

—ANDREW KEITH, MANAGING DIRECTOR AT SELFRIDGES & CO., UK

"Nathan has shared with us the magic he makes in authentically helping others create what they want for themselves. This book is a guide to getting comfortable with the uncomfortable and roadmapping the how-to, 'no matter the closet, open the door.'"

—WENDY LEWIS, CEO AND FOUNDER AT ALLYSHIFT®

"Beautifully combining the power of authenticity and resilience, Nathan Andres has crafted a winning combination of skills we all need in our tool belt as we face difficulties in life."

—ALISON MASSEY, GROUP DIRECTOR OF HEALTH AND WELLNESS PROPOSITION AT HSBC

"As a leader and a member of the LGBTQ+ community, I find this book to be a thoughtful and considered approach to help members of our community and the world at large, by sharing pragmatic tools that build lasting resilience and authenticity."

—MARTIN MASON, CEO AND FOUNDER AT UNLEASHED INTERNATIONAL, LTD.

"If you want to live on your own terms with greater understanding of what makes YOU unique, read this book. Nathan Andres's REAL framework helps us to get unstuck, and to find answers and the way forward—from within ourselves. Powerful and significant."

—MORGAN TAN, STRATEGIC ADVISOR, ADVISORY COUNCIL MEMBER, AND FORMER PRESIDENT OF SHISEIDO GROUP

"Nathan has an outstanding passion and energy for personal growth, and his authenticity inspires others to continually learn and grow. Superb writing."
—KATRINA WRIGHT, GLOBAL EXECUTIVE PEOPLE DIRECTOR AT THE BODY SHOP INTERNATIONAL LTD.

"Nathan Andres is generous with both his time and his ideas. Readers will undoubtedly gain the same insights I have been fortunate to glean through his live talks and one-to-one coaching. Nate walks the talk of authenticity and understands the importance of resilience in living your best life."
—PAUL ENGLERT, PHD, INDUSTRIAL-ORGANIZATIONAL PSYCHOLOGIST AND EXECUTIVE COACH

"Nathan Andres is a deeply nurturing and skillful coach who brings his model to life with personal stories and practical methods to help us all be a little more authentic and resilient in our lives. Accessible, insightful, inclusive, and important reading for all."
—DAVID LEE, PHD, PSYCHOLOGIST, SLEEP EXPERT, FOUNDER AT SLEEP UNLIMITED

"Nate Andres has included Love in the REAL model, and this really makes a difference in how we demonstrate our authentic selves with self-compassion—it's often left out of the conversation around resilience but is so crucial. A valuable read for all."
—EMMA BARDWELL, NUTRITIONIST, WELL-BEING COACH, AND AUTHOR OF *THE PERIMENOPAUSE SOLUTION*

"This book illuminates the core qualities that will help you get through the hard times and enhance the good ones: knowing ourselves, being true to ourselves, and connecting to our purpose and to each other. Resilience isn't toughing it out; it's human connection, and Nathan brings this to life with energy and joy."
—HELEN BARKER, CHARTERED PSYCHOLOGIST, EXECUTIVE AND LEADERSHIP COACH

YOUR REAL LIFE

YOUR REAL LIFE

GET AUTHENTIC, BE RESILIENT & MAKE IT COUNT

NATHAN ANDRES

NOTES TO READER

Unless otherwise noted, this book, models, tools, exercises, practices, tables, special terms, and practices, etc., herein are ©2023 by Nathan York Andres. No part of this book may be reproduced by any mechanical, photographic, or electronic process, or in the form of a phonographic or audio recording; nor may it be stored in a retrieval system, transmitted, otherwise be copied for public or private use—other than for "fair use" as brief quotations embodied in articles and reviews—without prior written permission of the author. The scanning, uploading, and distribution of this book via the internet or via any other means without the author's permission is illegal. Please purchase only authorized print, electronic, or audio editions as this aims to protect the author's rights and prevent piracy of copyrighted materials.

Every effort has been made by the author to ensure that the information shared in this book is complete and accurate. The content is based on the lived personal and coaching experiences of the author and his clients, colleagues, friends, and family, in addition to an extensive review of academic literature and research. Where possible the author has gone to great effort to document and build upon the work of others and any inadvertent extraction of material without citation is unintended, unpremeditated, and accidental. The author of this book does not dispense medical advice or prescribe the use of any technique as a form of treatment for physical, emotional, or medical problems without the advice of a physician, either directly or indirectly. The advice and strategies contained herein may not be suitable for every situation and every reader. The content of this book makes no guarantees for results whatsoever, either expressly or implied. The book should not be used as a substitute for professional services, evaluations, or medical treatment by a competent mental health or medical practitioner. By its sale, neither the author nor publisher is engaged in rendering psychological or other professional services. If expert assistance or counseling is needed, the services of a competent professional should be sought. In the event the reader uses the information in the book for themselves, the author or publisher assumes no responsibility for their actions. The intent of the author is only to offer information of a general nature to help the reader in their journey for physical, emotional, mental, and spiritual well-being as well as to build personal authenticity and resilience.

Some of the names and identifying features of people named in case studies, examples, personal stories, and other anecdotes have been changed by request in the name of confidentiality and in the spirit of protecting privacy.

COPYRIGHT © 2023 NATHAN ANDRES
All rights reserved.

YOUR REAL LIFE
Get Authentic, Be Resilient & Make It Count!

FIRST EDITION

ISBN 978-1-5445-4125-9   *Hardcover*
      978-1-5445-4124-2   *Paperback*
      978-1-5445-4123-5   *Ebook*

For my parents, Timothy & Carol Andres,
some of the most authentic, resilient, and REAL people I know.
Thanks for that little bit of "extra."

CONTENTS

INTRODUCTION 13
1. WHAT IS ADVERSITY? 29
2. WHAT IS AUTHENTIC RESILIENCE? 43
3. THE MODEL: REALITY 59
4. THE MODEL: ENERGY 89
5. THE MODEL: AUTHENTICITY 121
6. THE MODEL: LOVE 163
7. SELF-COACHING THE MODEL 197
   CONCLUSION 223
   ACKNOWLEDGMENTS 237
   ADDITIONAL RESEARCH 247
   NOTES 255
   INDEX 263

INTRODUCTION

IT WAS ONE OF *THOSE* DAYS; ANOTHER MANIC WEEKDAY dictated by Murphy's Law, where everything that *can* go wrong *does*. I woke up to realize that the dreaded *drip drip drip* sound of my kitchen sink leaking ferociously wasn't only a product of the dream I'd been having. On the way to investigate the source of the panic-inducing noise, I discovered our dog had thrown up all over the apartment during the night. I cleaned it, cleaned the kitchen floor, and then went to clean myself—but the shower head burst off the wall from the pressure that had been building up since a construction crew had been messing with the building's water the day before. Just what I needed before heading to work. I tried to calm down as I switched to the rain showerhead and used that to clean up instead. It almost worked, until I finished brushing my teeth only to find the bathroom sink was clogged. Now I had to clean that mess, finish up in a different sink, get dressed, *and* feed my dogs—I would *definitely* be late to work.

But all of that paled in comparison to the cherry on the rotten cake, the reason I'd had to deal with the mess and drama on my own: the country in which I was living doesn't recognize gay marriage and had just torn my nontraditional family unit apart by forcing my husband to leave the country and take up residence elsewhere (more on that later). Honestly, it felt appropriate that when I ran home from work to meet the plumber that afternoon, I found that our other dog had pooped on the rug. Sometimes, life kicks you while you're down...and plays out like some made-for-TV movie. Often, in the moment of experiencing adversity, the lines of reality blur and your brain can make you feel like you're outside of yourself, watching the events play out as if on a screen.

Adversities come in all shapes and sizes, occasionally more than one at a time. We all meet seemingly insurmountable obstacles in the way of our happiness and personal or professional success. Adversity can be a difficult or unpleasant situation (as simple as spilling hot coffee or running late for a meeting) or it can become a state of serious and continued difficulty (for example, feeling stuck in an unhealthy relationship). Further, various adversities intersect with one another. They can wreak havoc on our lives—especially when they remain unaddressed. When we don't face and respond productively to adversity, it disrupts not only our ability to succeed in our careers and relationships, but also our ability to know ourselves, find well-being, and experience joy.

When that happens, do you grin and bear it, or do you fight like hell? Fight like hell, right?! Okay, but *how*?

That's the point where people stall. After all, it's not easy to figure out how to be resilient. We hear all the time that when you fall down, you should just stand back up and dust yourself off. That's easier said than done. So I've dedicated my coaching career to figuring it out.

Over the years, I have coached people who came to me with a variety of adversities they wanted to overcome. Most frequently, people feel stuck. They don't know how to break through career challenges or relationship woes. Sometimes they feel unclear about what their next step in life should be. Many times they are searching for the deeper soul or "what makes them tick" out of a desire to steer their own ship toward a life with purpose and authenticity.

Often, people don't know their purpose. Sometimes, they don't yet truly know themselves. They want success, but more than that, they want joyful lives with deeper meaning. Their issues not only stem from adversity, but then become forms of adversity themselves.

Through thousands of hours of working with clients and employees, navigating my own collection of adversities, poring over research papers and scientific studies, and of course via professional and clinical training, I have developed the REAL model. It can be tailored to each individual, and it has been proven to help clients overcome adversities large and small, and live more joyful and fulfilling lives. The end goal of this model is to develop my version of *authentic resilience*. This book is a blueprint to help you become a more resilient person by learning to lead yourself from the power of authentic resilience.

Every adversity large or small that we experience anywhere in our everyday lives will remain with us, affecting our behavior and future life experiences. But when we have authentic resilience—which we gain by coaching ourselves through the REAL model—we can bounce back from adversity. In fact, it's more accurate to say we *bounce beyond* adversity. We diminish its negative effects, grow from it instead, and thrive in our own lives.

WHAT IS AUTHENTIC RESILIENCE?

In short, I'm talking about the combination of being authentic and resilient: being self-driven to evolve and learn, so as not to make the same mistakes, in a way that's based on genuine self-awareness of how you present yourself to the world. If adversity is an experience that triggers the brain to perceive a threat, then resilience is that which helps us get over the threat. Therefore, most people focus simply on building resiliency. But there is no cookie-cutter form of resiliency. Resilience will be different for every person. Your resilience skills are unique to you, based on who you are, the adversities you've faced (and how you respond to them), and the life's purpose that drives you. In other words, each person's resilience will be an authentic and individualized set of skills designed to overcome life's obstacles.

How *you* cope, react, and recover is different from how other people do. As we grow into adulthood, and our brains and bodies mature, we collect millions of experiences that shape how we respond to adverse situations—including whether or not we even choose to. How you responded to getting your first bad grade in school was different from how I responded, just as we certainly responded differently to the first time we were each rejected by a paramour. In fact, modern psychology is built around the individualism of our responses to life. How you react to and (hopefully) recover from challenges in life leaves fingerprints on you. Part of the magic of mastering self-identity is uncovering these fingerprints.

This is also part of how we build authentic resilience. To be truly resilient in life, you need to have a strong understanding of who you are on a deep and authentic level. The *only* way to bounce beyond adversity is by developing authentic resilience.

This book will teach you how to build and master your own unique skills that will be an authentic reflection of you.

A SNAPSHOT OF THE REAL MODEL

The REAL self-coaching model is built on scientific and psychological research, and has a proven track record of helping clients who've come to me for personal and professional development. It also worked in my life. It will help you too.

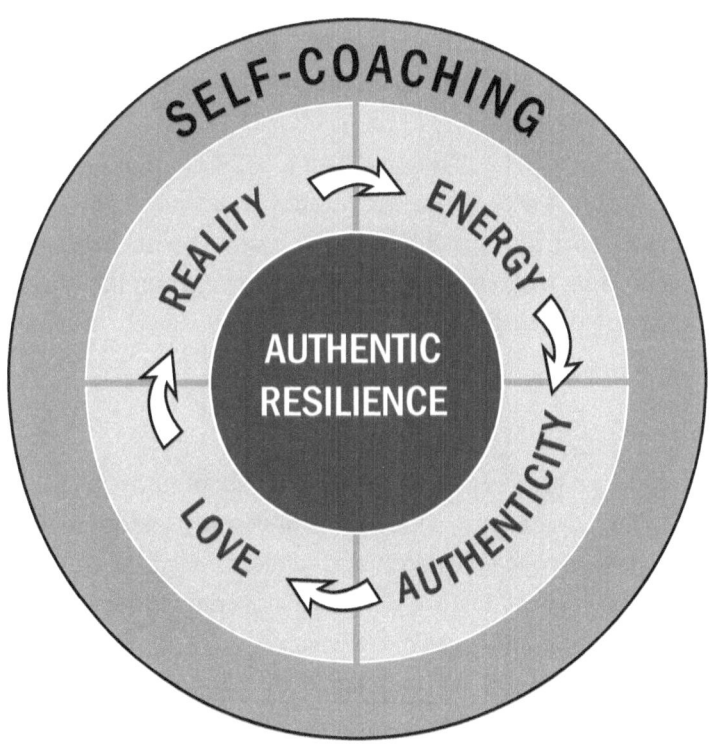

REALITY

The first step in getting REAL requires you to face Reality. In order to develop authentic resilience, you first need to understand how you typically respond to adversity and prepare yourself to change your habits.

I'll show you how to start by choosing to "Face It": acknowledge an adverse event you're currently facing and then ultimately accept that event (as well as adversity in general). Resilient people know how to move from acknowledgment to acceptance quickly.

Then, I'll tell you how to "Control It": adopt a growth mindset, understand your agency, and take control of the adverse event and how you will respond to it (e.g., by looking for the "advertunity").

Finally, you'll learn how to "Plan It & Take Action": identify obstacles that are making it difficult to respond to the adversity, and learn how to problem-solve around them, then go do it! The knowledge isn't helpful if you don't act on it, which I help you prepare for.

ENERGY

The second step in getting REAL is all about understanding and managing energy. Once you understand energy regulation, how to recover energy, and where to focus it, you will be able to *respond* instead of *react* to adversity by harnessing and allocating resources more wisely.

First, I want you to "Understand Your Energy Regulation": learn about the different energetic domains (physical, emotional, mental, and spiritual), identify your triggers that lead you to waste energy, and dismantle your energy habits so you can consciously regulate your energy use instead.

Then, you're ready to learn how to "Recover Your Energy": stop doing things that deplete you and start doing things that charge you up (including gratitude, self-care, and other interventions, such as yoga or journaling).

Finally, I'll help you think about how to "Use Your Energy": actively choose where to spend your energy; make sure that spent energy "counts" and is serving you; and remember to save some energy for the learning and growing that follows failure, mistakes, and adversity. Resilient people know how to manage energy and this is key to building a fulfilling life of well-being.

AUTHENTICITY

The third step in getting REAL focuses on Authenticity. It's important to learn to identify and nurture your authentic self because without true authenticity, you will never be able to bounce beyond adversity.

In this chapter, I'll prompt you with ways to get to "Know Yourself": define your core values, beliefs, and personal strengths. You'll use that information to help you find your purpose—when passion and purpose collide, and they're built on core values and beliefs, it'll be easier to get up when life knocks you down.

Then, you'll discover how to "Release Yourself": free yourself from everything that mitigates or denigrates your authenticity, including judgment, self-sabotage, imposter syndrome, tendencies to spiral, your inner critic, the walls you put up, and shame.

Finally, I want you to "Love Yourself": create space for yourself; develop healthy boundaries; practice self-care, self-compassion, and self-advocacy; and most important, love yourself. Resilient people draw on their own authenticity often, using it to love themselves inside and out, outside and in.

LOVE

The fourth and final step in getting REAL encourages us to Love wholly and completely. Love helps you build resilience because it makes you stronger and healthier, it helps you build an authentic community rooted in your core values that will support you, and it develops in you the capacity to respond to adversity with optimism and peace.

A key element to this anchor is developing the ability to "Forgive Yourself & Others": acknowledge hurts and mistakes of the past and choose to forgive and release them. This is the last obstacle to clear from your path before you can run free.

Then, you'll be ready to "Develop Authentic Community": build a support system based on love—instead of, say, money or career/reputation—including your birth family (if appropriate); your chosen family; your professional and social networks; and a support system of doctors, counselors, and coaches.

Next, I'll demonstrate to you how to "Communicate with Love": find a loving way to say hard things (e.g., I don't love you anymore or I don't want to work here anymore). Words matter; responding with love always leads to better outcomes, not least of which is the cultivation of more love.

Finally, "Have Fun!" Look for ways to have a little bit of fun; it can make tough moments easier and help keep you from spiraling into negative self-talk. Laughter leads to resilience and further enables your authentic self to emerge.

This book dedicates a full chapter to each of the model's four anchors. Then, after we've explored them individually,

I'll zoom back out and show you how to put them all together through self-coaching. When you know how to self-coach, you'll be able to take yourself through the model under any circumstances and at any time. You'll know how to bounce beyond adversity by leaning on your already-developed authentic resilience.

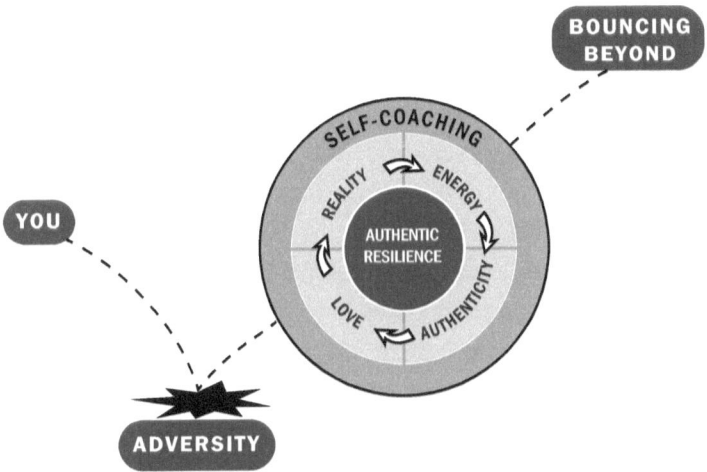

HOW AND WHY I BECAME A COACH

Long before I figured out the formula to bounce beyond adversity, I was doing it on the fly. I was bullied as a child for being "different"—something a lot of gay children know about themselves, but don't have the words for yet. The bullying continued into high school, and this is where I first understood the power of authenticity. I became involved in Key Club (a high school–level service organization) and the leadership roles therein. In the process of campaigning and running for a regional office, I realized I had to be me. In order to serve others, my community, and my school, I had to be 100 percent authentic. The empowerment that developed from that decision was profound and also directly related to my success—both as a leader and in my teenage relationships. It was as if I didn't even hear the bullies anymore. That was the first time I truly felt confident. The lesson stuck with me.

Next, I attended Marquette University, a Jesuit institution founded on the principles of St. Ignatius Loyola, which further instilled in me the desire to serve others. One of the school's founding principles is *Cura Personalis,* Latin for "care for the whole person." This is also a founding principle of my work as a person, leader, and coach. I dedicated my life to service when I was eighteen years old. This book is part of that. I want to give people the gift of learning how to help themselves and care for their whole person.

After college, I pursued a lifelong dream of living in Japan. The old expression "you have to go far away to find yourself" turned out to be very true for me. In my experience, nothing makes you question your grip on your identity faster than realizing everyone in a tiny foreign town is watching you, observing you as a representative of your culture. It was the adversities that came with this realization that led me to realize I'm gay, and eventually come out as such. During those five years, I also came to fully understand who I am and I learned how to live without apology or fear.

I returned to America even more confident and ready to take on the world. That's when I somewhat accidentally wound up working in human resources (HR) in New York City. It was the greatest gift that could've happened to me. Working in HR launched my curiosity about people and, ultimately, led me to coaching.

I remember the first time I had to coach an employee about their future career. They were battling themselves in the daily struggle to enjoy their job, perform to their (and the company's) expectations, and manage to care for family and an elder mother. This person was likely not right for the job and the job not right for the person. I was terrified. Immediately after our conversation, I felt devastated. Had I just helped someone decide to quit a good job at a great company? But a few weeks later, after the employee resigned, she was incredibly relieved. She thanked me. I had stumbled onto a career that would allow me to use my confidence and my abilities to drive conversations, connect with people, and care for the whole person.

In total, I've worked in HR for 20-plus years. Along the way, I've picked up even more coaching skills and, more important, I've clearly developed my purpose: to help people build authenticity and resilience. That's why I pursued coaching more specifically, as it allows me to more purely live in my purpose.

A teacher of mine once asked, "How have you jumped across so many different career paths; endured discrimination; lived through an earthquake, a tsunami, a typhoon, and a terrorist attack; *and* run marathons?" She wanted to know what special ingredient I had that other people don't. I wanted to know that too. That conversation and my work in HR sent me on a path of discovery that led me here: writing a book on resilience after realizing that other people *do* have that ingredient. Everyone does—some people just haven't learned how to tap into it yet. It's my job to change that.

I was certified as a coach in 2015, and in 2017, I earned my Master's degree in Coaching, Learning, and Development. Once I started coaching, I quickly locked onto the two main ingredients of my work: authenticity and resilience building. I wanted to make sure I understood these concepts from all 360 degrees. So I began a pattern of delving into research to critically think about these ingredients, and then meeting with clients again...then going back to the literature, and back to my clients again. (This is still my process today.) I will never stop reading and learning from clients.

A coach does not solve the problem and only rarely counsels or advises. Rather, a coach is there to hold space for a person, probe with the right questions that enable a person to access what they need to solve a problem, and then play back for a person what they've accessed and seen. I help people create what they want for themselves. It's magical every time, and often reminds me of that first taste of confidence and authenticity I felt back in high school.

As for the model, the "aha" moment finally came to me one night while talking about life's challenges with my best friend, Steve. During that conversation, I told him about the model I was developing for my clients and how the core of it was built around facing reality, managing well-being energy, finding self and authenticity, and components of love. I shared extensively that I wanted to bring the research—the genius of scholars and scientists, and my own coaching experiences—to life, and make it easy and accessible to understand and digest.[1] I said I wanted to tie all that information together, make it relevant and "real" for others. I'd gone back to my notes and research and saw that the acronym was already there and had been staring me in the face. When I shared this with Steve, he said, "Nate, you've been telling me to 'get real' for 30 years now." That's when I realized that although I had only been a professional for a few years, in a way I've actually been coaching my whole life.

I consider myself a well-being activist. The REAL model is a tool whose by-product results in a greater sense of joy and well-being. Authenticity and resilience are the bedrock. On my own path, I fought hard first for myself, by developing and using the tools I share in this book. Then I expanded my vision and started fighting for the mental health and well-being of others. Many of us start as accidental activists, slowly growing our cause and momentum. But whatever your struggle, when you bring the best of who you are into the world, nothing can stop you.

EMBRACE YOUR ADVERSITY

Yes, adversity is hardship, trouble, distress, suffering, and pressure. But it is also opportunity. It forces us to stop in our tracks and investigate how we live our lives. It forces us to evolve. It enables us to understand ourselves, including our beliefs and core values. Adversity can become a power that propels us forward. We can accept it as a gift and use it to our benefit. It's often in moments of adversity—even the small moments—that we make our biggest, most bold choices.

This book is a blueprint for how to do that: by developing authentic resilience and tools meant just for you that have been built by your own experiences. Yes, this blueprint has been built on psychology and neuroscience but, to be clear, this book and the REAL model are *not* psychological theories in and of themselves. And, certainly, they are not designed to help you solve the kind of problems requiring professional psychological help, such as issues that arise from deep trauma. For that, please seek help both from a medical professional and from your trusted community. My goal is not to provide a panacea but a guide to help you on your journey of self-discovery to the "more" in your life—the lessons, good and bad, that make your life count.

This book is the combination and culmination of knowledge gathered from thousands of hours spent with my clients and employees; poring over hundreds of studies and research papers on adversity memory in the body, adversity in the brain, and somatics in the body; and living through my own experiences. Hopefully, I can prove to you that when you combine authenticity with resilience, you can overcome any obstacle and bounce beyond any adversity—and do so feeling stronger and happier than you were before.

If you think that sounds hard or you feel a little afraid, that's natural. But I can tell you from experience that you're stronger than you think you are. We will start small and build from there. Turn the page and let's get REAL.

CHAPTER 1

WHAT IS ADVERSITY?

IN THE FALL OF 2000, I RETURNED TO THE UNITED STATES after fulfilling a lifelong dream of living and working in Japan. I discovered so much about myself while I was away, I was excited to return to my home country and see how the new, more open Nate would show up in the world.

My criteria for successfully reestablishing myself in America were few and simple: I wanted to live in a big city and find a job that paid at least $35,000 annually—which was a living wage back in 2000—and utilize my knowledge of Japanese culture and language.

I never could have dreamed the job that met those criteria would lead me to New York Fashion Week in Bryant Park. What started as a trip to New York to visit my aunt and uncle, Jo Andres and Steve Buscemi, quickly turned into me working for my aunt's high-fashion women's wear designer friend, Nanette Lepore—who just happened to be opening a branch of her business in Japan.

The stars could not have aligned more perfectly for me. I'd accidentally fallen into not one, but *two* dream jobs in my lifetime. After the fabulous events of fashion week, I was back on a plane to Tokyo to help launch the business there. I went back and forth several times, wheeling and dealing through the company's licensing deals. I was young, hungry, and succeeding in an exciting, glamorous industry.

In just over a year, it would all come crashing down.

I woke up in my New York apartment on the morning of September 11, 2001, turned on the TV, and learned that a plane had hit one of the World Trade Center towers. I ran outside the building, saw the smoke, ran back inside, and watched the second plane hit live on TV. I couldn't believe what I was seeing. My brain asked me if this was real or a movie.

The rest of the day happened in slow motion. My brain was like, "Panic! Panic! Panic!" What were we going to do? Death and destruction were everywhere. Phones were knocked out. There was no communication. Thousands of people were missing. The man I was dating worked downtown as a banker. It would be days before I knew whether or not he was alive.

Meanwhile, my job fell apart. The company's prospects in Japan hadn't been what they'd expected. The dot-com bubble burst and retail sales became unbearably sluggish. I was developing exhaustion from the travel. And then, over the course of a couple of hours on the morning of September 11, international travel became questionable altogether. It was no longer what I wanted. The company and I mutually agreed to part ways.

During the weeks that followed, I spent a lot of time at Jo and Steve's place. Together, we processed the nightmare: the makeshift kiosks searching for missing friends and colleagues, the body parts, the funerals, the parades. As a former firefighter, Steve went down to "the pile" every day. We attended many funerals that fall. We all tried to find meaning in different ways. We did a lot of soul searching. And drank a lot of wine.

My existential crisis resulted from a cocktail of adversities: emotional, physical, mental, and financial, too. I felt low self-worth and high self-doubt. I realized how lucky I had been in life and in my career—I had landed two dream jobs, for goodness' sake! Now, multiple adversities were intersecting with one another at once to keep me down. I didn't know what would happen next, but I knew I needed to start moving forward with more purpose.

THE SEVEN TYPES OF ADVERSITY

When I talk about intersectionality of adversities, I'm referring to interactions between different types of adversity. Specifically, researchers have categorized these under seven umbrellas. You might be more familiar with their counterparts: the seven dimensions of well-being.[2] These categories make up the main areas of wellness we are all working to fulfill every day: physical, emotional, mental, spiritual, social, environmental, and financial. Think of adversity as the challenges that block us from meeting the needs of those areas. Those challenges can usually be categorized as one of the exact same seven areas.

Physical adversity is something that affects the senses or the body. When someone's been in a car accident, has a medical condition that causes chronic pain, or is born with a physical disability, that person experiences physical adversities. Every single one of us has experienced forms of adversity that affect us in a physical way.

Emotional adversity affects our feelings and has to do with our state of mind (the right side of the brain's frontal lobe). These adversities disrupt our emotional selves; they interrupt or distract us from building positive feelings of self-worth and self-love. They can also lead to things like rage or sadness in response to emotional events. Emotional adversity isn't a negative event itself so much as the feelings that emerge from that negative event, which can prevent or disable us from having control over our emotional selves.

Mental adversity is the other dimension that affects our state of mind (typically on the left side of the frontal lobe). It's often connected to mental problems, whether that's a mental illness or just something that interrupts our mental processes. This type of adversity is associated with deeper psychological developments: things that affect our mindset, our flow of logic, and even our neurotransmitters, the chemicals our brains use to tell our bodies how to respond to things.

Spiritual adversity, for a lot of people, brings to mind their relationships (or lack of) with a higher power, or their faith (or lack of) in a deity of some sort. And certainly for some of us, adversity can come from questioning those beliefs and faith. But how I look at spiritual adversity—and how I teach my clients to think about it—revolves around the faith that you have in yourself. That's important for all of us to have, regardless of our religious or spiritual beliefs. Faith in yourself is connected directly to purpose—whether you believe your life has a purpose and choose to pursue that purpose (and pay those costs) if you do. Spiritual adversity often stems from not being clear about your sense of purpose, your values, or your core strengths.

Then we have the external types of adversity: social, environmental, and financial.

Social adversity is probably the category we face most often in today's society of being socially connected in all kinds of different ways. As humans, we require social connections—they are critical to sustaining human life. Adversity in this area is a conflict of not being able to have those meaningful human connections, whether personal or professional. When someone doesn't know how to show their empathy, or how to communicate with others, or maybe gets cut off from their circle of friends or a professional network, social adversity is sure to follow.

Environmental adversity is exactly what it sounds like: it stems from aspects of the environment around you. Even though it's an external factor of our state of being, the environmental area of wellness is especially important to us because it heavily affects the base levels of our hierarchy of needs (food, water, shelter, safety, etc.). Access to clean water, the quality of the air we breathe, and the climate of the area we live in are just a few examples of this dimension of well-being in our lives. Natural disasters, shootings and bombings, and unsafe home situations are some of the environmental adversities that can stand in the way of meeting these needs. And as the hierarchy of needs demonstrates, when we don't have the most basic of our needs met, it can be extremely difficult to overcome adversities in other areas of our lives.

Financial adversity is the last of the seven dimensions of adversity. This refers to any situation that impacts your ability to pay for the things you need. A financial adversity is any that disrupts your financial security. This can affect people of any socioeconomic status; if you're living from paycheck to paycheck to survive, the adversity there is obvious. But even if you're more secure, yet still unable to afford the lifestyle you want, that's a form of financial adversity too. Adversities in this area can take the form of poor money management, overspending habits, or just not knowing how to invest or plan for the future...which can all lead to further financial adversity.

INTERSECTIONALITY OF ADVERSITIES

The frustrating part about the adversities we face is that they rarely affect us in only one area at any given time—and rarely do we only experience one adversity at a given time. We often deal with intersectionality of adversity because of, as I mentioned earlier, the interconnected nature of our bodies, minds, and external environments in these seven areas of well-being (or adversity). We are complicated creatures; the human experience varies across cultures, ethnicities, races, sexual orientations, and genders (to name just a few). Adversities (which tend to hit us in multiples at any given time) affect us all in different ways based on this three-dimensional intersectionality of individual experiences.[3]

Here are a couple of examples, one ancient and one all too modern. First, imagine what it would have been like to have leprosy before it was treatable. The disease itself is a physical adversity you would live with day in and day out. On top of that, since leprosy was once a highly contagious and devastating disease, anyone who had it was completely shunned by the public. Not only is this isolation a social adversity, it's also a financial adversity because you couldn't find work. Lack of income and connection leads to lack of stability, which can cause mental adversity in the form of metal health crises. All of these different areas of our lives can be affected by a single event or a chain of related events.

Here's a more modern example. A big workplace issue for women (or at least, people assigned female at birth (AFAB)) is the stigma surrounding perimenopause and menopause. For some reason, this topic is considered taboo to talk about, even though it affects working women everywhere. Not enough people talk about it, so there is a sense of shame surrounding the women who experience it. It's a physical, mental, emotional, and social adversity. For those who experience more severe symptoms, it can also cause financial adversity; studies have shown that in some places, a large percentage of women leave the workforce due to menopause symptoms.[4]

The adversities we experience are also affected by the intersecting prejudices people in society face. Menopause is only experienced by women and AFAB people, but a white woman and a black woman are going to face different social circumstances while going through menopause. Our experiences are layered through so many variables, which is why it's so common for adversities to wind up impacting us differently at every level.

HOW & WHERE ADVERSITY LIVES IN OUR BRAINS

We can't successfully write a book about authentic resilience without saying a bit first about adversity, as this is the birthplace of resilience and learning. Each adversity affects our brains and our bodies differently—but together they do so in tandem, simultaneously impacting intersecting parts of our well-being. This is because of the interconnected nature of our bodies and our minds. Everything we experience is processed through our brains, whether it's physical or psychological, conscious or unconscious. The brain is where adversity lives in our bodies. Without recognizing which parts of your brain an adversity is coming from, it's difficult to build authentic resilience in response. So let's dissect the "biology" of adversity.

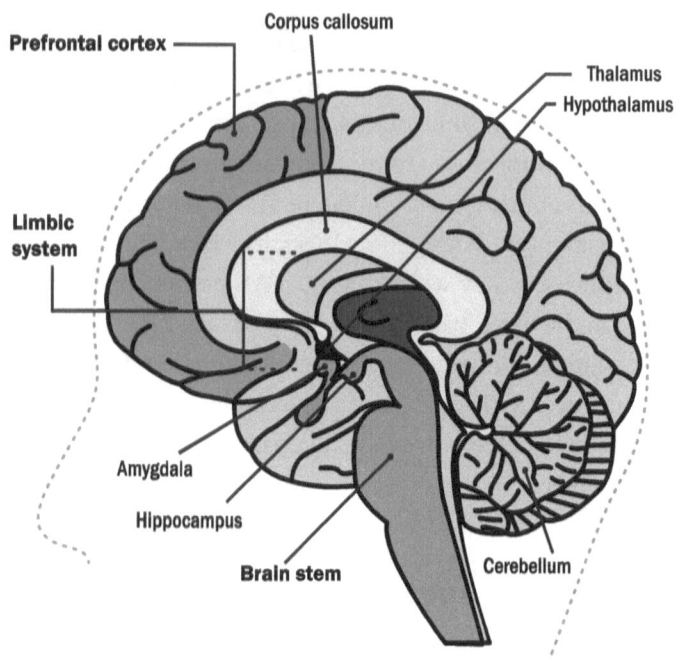

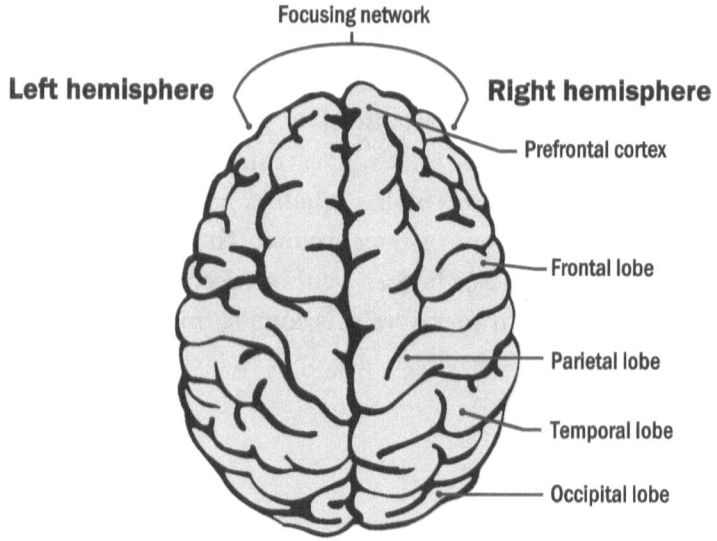

The brain is made up of several different parts, each of which can be generally categorized into the upper or lower brain. The lower brain is what I call "caveman brain" (and I'm sure neuroscientists hate it when I do, so from hereon, I'll refer to it as "prehistoric" to keep things simple); it contains the hippocampus and the amygdala. The hippocampus is the part of our brain that translates our experiences and learned information into memory. These can be stored in explicit conscious memory (think the memories you draw from to inform decisions) or in implicit somatic memory (think muscle memory and physiological responses).[5]

The amygdala is the unconscious part of the brain that's driven by instinct to go into fight, flight, or freeze mode in response to threats. The good news is this means we're hardwired for survival. The bad news is since we're no longer cavemen, the modern situations we face today can often be misinterpreted as threats when, in reality, they aren't. Our brains just aren't very good at distinguishing actual threats from psychological or perceived threats; the "prehistoric brain" works too fast for our conscious mind to prevent these instinctive reactions.

The upper brain is more suited to the modern human experience. Over time we have developed a frontal lobe that contains a prefrontal cortex connecting the left and right hemispheres of this lobe. The left hemisphere is where functions happen such as logic, rationality, synthesis, analysis, and patient judgment planning. The right hemisphere is the more creative side; this is where emotional processing, visualization, and interpretation of verbal and nonverbal communication all happen.

Connecting these hemispheres is the prefrontal cortex, the central processor for the whole body. It ties these two sides together to form what makes each of us unique. It's basically the place where we as humans are involved with our own complex thinking. It's where we problem-solve, express our personality, moderate how we behave, and think about the past, present, and future. This is the part of the brain that makes the human experience so unique. It is generally accepted that we are the only species that can ruminate on the past and visualize the future.[6]

Think about how much time you spend thinking about past decisions or hopes for the future. Researchers have found that people actually have a hard time living in the present moment; of the millions of thoughts each person has every day—that's right, I said millions—about half of them are ruminations on the past while the other half are predictions of the future. And it all happens in this one major part of your brain.[7]

When you experience an adverse moment, it's bound to be processed by all these key components of the brain. Then, your response to that moment shows up as behavior. The combinations of events and resulting responses are practically infinite due to the complex nature of the brain, so the patterns you develop are uniquely wired to you.

You might be thinking, "Okay, Nate. I didn't pick this book up for a middle-school brain anatomy lesson. What does this have to do with building resilience?"

Adversity isn't the only thing residing in our brains—resilience lives there too!

HOW WE CHANGE

So we've talked about the anatomy of the brain, the seven types of adversity, and intersectionality of adversity. How do all these concepts come together? When we realize that the dimensions of adversity mirror the dimensions of our well-being, it becomes easier to identify the origins of the perceived threats that our lower prehistoric brains are constantly picking up. This helps us determine whether they're actually threats (even if just internal ones), which then allows us to direct our energy to conditioning our brains to respond appropriately (which we will discuss in Chapter 4).

Condition is the key word here. Every one of us has a different idea of what success looks like in each of these seven areas of well-being. And our brains have been wired by our individual experiences to respond to specific stimuli in certain ways, both through explicit and implicit memories. In other words, our individual experiences condition our brains to respond to things in a unique way, whether we're conscious of it or not. This "hardwiring" is our resilience! Our ability to adapt, go into fight/flight/freeze mode, make split-second decisions or think things out and try new approaches—all of these are manifestations of resilience.

The thing about conditioning is that it can be a double-edged sword. It allows us to build resilience, but it greatly depends on how we are able to learn from our experiences and where that learning is patterned into our brain. So depending on our experiences, conditioning can be used to develop patterns of giving in to adversity rather than overcoming it. It's easy for a person to become "set in their ways" because habits (physical, psychological, or even physiological) are formed through repeated experiences that reinforce existing beliefs. And the brain is wired to learn and repeat patterns of behavior in this way, even if they're actually harmful patterns.

But once again I've got good news for you: like the seven dimensions of being that make up a whole person, this learning style of the brain also has a counterpart: neuroplasticity. If conditioning is learning to form patterns, then you can think of neuroplasticity as the brain's complementary learning style to conditioning—it's essentially our ability to rewire our brains in order to change those patterns!

Dr. Richard Davidson, a prominent neuroscientist who has studied the effects of meditation on the brain, explains this concept well. He's written that based on everything known about the brain in neuroscience, "change is not only possible, but is actually the rule rather than the exception. It's really just a question of which influences we're going to choose for our brain."[8]

Neuroplasticity is what makes building resilience a completely unique experience to every individual. No two brains are the same because no two lives are the same, and that's why you have to build resilience patterns that are completely authentic to you—the entire being that is stored in all those different parts of your special brain!

That's why I created the REAL model. This model is a vehicle that's going to help you cross the bridge from the adversity dimensions into the dimensions of wellness, no matter how complicated the intersections of that path get for you. I've helped countless people learn to make this journey, including myself. I know you can do it too. Use this model to build resilience and push yourself through any adversities you encounter. I promise you'll come out stronger on the other side.

KEY TAKEAWAYS

- Adversity can be generally categorized into seven types: physical, emotional, mental, spiritual, social, environmental, and financial.

- Adversity is intersectional, which means a single adverse event can affect you in any combination of these seven categories and be further influenced by intersecting variables such as race, socioeconomic status, gender, sexuality, etc. This is why negative events tend to have a compound effect on us.

- The brain is a complex organ that houses adversity as well as resilience, which is why we're all wired to manage it in our own unique way.

- It's the nature of the brain to be conditioned to repeat patterns of behavior. It's *also* the nature of the brain to build new patterns via neuroplasticity. This is the function you are utilizing most when building your authentic resilience.

CHAPTER 2

WHAT IS AUTHENTIC RESILIENCE?

"ATTENTION IN THE BUILDING! ATTENTION, NATHAN Andres, Major League Baseball. Your family is safe in the lobby of the building."

I'd never heard the emergency loudspeaker at 245 Park Avenue before—but what a relief it was to hear this announcement at work on August 14, 2003, the start of what would go down as one of the biggest blackouts in U.S. history.

Of course, I didn't know that at the time. All I knew was my name was on the loudspeaker in our building, which was running on an emergency generator after more than an hour of no power. The announcement caused this massive stir in my office; my colleagues suddenly all clapped and cheered, yelling down the hall, "Happy for you, Nate." It was actually a little embarrassing, but I was just happy my sister Jules, who was visiting me in New York for the first time, had figured out a way to let me know she was okay while no phones were working.

I'd seen Jules a few hours earlier when she'd arrived in NYC. We met for lunch, after which the plan was for her to go shopping while I finished my workday and then she would come back to my office and we'd take all her stuff back to my place. We had a whole long weekend of fun New York activities planned, but then the power went out. On August 14, 2003, at about 4:15 in the afternoon, power in the entire Northeastern segment of the United States went out. Of course, at the time we didn't know what it was. To recall the movie analogy, at this moment I felt like the character in a thriller who's on the verge of realizing something worse is about to happen.

First the lights shut off, then the computers, and then it was dark. Air conditioning went out. It all stopped. At the time, many of us thought it was a building issue or a generator that crossed wires or something. I remember thinking that I wished I'd known the elevator would stop working before I let Jules leave her big ass suitcase with me on the thirtieth-something floor. My sister is not a light traveler.

After a few minutes, we realized this was happening all over the city and began to fear the worst. Some of the executives wandered out of their offices and people started to poke their heads around the cubicles. We gathered to ask, *What's going on? Do you think this is terrorism?! Is this another attack?*

When you've lived through an event as catastrophic as September 11, going through a massive blackout can understandably bring up some posttraumatic responses. As the minutes turned into hours and the power didn't return, many of us who had been in New York two years earlier started to worry. I specifically remember one colleague who completely panicked. She said something like, "I've gotta get out of here, I can't live through this again." She didn't think twice about running down the 100-plus flights of stairs to get to the ground.

She was wearing white, and I recall thinking she was out of there so fast it looked like a flash of lightning through the door.

It was a tense wait; some people were crying and having panic attacks like the lightning lady had. Everyone was thinking about what we'd experienced in 2001, and it felt like we were sitting ducks for terrorists again.

But the MLB chief of security at the time, Kevin, happened to be in the office that day. At first, he was adding to our nervousness because he kept moving all over the office, standing by the windows and fiddling with something we couldn't make out in the dark. He didn't inform anyone he was looking for batteries and trying to get a good signal for the battery-operated radio he had on him until much later. Eventually, though, he got it working, and it was through this device that we heard officials assuring everyone that it was just a huge power outage, not an attack.

The relief in the room was palpable. Once I heard that it wasn't terrorism, I was able to completely refocus my energy on planning for the aftermath of the blackout. I was still concerned about my sister out in New York with no power, but I was certain she'd be okay. She's smart, and it wasn't like she'd never been in big cities before. Worrying about her wasn't going to help anything. I needed to redirect my energy into some kind of plan, something useful.

Jules wouldn't know anywhere else to look for me, so I decided to stay in the building and wait for the power to come back on. I considered moving to wait for her in the lobby, but then the generators kicked in and soon the announcement for me played on the loudspeaker.

While I made my way down to her, I kept thinking, how can I show my little sister some strength and help her remain calm? Did she know this was an outage, not a terrorist attack?

This certainly wasn't anything out of her playbook. I gathered my control, went back to my own values, and decided we would get through this together by finding the humor in the situation, big ass suitcase and all.

It turns out she had been just a few floors below me the whole time—stuck in the elevator two or three levels below the Major League Baseball offices. Unfortunately, my sister is claustrophobic, couldn't get her cell phone to work, *and* needed to go to the bathroom. But she made it out "alive" (if very frazzled). It had only been a few hours since our lunch, but it felt like an eternity had passed.

After our happy little reunion on the ground floor, we walked from Park Avenue in Midtown Manhattan all the way to West Village. To this day my sister and I still laugh about some of the wild things we saw on that trek: a lot of people still in disbelief, but also people laughing, and people drinking. We saw an entire beauty parlor standing around outside chatting in their gowns and curlers, like something out of the "Beauty School Dropout" number in the movie *Grease*.

I think what makes this memory so fond for me is that it felt so easy to adapt to a blackout after experiencing the horrors and aftermath of September 11, when I'd spent my days struggling to take things one step at a time, and had faced new traumas as bodies were found and fires raged on. Therefore, as worried as I was for my sister at first, this blackout weekend didn't feel like a big deal in comparison. After September 11, if anything, we learned that we need to ride it out a little bit, to wait and see what the aftermath will be following a major event. The adaptation was to go step by step, to focus our energy, put a loose plan together, and go day by day. So that's what I did in the office following the blackout. I stayed calm. I faced the reality, realized there wasn't much I could do in the moment, and decided to wait it out. I felt resilient this time. That resilience was authentic because it came directly from my unique lived experience. I was drawing on past personal experiences—those learnings that move from implicit to explicit memory (thanks to the hippocampus)—to drive my authentic decision-making. This was the conscious wisdom I brought with me to the blackout. It was this wisdom that fed my ability to draw upon my resilience in this situation.

Once my sister and I were out on the streets, I could see I wasn't the only one bouncing back quickly. During that walk to my apartment, my sister and I saw the first of what would become impromptu, weekend-long festivals with candles, picnics, block parties, and other events of people just coming together and making the best of the situation. After living through something so horrific not even two years earlier, I could see that New Yorkers had all been rewired to look on the bright side and be kinder to each other through times of adversity. It was New York City at both its chaotic best and finest worst.

There's a reason New York has the reputation it does: every aspect of living in such a massive and busy city is a battle. You're always fighting for tickets, parking spaces, jobs, homes, taxis, a place in line at venues, and much more. The whole city is a battle royale of daily adversities. So, the residents' threshold for stress is already high, which creates a baseline resilience that comes from constantly adapting to those everyday stressors.

Lots of people love living in New York, and those people tend to have a reputation for being the stereotypical rude New Yorker who is always too *something*—too loud, too rude, too rushed, etc.—at least to outsiders (or to people who love to hate New York). But not everyone is suited to this environment; you need to have a lot of authentic resilience to be comfortable in this city. And during the blackout, we learned that the city itself had also developed some authentic resilience.[9]

DEFINING AUTHENTICITY AND RESILIENCE

You might be wondering what I mean by "authentic resilience." Is there such a thing as inauthentic resilience? Not necessarily, but I do think people often mistake resilience for its cousins, endurance and perseverance.[10] Don't get me wrong, these are important traits on this journey—but they alone aren't enough to get you through adversity and coming out stronger on the other side. So, to truly understand the process of the REAL model and gaining that strength, first it's important to get clear on a few definitions. Let's start with authenticity.

AUTHENTICITY

When I talk about authenticity, I'm talking about being true to yourself. Specifically, being true to your own personality, spirit, or character. Authenticity draws on the deeper set of your core beliefs, values, and strengths that you develop over your lifetime; it's an actualization of those things manifesting in your behavior. Rather than a trait, think of it as a process—a journey to understand yourself down to the core. Authenticity comes from deep within yourself; it's an understanding that works from the inside outward.

Think of the popular iceberg analogy. If your authenticity as a whole is an iceberg, then the massive chunk of ice people can see above the waterline is your behavior: actions, words, expressions, and body language. The ice beneath the surface represents your core values and beliefs, the ways you think and feel, and your strengths and philosophies. These aspects of you that people can't see are the pieces you need to understand to activate your authenticity from the inside outward.

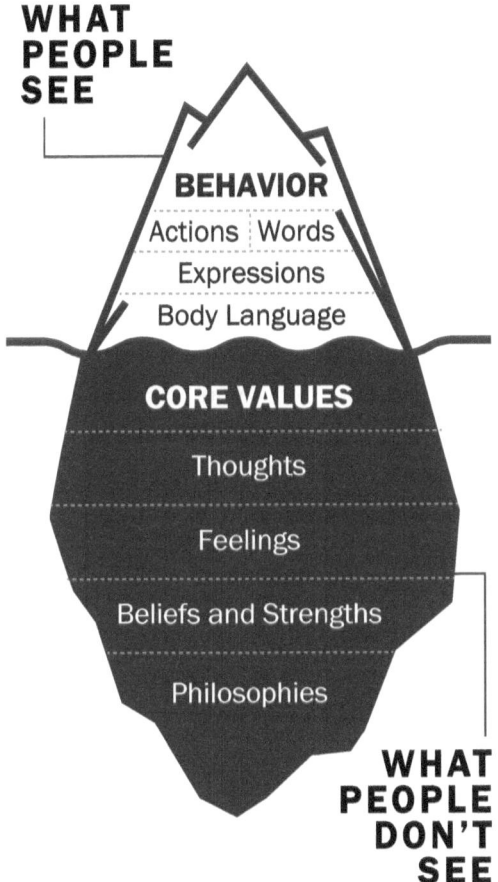

But again, authenticity is refined over a lifetime. Just as much as it's an inside-outward journey, it's also a journey from outside inward. Our reactions to things outside ourselves in life—whether it be positive experiences or adversities—ultimately leads us to develop these inner strengths, ways of thinking, values, thoughts, feelings, and all the other inner components of the authenticity iceberg. It's a cycle of evolution. Both authenticity and resilience evolve from this cyclical pulsation of learning and adapting.

Just like your brain, with its physiological "wiring" that comes from your unique combination of life experiences, your authenticity is completely unique to you. This uniqueness is what makes it so hard to define authenticity in a universal way; it's not really a universal concept because there are an infinite number of developments that go into building our authenticity, just like with our brain patterns.[11] There is no one style of authenticity—it looks and feels different for everyone.

Let's talk about things that get in the way of authenticity. To have true authenticity, you have to look at your core self. And a lot of people are afraid of what they'll find there, so they don't want to look. It's not uncommon for people to use things like swagger, bravado, or even insecurity to avoid this exploration and cloak their authenticity. Some even go so far as to convince themselves that this cloak is what their authenticity looks like. I think the author Mike Robbins said it best when he called this a "resistance to authenticity."[12] The source of this resistance can come from anywhere: feeling embarrassment or trying to save face; self-preservation; learned behaviors; family, social, and cultural influences; etc. The list goes on.

The attack in 2001 forced a journey to authenticity for the entirety of New York. The destruction, chaos, and grief that came from that event caused New Yorkers to reexamine themselves. It made us realize that we're vulnerable, not as tough as we think we are, and each day is a gift. I remember in the weeks following September 11, people were kinder. There was less bravado and confrontation coming from people dealing with the daily adversities. I think we all learned that with a little sense of humor and by reflecting on where we've been, we can work our way through just about anything—because these are among the things that help us be authentic to our true selves.

Finding this authenticity is what equipped New Yorkers who lived through September 11 to draw from their resilience and rebuild. This discovered resilience is what made the blackout that followed two years later no big deal for so many of us.

RESILIENCE

My definition of resilience (which I've adapted a bit from the American Psychological Association definition) is the ability to adapt well to adversity, which can come in the forms of trauma, tragedy, threats, and other significant sources of stress. Resilience is how you process, react to, adapt to, and cope with challenges in your daily life. Simply, it is the art of taking back control from an adversity and learning from that experience—not allowing the adversity to dominate you, but rather, gaining dominance over the circumstances of that adversity and those that follow.

As I mentioned earlier in the chapter, many people mistake resilience for endurance and perseverance. While these can be important parts of the process of building resilience, they're by no means the same thing. Perseverance is the ability to continue working at something, never losing sight of the goal in the face of obstacles. Endurance is being able to keep going at something for long periods of time. These are very different from resilience (being able to adapt and learn from events, and from using that learning to cope in the next instance and the one after that). These traits are more like cousins than different sides of the same coin.

Another distinction I want to make is between resilience and numbness. Becoming numb in response to adversity *can* be part of building resilience in some situations (mainly in the "freeze" response triggered in the brain by the amygdala). However, this should not be conflated with long-term numbness. If someone is still feeling numb after processing an adverse event—if the adaptation to the event *is* numbing—then that's no longer a prehistoric brain instinctive reaction. It's an upper-brain, emotional response, and not generally a healthy one. This is usually an indicator that something in the psyche needs to be looked at and addressed. Therefore, numbness is *not* another cousin to resilience.

HOW WE LEARN RESILIENCE

The scientific community has been studying resilience since long before it became the post-pandemic buzzword it is today. In a wide longitudinal study of resilience in twins at Virginia Commonwealth University in 2014, researchers found that roughly 30 percent of resilience comes from genetic makeup and is heritable.[13]

The remaining 70 percent of our individual resilience is developed from how we're raised, how we live our lives, how we experience the challenges of our lives, how we learn, how we grow, and how we continue to adapt. All of these things influence the infinite combinations of neurotransmitters in our brains that form our responses to threats, stresses, traumas, tragedies, and so on.

We learn resilience the same way we learn most things: by observing as children. We watch people around us in our families and communities and learn from the environment that we live in. In modern culture, many young people also learn resilience skills from figures in pop culture and media.

For me, I credit my dad Tim with showing me how to experience adversity with strength and hardiness. Thinking back,

I can apply the REAL model to my dad's ongoing adversity with heart disease.

When I was a child, my father was diagnosed with cardiovascular disease. He had to lean into *reality* when he had his first open-heart surgery at thirty years old in 1979. My siblings and I were too young to know what any of that meant, but my mom was scared to death, so we little ones figured out that Dad was sick enough to need to stay in the hospital.

When he came home from that first operation, I was struck by his approach to recovering his *energy*. He would always say, "If you want to get energy, you gotta spend energy." My dad is kind of a busybody, so he hated being prescribed so much bedrest. Resting that much didn't suit his idea of productivity, so he was always finding ways to focus his energy into little projects around the house. It was a key part of his resilience.

After that first surgery back in 1979, the doctors told him he wasn't going to live past fifty. But he had children to raise and a life purpose to fulfill, and that *authenticity* drove him to keep going. He made the changes he needed to improve his diet and his habits so that he could be healthy. This started when I was pretty young, and then, out of his deep *love* for us, he instituted life changes for the entire family. Our diet was basically pescatarian for at least two years. And we found it to be a positive humorous sign of Dad's love when he had us start cholesterol testing at age ten. Plus there was this drink that tasted like liquid sand. Long story short, we were a really healthy family.

Seven years later, my dad needed a second open-heart surgery. The doctors told him they could potentially extend his life for twelve more years at most. Another eight years later, he went in for a third open-heart bypass, and the doctors predicted even more time.

My dad is seventy-four years old now, and it feels like he's had every medical technology put into his body. We can laugh about it now, but there have been some real freak-outs over the years.

He has surpassed every expectation medical professionals held for his life span. They did the physical work (the rewiring around his heart) and my dad rewired his brain. It was a partnership each time. My dad evolved his own resilience. In his own authentic way, my dad is extremely focused. He's constantly setting goals and redefining the purpose that drives him every day. By the time of his third bypass, when I was in college, he wanted grandchildren and to continue his retirement. Now, he wants to improve his golf game. He's constantly re-tweaking his energy and focusing it in different places.

I think a big part of my resilience comes from having him as a great role model. I grew up watching my dad acknowledge, suffer, accept, and rebound from medical challenges continually through forty-five years of heart disease, which is nothing to sniff at. But even through the bad times, he defied the odds because he was constantly rethinking his own resilience. He did that by facing reality, managing energy, constantly engineering purpose, and surrounding himself with love (all of which will be outlined as tools in this book).

And that's just one of loads of examples in my life of incredible resilience. I'm very blessed—but I know not everyone is so lucky. So I want you, the person reading this book, to know that if you can't see this kind of resilience around you, you have to go look for it. One of the best things you can do for yourself is seek out great role models in people who are practicing resilience.

Two great places to look are in child psychology and with your chosen family. Child psychologists help build resilience in children by focusing on practices such as demonstrating calmness when there's a mistake, not panicking when there's a failure, and exploring what kids can learn from certain experiences.

Current research also shows that a sense of community is vital to learning resilience. In the '80s and '90s, when the AIDS epidemic was happening, the concept of chosen family was tantamount to the success of gay men's resilience during that time. The community had to fight for self-advocacy and created HIV testing centers around the world. These were absolutely places to learn resilience for gay men going through the challenges of discrimination in healthcare. Resilience comes from a multitude of people and places—you just have to look for it.

The important thing to remember is that building resilience takes time. Just like your role model bodybuilders, tennis stars, and marathon runners didn't develop their amazing skills in a day, neither can you build amazing authentic resilience overnight. It takes work, building up strength, and repeating resilience habits over and over again to wire (or unwire) those neurotransmitters in your brain until what you've learned has become so embedded that it becomes second nature.

Resilience and authenticity are embedded from every experience we live through. So if you want to hijack those patterns and rewire your brain to be more resilient and authentic, you have to undo that previously embedded learning—undo those synapses and break those neurotransmitters in order to rebuild in a new way.

AUTHENTIC RESILIENCE IS YOUR MAGIC POWER

I've shared all these anecdotes of my life with you because they all illustrate the same point: when you combine resilience with authenticity, you can get through anything. You'll get through anything because it will all come from your most genuine inner self.

If we go back to the definitions, authenticity is being true to one's own personality, spirit, or character, and resilience is being able to adapt well to and take back control from adversity, trauma, and significant sources of stress. So if you're authentically resilient, you're in your own skin, dealing with challenges the way that you do. And *that* is a magic power.

When you can turn it on, regain control, and get back to your core values, strengths, and purpose, you can use those things to get over *anything* that you encounter in your life.

Here's what a real, authentically resilient person looks like: They can pretty much face anything. They understand their boundaries, and they usually have a plan to get through tough times. They usually know how to focus their energy. They're confident in the things that they pursue as a result of having gotten over adversities in their own life. And they're not afraid to face those things—they're less inhibited by fear. An authentically resilient person is more open to freedom and less controlled by worry. This person is better balanced in their energy and their well-being, because they know themselves inside-out and outside-in.[14]

It all comes back to that cycle. I call it a circular reference, when we experience the world on the outside, process it on the inside, use the outcome to learn and adapt, and then go out and do it again in the outside world. We've all known someone who gets stuck in a circular reference, looping the same complaint over and over. On the other hand, the authentically resilient person bounces out and beyond this process, and thereby experiences a higher connection in their mind, body, and soul. There is always more to draw from, even if authenticity and resilience levels seem low. They can always pull it out in order to get through any kind of next big challenge.

That's why these two things are important. The REAL model is about helping you get authentically resilient so that you can live your best life and get over troubles you encounter in a way that benefits your well-being.

The REAL model will help you develop the skills of authenticity and resilience by facing reality, learning energy management, exploring your own authenticity, and dancing with all the elements of love.

KEY TAKEAWAYS

- Authenticity is about being true to yourself: your unique personality, spirit, and character. It's a journey to understand yourself down to the core.

- Resilience is adapting to and reclaiming control from adversity, trauma, and significant stressors. It's refusing to allow adversity to dominate you and your life, and instead establishing dominance over the circumstances.

- A key way we learn resilience is through watching others (particularly as children). That's why role models are critical to building resilience.

- Combining authenticity and resilience empowers you to overcome anything that life throws your way.

CHAPTER 3

THE MODEL: REALITY

THE PALAIS GINZA OFFICE BUILDING WAS A STOUT, semi-derelict, eight-floor building that smacked of Japan's 1980s' bubble-economy heyday. My office and the unique offsite stockroom were on the fifth and sixth floors of the building, sandwiched between a dental office above and a bunny club for Japanese salary men below. No one was wise to the building's various comings and goings because its three-story facade was anchored by a famous Italian fashion brand, making the building appear more glamorous than it was. It sat among other flashy luxury brands that lined both sides of the street in a flamboyant shopping district.

In contrast to our office building, our retail space was directly across the street and it still sparkled and smelled brand new. It was a custom, eleven-story-tall tower that stuck out in its own right. Scintillatingly sexy with onyx-colored glass, black stone masonry, and deep oak interior finishes, it stood proudly as the newest peacock on the block across the slick Ginza skyline. Up the street on the corner of Harumi-dōri and a Chūō-dōri—in the heart of Ginza, the super elite

"Rodeo Drive of Tokyo"—is the Wako clock tower, one of the most iconic clocks in Japan.

Just after lunch one Friday afternoon, I scurried past the tower on my way back to the office. My office had a floor-to-ceiling glass window overlooking Chūō-dōri that allowed me to look out across to the pride and joy of the newest flagship in the company's retail fleet. Not long after I settled back into work, the windows creaked. It was about ten minutes to three. I poked my head out of my room and asked my colleague Leina if she'd heard it too. Suddenly, the windows began to rattle loudly and shake. The building swayed back and forth. I looked out the window again to see our new magnificent tower also starting to sway. Leina and I simultaneously shouted, "Jishin!" Earthquake.

The building now moved violently. I asked the team on my level to take cover under the front desk and stay away from windows. I stood in my office doorway. From my perch of false stability, I continued to peek out the window and watch our retail building sway. I grew increasingly concerned for our employees in both buildings. This was clearly a massive earthquake, like none I'd experienced in Japan before.

What came next, no one could have foreseen. It was a three-peat disaster. Unbeknownst to us, news of the 9.1-magnitude earthquake spread around the world fairly quickly. It was the most powerful quake ever recorded in Japan, and the fourth-most powerful in the world since record keeping began in 1900. The quake seemed to go on forever. We learned much later that it lasted about six minutes. There were days and days of aftershocks. Some of the biggest aftershocks were in their own right 6.0 or bigger.

During the first quake, once it seemed to slowly peter out, the regional manager and I radioed each other and decided to evacuate the office building, which had not been retrofitted for disaster since the early '80s. We believed we'd be safer if we huddled both teams in the ground of the new retail tower while we made our next plan and got further information.

After living through September 11, I knew this type of urgency; my body knew what to do. The building began to shake again, file drawers rattled, and our clothing racks in the back rooms with their roller wheels began to clunk back and forth.

The teams were frozen in fear. We calmly asked them to all head down the emergency stairs. Then the building jumped and bumped again. As I heard many people screaming in fear, I was calm. I instructed everyone to exit through the stairwells at the ground level and proceed to the store lobby. I insisted that our asset protection manager go before me into the stairwell as we locked the door behind us so I would be the last one out. Everyone moved across the street.

The alarm systems were loud and screeching. I could hear panic in people's voices. The language of fear all fused; English and Japanese mixed like music playing the symphony of uncertainty. Mother Nature's orchestra of adversity was working its way through the overture.

It was my turn to exit the building and go down the stairwell—not my first time wandering down a long stairwell in the middle of a disaster. I could actually see cracks emerging as the building kept moving and shaking. Dust and chunks of plaster popped off the walls.

This time, I felt trapped in a disaster movie. But it wasn't. It was March 11, 2011, the day that became known as the great Tōhoku earthquake and disaster.

The earthquake triggered the tsunami alert system. People in parts of Northeastern Japan had about thirty minutes to take cover. With no playbook, and aftershocks continuing in Tokyo, we also decided to seek bigger shelter up the street at the evacuation site, just north of the building. We had 200 employees on duty that day. We emptied out onto the center of Chūō-dōri, Ginza, where time, even that clock tower at Wako, seemed to stop. Cars were stopped. People were cluttered on the street, frozen. Aftershocks began and ended. The trembling continued further, and we saw the traffic lights and signs quiver and sway over our heads.

Rumors quickly bounced around that Tokyo Bay would be flooding and a tsunami was on the way. We knew that getting the bulk of our team to higher ground and shelter would be best. The regional manager took the helm at the front. I stayed behind to ensure everyone got there.

Although the exact number is disputed by researchers, somewhere around 221 aftershocks of 5.0 magnitude or greater filled the days following. All of them were accompanied by tsunami warnings. A tsunami never arrived in Tokyo as predicted, luckily, but liquefaction was evidenced all around the greater city area. The destruction and devastation only a few hundred kilometers north of us was unparalleled and humbling. Within the next four days, Fukushima Daiichi Nuclear Power Plant exploded, and its reactors went into full nuclear meltdown. It was the most severe nuclear accident since Chernobyl in 1986.

I remember sitting in refuge with my Japanese chosen family, watching it explode one reactor at a time. Three nuclear meltdowns and three hydrogen explosions. This was reality. Perhaps one of the biggest disasters of my lifetime at that point, despite living through the horrors of September 11. Within four days, an earthquake, a tsunami, and a nuclear accident. On that first day, the world literally shifted. I mean that—the Earth's axis actually shifted between estimates of ten centimeters and twenty-five centimeters. And it actually moved Honshū, the main island of Japan, by about 2.4 meters eastward.[15] *That's* reality.

So, if you've been keeping score, adversity in the shape of catastrophe and I are familiar. I wouldn't call us friends, but we know each other well. At this point, I had been through September 11, a great blackout, the anthrax scare, and a few hurricanes in Florida. Devastating events such as these don't scare me the way they used to. I've had the *opportunity* to develop resilience to them.

Facing reality is a key part of building resilience. This is the best way for anyone to begin the process. In simplified terms, when we face reality, we are working to access the prehistoric brain, so we can tap into memory and the wisdom of our resilience and use them to take action. We've already talked about that. So now, let's get into how to get REAL and begin to bounce beyond. It starts with reality.

THE CORE TENETS OF REALITY

In your quest to build authentic resilience, you must begin by investigating how you typically respond to adversity. Only afterward will you be able to change your habits. That work is the focus of the R portion of the REAL model. This chapter breaks down exactly how to do it, specifically, by following three core tenets: Face It, Control It, and Plan It and Take Action.

When an adverse event occurs, the first step to overcome it is to acknowledge that it happened, to face it. The faster you can acknowledge and move to accept the situation, the faster you can begin adapting. At times this is easier said than done, like when experiencing an adversity that your body and brain have never gone through before (such as a catastrophic terrorist attack or an earthquake). These types of adversities can send people into shock, which delays the neuroplasticity process (rewiring/adapting/bouncing beyond) from kicking in. In cases like these, facing reality can itself be more than half the battle.

That said, your brain is already adept at processing adversity and adjusting accordingly. It's already been conditioned by the mundane adversities that arise in everyday existence. It's also been rewired before—that's why it gets easier to cope with forgetting your car keys or stepping in dog poop on the way to work. Your brain and body have already built that resilience.

It's important to understand the brain processes and adversity types discussed in the previous chapters. Being aware of and able to identify what exactly is going on in your brain and body while you're processing an adverse event will help you embrace reality faster. The goal of learning to face reality quickly is to build the self-awareness required to access certain parts of your brain (such as the hippocampus, where your memories are, and the prefrontal cortex, where you process what's happening at the present moment). Once you've built that self-awareness, you can start developing a plan to overcome the adversity itself by accessing the resilience already conditioned in your brain and body.

The Reality anchor of the REAL model is illustrated in the common J-curve below.[16] I call it the Reality Curve. To build your authentic resilience, you need to progress through the stages displayed in the curve using the Reality anchor's three core tenets.

REALITY CURVE FOR AUTHENTIC RESILIENCE BUILDING

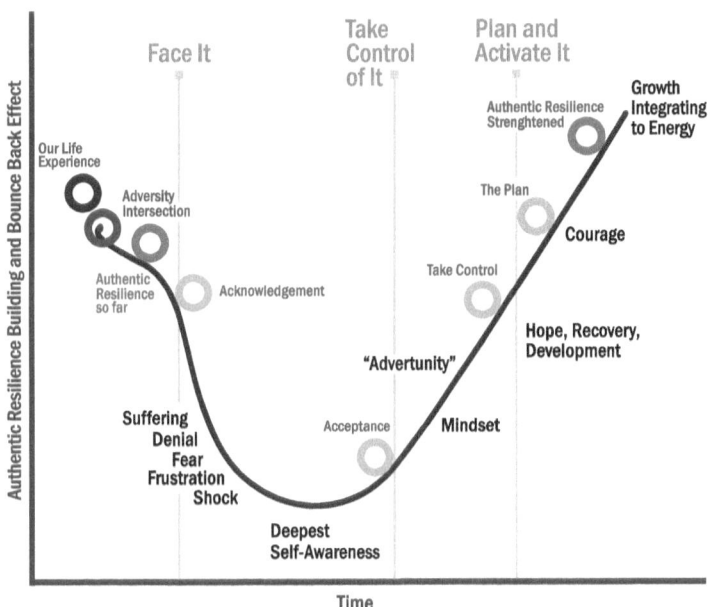

At the top of the curve, the adverse event occurs. I call this spot the adversity intersection—where life and adversity collide. These are the moments when you're asking yourself, *What was that? What just happened?* Your brain and body begin accessing your authentic resilience by tapping into what *you've* already experienced so far in your life. (This is what makes it authentically yours.) This leads to the first step of processing the new adversity, acknowledging it—which is at the heart of the first core tenet, Face It.

The curve then slopes down as this acknowledgment leads to any suffering, denial, fear, shock, or frustration you feel in the moment. At this point, your brain is processing the event in the slower upper brain. This is when you're facing reality by asking yourself (consciously or unconsciously) questions such as, *Is it logical?* and *How do I feel about it?*

At the bottom of the curve, you land at a place of questioning and enter the stage of self-coaching. This is when you're asking yourself, *What am I going to do about it?* Starting to answer this question is what leads to the rising slope of the curve—and that begins with acceptance. Your conditioned mindset is crucial at this point because how you use that acceptance determines whether or not you'll be able to take control of reality.

Then we move into the second core tenet, Control It, when we see the adverse event as an advertunity. *Advertunity* is a term coined by Dr. Paul Stoltz, who argues that people who respond to adversity as an opportunity—and do so with purpose and control—remain strong.[17] Those who are more victimized by the adversity, who respond helplessly, become weak. My definition is inspired by Stoltz but remains simple in this context of facing reality: advertunity is seeing the opportunity in adversity. It's always there; you just have to find it. And in the REAL model, it's one of the most important parts of the Reality anchor. When you get to a place where you can find advertunity, you're practicing resilience—because you're taking power back rather than relinquishing it to the adversity, as you may have done in the past.

At this point in the curve, you're able to feel hopeful; you're no longer heading in a downward direction. Feelings and emotions have diminished and perhaps stabilized. Now work your way up the curve by accessing positive energy and learned optimism through rewiring and neuroplasticity in your brain. You'll need that energy to execute the final core tenet: Plan It and Take Action.

Building a courageous step-by-step plan to overcome the adversity will help you change your current reality. At this point, you've pushed your brain to rewire itself so that you can pull yourself out of the adverse moment. As a result of that, your authentic resilience is strengthened. You've faced reality and pushed through adversity, in your own unique way, and are beginning the journey of bouncing beyond.

CORE TENET 1: FACE IT

When we learn to face reality, we trigger the brain to move its signals from the amygdala in the lower brain to the prefrontal cortex in the upper brain. Otherwise, during an adverse moment, your prehistoric brain is behind the wheel, immediately choosing flight, fight, or freeze in order to keep you alive. In the seconds that follow, your upper brain works to process what's happening. This is where it begins tapping into the previously embedded conditioning (or rewiring via neuroplasticity) that is your existing authentic resilience. The left and right hemispheres of your prefrontal cortex seek meaning in what's happened and determine the logical and emotional responses to the adversity so you can start to move toward acceptance.

This is all happening when you acknowledge an adverse event, which is why "Face It" is the first of the core tenets of the Reality anchor. At this stage, you're sliding down the Reality Curve into the place of suffering. If the journey of bouncing beyond starts by acknowledging that you must suffer to get to acceptance on the other side, then what makes us suffer?

Often, the answer is change.

Change is the one constant in life. It's one of the fundamental laws of nature. Our bodies and brains change from the time we're born to the time we die; the earth changes; the weather changes. This is an inescapable part of the human experience, which means adversity and resilience are also constant. So change is the cause of much of our adversity—but in a beautiful ironic twist, change is also a big part of the solution.

We've just established that this resilience journey requires a flexible brain. How do you begin this rewiring process? By changing your perspective! Changing your point of view helps you rewire your brain by tapping into both sides of your prefrontal cortex via critical thinking. Over time, the act of changing perspective interrupts the amygdala's instinctual response. Linda Graham explains, "sending the brain in another direction gives it a few moments to recalibrate itself."[18] This moment is when we can shift our perspective.[19] This is where we move into the second phase of Face It: acceptance.

Acceptance comes from understanding that flexibility is needed to face change, which is the main adversity in life for which we need resilience.

When you're experiencing suffering, if you can think of something in a different way or introduce a new concept, it can help you think through adversity differently and build a more flexible brain. But that doesn't make it easy to do. So now let's practice what we preach and change perspectives for a moment, by discussing ways to cope and handle the suffering related to adversity.

The Three Marks of Existence

In Buddhist practice, there is a concept called Three Marks of Existence, which offers a way to understand reality. It argues there are three characteristics that apply to and define literally everything. They are suffering, impermanence, and "no soul."

The first mark of existence recognizes that bad things happen and suffering occurs. Everyone goes through hardships. Because things are constantly changing, people don't always feel like they achieve the complete satisfaction of getting everything they want in life.

I think those who keep this first mark in mind have it right. If you're aware that suffering is inevitable—and have that embedded in your brain from the beginning of an adverse event—you're going to move way faster toward acceptance.

The second Buddhist mark of existence is impermanence: nothing lasts forever. This ties back to the inevitability of change; nothing stays the same because everything in life is subject to change. This is where many people struggle with adversity. A lot of us don't want to acknowledge or accept that everyday changes happen in our lives, let alone adverse moments. We've all heard the phrase *humans are creatures of habit*. Think about what drives these habits; we're always trying to make ourselves comfortable. Routines and habits are part of those pathways that have been beaten into our brains through conditioning. We are instinctively driven to eliminate our suffering in order to live more comfortable lives. But because even good things can't last forever, we wind up battling constant change in our efforts to stay comfortable.

The instinct to fight it makes sense, but it's actually counterintuitive. If you can accept that change and adversity (after all, the terms are nearly interchangeable) are fundamentally part of your life, then building a tool like authentic resilience to confront and adjust to change can be one of the keys to living joyfully.

The third mark of existence is a bit more controversial for those who don't practice Buddhism (including me). But hear me out before you write it off, because you need not subscribe to this belief literally to take an important lesson from it. The third mark of existence: there is no soul.

Like I said, hear me out!

While I personally disagree with the idea that there is no real soul, I think we can benefit from considering the simpler idea behind this belief: our egos make each of us the center of our own world when in reality we are all much more connected to each other and the universe than we typically perceive. In truth, we are not the center of everything. We all know this on a logical level, but the ego makes it difficult to internalize this truth. If you can rewire your brain to accept this wholeheartedly so that it's part of your authentic resilience, this can help you get to the acceptance phase much, much faster.

Realizing that you're not always the center of suffering in the world—and that no suffering can last forever, because change is inevitable—enables you to acknowledge reality in a way that leads to resilience. More important, it will be a resilience that intentionally responds to the world around you, rather than instinctually reacting to it based on patterns instilled from past threats.

Don't let the simplicity of this description mislead you. The path to acceptance can be scary. There's a reason it's the downward part of the Reality Curve graph: shock, fear, pain, frustration, and other suffering are all powerful negative feelings. But if you acknowledge that experiencing these emotions means that you're moving *through* the suffering, you can feel secure in the knowledge that you are inevitably headed for that curve on the other side.

This acceptance allows you to deeply connect to how you feel and brings more clarity to your self-awareness. When you're in this state, you first realize that acceptance can be productive, that living your most joyful life involves accepting reality as it is and working with whatever that brings you. Life is full of choices. Acceptance doesn't mean complacency or giving up; we can accept something while at the same time trying to make it better. What's important is the mindset you create. When you accept the opportunity to grow and learn, you enable resilience.

Coping with Suffering: Avoid Learned Helplessness

Why is it so important to reach the acceptance stage of the Reality Curve? If you don't face the adversity in front of you, you can quickly lose all sense of control in your life.

When it seems like bad things keep happening to us—especially events over which we have no power, such as a terrorist attack or earthquake—we feel out of control. Over time, we begin to feel helpless, powerless to stop what's happening to us, even when later situations are more controllable than the scenarios described above. Our minds can get hijacked by these thoughts and fall into what psychologist Martin Seligman calls learned helplessness, the idea that we can be conditioned to be helpless. Learned helplessness is the passivity that often develops within us after we have faced adversity or changes that we can't control. We learn to tolerate pain and respond by being helpless rather than by working to change it. Further, we can get stuck in a spiral state of learned helplessness that can lead to depression, which can be conscious or unconscious.[20]

The way out of this spiral—the way to immunize yourself against learned helplessness—is to regain awareness of your "locus of control."[21] This refers to your agency: your ability to meet the world on your own terms, choose your mindset, and choose your actions. Those who are immunized against learned helplessness never give up.

That's what you see at the bottom of the curve; you've faced reality, acknowledged your suffering, and accepted that you lost control of your reality. Now you're ready to take it back.

CORE TENET 2: CONTROL IT

To take control of your reality, you need to shift your mindset from a place of suffering to a place of advertunity. This is the whole point of building resilience: it minimizes unnecessary time spent suffering before bouncing beyond.

Coping with Suffering: Engage a Growth Mindset

As you accept the reality of change and adversity, you shift from what Stanford psychologist Carol Dweck describes as a fixed mindset into what she's dubbed a growth mindset. The growth mindset enables you not only to face reality, but also *do something* about it.

Dweck explains, if you believe that you're not able to change, and that your qualities are unchangeable—that is, you're fixed—then you're going to prove yourself right repeatedly and you'll stay fixed. On the other hand, a growth mindset understands the self as in flux, able to shift and adapt. Adopting this mindset allows you to persist in the face of adversity and setbacks as you move through reality. The growth mindset is also fundamental to how you look at energy (and how much effort you put into building resilience). This mindset enables your mind to bend and learn from criticism and different alternative inputs to help with the rewiring process.

The growth mindset also enables you to learn and uncover inspirations in the success of others. It gives you a stronger sense of free will and control in your life, which are necessary to take back control of your reality. Your view of yourself and your mindset as you move into this stage can make or break everything.

When building resilience, you have to combat previous conditioning and rewire your brain. Trying to do this with a fixed mindset is a heck of a lot harder to do. But if you've got a growth mindset, you're going to be able to build that resilience faster, because the growth mindset enables advertunity, which enables you to then take control. It empowers you to use that neuroplasticity to change perspectives and keep your mind open while you learn.

The growth mindset is based on the belief that your basic qualities—which include your sense of self (your authenticity) and your ability to overcome adversity and take back control (your resilience)—can be grown, cultivated, and developed through your own efforts. Growth mindset basics for building resilience start not by asking *can* I be resilient, but asking *how* do I build my resilience. Looking at how to engage, how to persist, and how to learn from adversities is a step in the right direction. People with a growth mindset are in control of the "how" while those with fixed mindsets often merely never ask how. (For the record, reading the book in your hands and practicing its recommendations are growth mindset-building activities!)

You are more in control of things than you think. Daniel Kahneman, award-winning psychologist and Nobel Laureate, talks about this sense of control in his research on experiencing ourselves versus our memory of ourselves.

He suggests that people make choices using two systems

of thought. System 1 is fast, instinctive, and emotional while System 2 is slower, more deliberate, and more logical.[22] He explains the concept of two selves—the experiencing self and the remembering self. The experiencing self does the living, but it is the remembering self that ultimately "rates" the experiences we face by the "maximum or the minimum of the experience." In Kahneman's research, the remembering self dominated his patients' ultimate conclusions of experience in life.[23]

In other words, our experiencing self tends to feel out of control in the moment, but our remembering self, looking back over the summation of our pleasures or pains, usually realizes that in fact we had been mostly in control.

Having a growth mindset and taking control enables you to be more comfortable with the risk and effort of making things happen for yourself. This then opens the possibility to advertunity. Mindset and advertunity go hand-in-hand. Without a growth mindset and its related thinking, it is harder to look for those opportunities that build resilience. No doubt, without a growth mindset, it's also challenging to make decisions that are unique and authentic to you.

Coping with Suffering: Develop Learned Optimism

When we shift to a growth mindset, it can often lead us to develop a new optimistic lens, which is vital to regaining agency.

To understand this, let's consider what stunts recovery. Author and business executive Sheryl Sandberg categorizes such challenges into "the Three Ps": personalization, the belief that we are at fault; pervasiveness, the belief that the adversity will affect all areas of our lives; and permanence, the belief that aftershocks of the event will last forever.[24] (I guess the "impermanence" mark of existence means that Buddhists are optimists!)

All of these beliefs are pessimistic. More important, they're *false*. These are internal responses to adversity based on learned helplessness. According to Seligman (the one who coined the term "learned helplessness"), the way to take control back from challenges such as the Three Ps is to foster a more optimistic mindset. That doesn't mean you have to be happy-go-lucky all the time (Buddhists aren't!) or always expect the best of circumstances. It simply means releasing that internalization of helplessness.

Spiritualists and scientists agree: optimists respond to adversity as external (not personal), limited (not pervasive), and temporary (not permanent). When we look at an adverse event and optimistically believe that we are not at fault, it won't affect all of the areas of our life, and it won't last forever, this will actually lead us to an easier way of handling adversity. It leads us to be able to control and take back the power of choice.

When we take an optimistic approach, we are able to perform better, build better results, and persist (and live) longer than pessimists. In contrast, people who don't respond favorably to adversity often suffer in all aspects of their lives. In a thirty-two-year longitudinal study of children in Kauai, researchers discovered that, among high-risk kids experiencing trauma, a certain number were nonetheless able to succeed in adolescence and adulthood. It was those who displayed resilience, those who believed *they* (not their circumstances) affect the outcomes and achievements of their lives. This ability enabled them to further develop an internal locus of control and positive social orientation, which enabled them to flourish. They felt they were the ones controlling their own fate.[25]

There are numerous examples proving that reframing and using an optimistic approach *does* help us get through the Reality Curve faster. It empowers us to identify the best options to control the situation and fire up the courage within us to build the resilience we need to get through life's hard stuff.[26]

RESPONSES TO ADVERSITY

	Pessimists	Optimists
Response to Adversity	Personal	External
	Pervasive	Limited
	Permanent	Temporary

Adapted from *Adversity Quotient*, Paul Stoltz

Growth + Optimism = The Advertunity Mindset

If you can coordinate your mind to be optimistic, open, and accepting, you're moving up the Reality Curve and are now able to see the opportunity inside the change or struggle you're dealing with. If you can embrace that mindset, you can propel yourself forward into the solution. This is when your brain starts using neuroplasticity to build stronger authentic resilience, because you're finding those answers for yourself. You are seeing opportunities in the adverse moments for yourself in a way that is your own. Inside of that is hope, because when you take control for yourself again, you give yourself the opportunity to start the recovery process and institute a plan for solving the problems you face.

You always have more control than you think. A great example of this is in *Man's Search for Meaning* by Viktor Frankl, an Austrian neurologist who was a survivor of the Holocaust. In his book, Frankl discusses his experience in a Nazi concentration camp. Frankl describes the loss of control apparent in prisoners who succumbed to ominous warnings they heard upon entering camp. Guards told all the prisoners they'd never leave. Those who believed it died shortly after arriving. Those who rejected the guards' warnings and retained a belief "that this too shall pass" usually survived. Even for Frankl himself, he continued to remind himself that despite the horrific conditions, he had greater control of himself than did the guards who tortured him—because he had "the last of the human freedoms—to choose one's attitude in any given set of circumstances, to choose one's own way" when responding.[27] This is an early illustration suggesting that when we stave off helplessness, we have far more internal control than we think we do at the time of an adversity.

This is the power of authentic resilience. There's personal power in taking control back. You get to move forward in the Reality Curve and bounce beyond. This is the birthplace of hope and courage; now you have the power to plan and take action.

CORE TENET 3: PLAN IT AND TAKE ACTION

Now that you've consciously realized you are in control and have agency over your choices, and have activated a growth mindset, you have one thing left to overcome before you're ready to take action: brain distortions.

Annoying Brain Distortions

When you're at the point of thinking through how to control your reality and building a plan of action, you can expect to run into some problems that will make this phase more challenging. This is due to what I call "brain annoyances."[28] Brain annoyances are tendencies of the brain that can lead you astray; they're distortions that get in the way of your ability to accurately identify and respond to a situation. There are a few common ones people encounter in times of adversity, but they can all be characterized in one sentence: the brain has a tendency to believe things that aren't true. And when these false beliefs turn up, they need to be dealt with before you can move on to the planning tenet of the Reality anchor.

This chapter has already discussed the insidious overarching driver of these brain distortions: learned helplessness.

Remember when I talked about having more control than you think? This is the stage where your brain likes to tell itself that you have no power to change anything. But you already know that's not true; at this point, you've regained awareness of your agency. As long as you never give that up, you can push yourself to never give up on other things. This tenacity is an immunization against learned helplessness.

So how do you gain that tenacity and take control back? Reframing. Again, we see this concept of changing perspectives. It matters. To reframe a problem is to reconceptualize it by looking at it from a different perspective. This alters the perception of the level of difficulty the adversity presents. That in turn may open up new avenues for action.

Let's talk about some of the most common false beliefs people encounter and how to reframe them.

- **The all-or-nothing distortion:** Binary thinking around the adversity that paints a black-and-white picture of success and failure or of right and wrong. This thinking is problematic because if there's no room for gray when dealing with the issue, then we will wind up believing that the plan for overcoming it *has* to be perfect. We'll think, "If it's imperfect, it won't work." This kind of thinking is paralyzing. How to reframe: Leave room for imperfection. By operating in gray instead, you leave room to try different things, to tweak and revise the plan, and to tolerate initial failures. Humans are not perfect. Solutions are not always perfect. Accepting this enables you to actualize your plan.
- **The fortune-telling distortion:** Trying to predict the outcome of the situation (and usually getting it wrong). The human brain tends to easily fall into making bad assumptions, which can cause misfired signals in response to a problem or outcome that doesn't actually exist, because our strongest intuitions are often wrong and we sometimes use the wrong data to make decisions.[29] How to reframe: Try to think positively instead of planning for disaster. When you're trying to push your way through a stressor, it's helpful to make positive assumptions. Doing so will help lead to positive outcomes.
- **The personalization distortion:** Thinking, *Why me?* Think back to the third Buddhist mark of existence; people can't help but (falsely) see themselves as the center of everything. This ego-centric thinking is a natural distortion of the brain that leads us to the belief that people around us are behaving the way they are—or things in the environment are happening around us—because of something that we did. We tend to blame ourselves or take things personally and it gets in the way of being able to objec-

tively identify the adversities we face. How to reframe: Try to objectively think about what is and isn't your crap to deal with. Someone else's actions are never in your control, so don't take them personally. Try to internalize that you really aren't the center of the universe—and that's a good thing!

- **The magnification distortion:** Drawing conclusions and misfiring on wrong or incomplete information. Also, generalizing things or blowing details out of proportion. These lead us to make choices that aren't well-informed because even though we think we have the whole picture, we actually don't. How to reframe: Be objective and look at the facts. Think about how the current situation resembles adversities you've faced in the past and apply the knowledge and resilience you gained from those experiences to the present. Make sure you have all of the information you need to see the full picture.

Reframing can shift your experience of adversity or change in ways that will not only let you see problems differently, but also allow you to experience and manage them differently, too. When we understand our brain distortions and the often-wrong beliefs that lead to learned helplessness, we can flip them on their heads—turning helplessness into optimism, reminding us again that with a growth mindset we have choices.

Now you're ready to develop a road map to build your resilience and get through this adversity. There are three steps: identify and reframe the hard parts, build solutions, and take action.

Step 1: Identify and Reframe the Hard Parts

Look at the continuum of your control and identify the hard parts. By hard parts, I mean whatever is going to be most challenging for you to overcome as you work through this adversity.

The hard parts are found when you reflect back to the suffering. Think about what you're up against. What type of adversity is it? Is it the internal or external kind? Is it one of the seven types or an intersection of those different categories of adversities? Where's the hard part inside of that adversity that you have to overcome to move forward?

The next part of this step goes back to reframing. In addition to reframing distorted thinking from false beliefs, you're going to need to reframe the adversity itself.

To visualize reframing, draw from your past experiences. Think about challenges that you've overcome before, or that you've seen others overcome. What worked well? What didn't? Doing this will also help you be more present in the moment. By taking your mind away from disaster planning for the future, you are intentionally stopping the negative thoughts about the adversity you're facing and choosing to think positively. Looking at the situation differently may then give you new options to explore in the next step.

For example, let's turn to a former client of mine who lost his job and its benefits. This happened not because of his performance, but because of internal politics. He was forced to resign because the new boss who beat him out for the top seat was uncomfortable with him still being around.

This is a social, environmental, emotional, and financial adversity that intersected at the point of the conversation when he was asked to resign. There was both internal and external adversity and with many hard parts to overcome:

telling his family, losing income, losing health insurance, and worrying about the future without a job, to name a few.

The reframe here was knowing that his partner had a solid job, health insurance, and stability. He used this knowledge to remind himself that he would be okay and find a way to work through the shock of being unemployed. The major underlying element that needed solving was how to communicate what happened to his partner and family. The advertunity for him? Maybe this would be the moment he decided to become a stay-at-home parent, something he'd secretly wanted for a long time.

At this step, it's important to clearly identify the underlying issue at the heart of the adversity; it's the one that, if solved, would have the biggest impact on the situation. Use that to move to Step 2. Is there an advertunity? If so, how can you seize it?

Step 2: Build Solutions

Now that you're thinking with a more optimistic outlook, you're ready for the ideation step. This is where you're taking all the information you've gathered in Step 1 and using it to develop solutions.

Most of the time, the primary goal here is to get out of the adverse moment, with a secondary goal to build resilience and learn from that adversity. This step is where you figure out *how* you're going to do that by generating as many ideas as you can to look at the problem from different angles and solve it. It's one of the best ways to weave your left and right brain together, activating that prefrontal cortex in the process.

The developmental stage of this step is known as **divergent thinking,** a thought process that often occurs in a spontaneous, random, free-form, free-flow, non-structured way of grabbing ideas that may enable solution generation.[30] The obvious first method to ideating solutions is to try brainstorming or, as its sometimes known, blue-sky thinking. Simply throw your ideas on a piece of paper and use that to consider what you want to do. You can do this by making lists or mind mapping to see what comes out. Don't attach judgment to anything you write. List every action you can possibly do and go from there without trying to get it right the first time.

Another method is to try proposing a solution in the form of a "what happens if I do X" question and working from there. This is a good way to practice the "yes, and" concept—saying and thinking "yes, and" instead of "no, but." When you say "yes, and," you can expand your thinking with more positive language. If you say, "no, but," you'll limit your options by failing to consider some.

The next stage is **convergent thinking,** which is when you diagnose and evaluate the ideas that you put on the lists or mind maps or whatever you made in the first stage. This is a more structured, categorical, systematic, logical, and "linear" approach. For example, take all the ideas you first generated and now list them in columns of "pro" and "con" or "advantages" and "disadvantages."

An interesting bridge between these two modes of thinking is the theory of appreciative inquiry, developed by David Cooperrider and Suresh Srivastva.[31] In short, appreciative inquiry is a method of consideration whereby one looks to things that are working and then builds on those in order to solve problems. (This is the flip side of the more conventional approach to solving problems, which is to look at what's not working and focus on fixing that.) Ask yourself, *What's always worked for me in the past? Can that help me in the present?*

While there are modern theorists and business leaders who like to say, "What got you here won't get you there," this is still a useful exercise for expanding your thinking—and by hinging on personal experiences, it also helps you explore and develop authenticity.

You've probably already realized how this ties back to our earlier discussion about times in the past when you used authenticity to triumph over adversity, which developed a resilience you can continue to draw from in the future. The right mindset is so important; building on positives is vital to making a well-informed plan to get through adversity and build resilience.

Step 3: Take Action

At this stage, you've chosen a solution. Now it's time to act. Go make that happen! And if it's not going the way you thought, tweak it. Edit and revise. Course correct. Then adapt with that new information. This step requires the courage and awareness to accept that you're going to have to learn by trial and error as you go.

You have to keep adjusting the plan to make sure you get to the other side of this adversity. Continually ask yourself: *What am I learning from this? What am I gaining? Am I able to rewire or learn new wiring from what I'm doing? Am I getting through the hump of the adversity?* It's as simple as that.

FACING REALITY IN ACTION

That fateful day in Tokyo, the three-peat catastrophe—earthquake, tsunami threat, and nuclear meltdown—cascaded into innumerable smaller adversities for everyone in the city. Personally, I had to face the fact that I was suddenly responsible for the 200 teenaged employees working in our retail stores that day. My business partner and I had no playbook for three-peat disasters. Initially, she was more in a shock-like panic mode as her body was experiencing this type of adversity for the first time. We quickly had to acknowledge this massive event and figure out how to take control of it (and accept what we couldn't control).

Then, after we sent the employees home, I had to figure out how to get home myself—and handle whatever was waiting for me there. I actually was closer to a friend's house and thought maybe that was a better choice. But along the way, I realized the cell phone towers were knocked out. Luckily, Japan's system of phone booths was still operable. But then I didn't have a phone card. Once I got to my friend's neighborhood, I could use coins to operate the phone to confirm his address. But he was not answering his apartment landline and I ran out of coins. It was one tiny adversity and challenge after the other for millions of dazed and confused Tokyoites wandering around that night. And, of course, we were the lucky ones.

Eventually, I was able to reach my apartment. And by Sunday, phones seemingly were restored, but this only led to more adversities. We needed to address the expat managers who wanted to return home. We had to address the damage to our buildings and structural integrity. We had to face so many realities that follow a major disaster. But inside of these challenges and emotional exhaustion were loads of advertunities.

There were advertunities for us to rise in our leadership and rise as humans to help people. These are just some of the questions that consumed me while I was living through this. I had to address each adversity as it came up, and figure out how to take back control and approach it with a growth mindset and open arms.

My journey through the Reality Curve started fresh with each new adversity. I got through it by constantly asking myself, *How can we learn from this? How do I want to show up for myself?* I took a good, hard look at what kind of leadership I needed to bring—for myself and for the employees I was responsible for. I helped create an old school telephone flow chart to help our employees communicate with their team members and families. We used it constantly, at first just to make sure everybody was okay, then every week to make sure everyone was updated on what the company was doing to take care of them while we figured things out.

It was an opportunity for me to advocate for them with the senior leadership of the company. When things were a little more settled, the CEO came to Japan to signal that we could reopen the store. That was an opportunity for me to be present in that space, not only positionally as the HR leader, but as a human who stayed.

And then there was the adversity of the people who didn't stay because they were afraid of the radiation. So many expats who had the privilege to go back to their home country left the natives of their Japanese community behind to deal with all of this. It still makes me mad because my values would not allow me to leave, even if I'd wanted to. Why would I ever abandon my chosen family and my chosen home in a time of crisis? There were a lot of us who felt that way. Some people even made a T-shirt that said, "I stayed! Tokyo, March 2011." (Only natural-disaster survivors could make a joke like that.)

If they had been strong enough to stay and face reality head-on, take back control, and make a plan, those people who left would have gotten through it. I know, because that's how I've gotten through it, every time. Looking back, I realize the real adversity there wasn't them leaving, but my judgment of them leaving. Those people left because their values were different than mine—and I was angry about it. My judgment of their choice was causing yet another adversity amongst all the other crap.

Staying in Japan after living through this catastrophe taught me how to hope again, and introduced me to the patterns of learned helplessness. I learned how to recover, how to help others find hope, and how to rebuild—both literally in the environment and figuratively within myself. Oftentimes when you get through a shared adversity like these large-scale disasters I've been through, a great learning happens. A brilliant hope is born and through it you form a stronger bond with the people experiencing it with you because everyone had to adapt and collectively push to the other side. It makes everybody stronger. And that's quite a beautiful thing.

When you find the courage to take control and act, you're taking the first steps to building resilience. These are the first steps to hope, recovery, adaptation, and reinforcing courage. And that enables self-confidence and self-worth, which then empower you to drive your resilience to get through adversity. It's really magical when you can activate them all.

KEY TAKEAWAYS

- The Core Tenets of the Reality anchor are Face It, Control It, and Plan It and Take Action.

- Reality Curve is a useful mental mind map of how to begin to tackle an adversity; craft your response, take back control, and learn and grow from hardship.

- The journey of bouncing beyond starts with acknowledging that you've got to go through some suffering to get to acceptance on the other side; understand that suffering is impermanent.

- Recognize that change is inevitable. It's part of everyday life. Changing perspectives is a tool that can help you embrace change and open your mindset.

- You're in control. Authentic resilience building is all about how you take back control from adversity. It's accomplished by facing reality, controlling it, and building a plan to overcome.

- Learned helplessness is the passivity that often develops within us after we have faced adversity or changes that we can't control. It often explains why people give up when facing adversity. Avoid falling into its trappings.

- Advertunity is a key part of reframing and reframing is the key part of advertunity. Using reframing to shift your experience of adversity or change will not only let you see it differently, but will allow you to experience and manage it differently, too.

- Developing an open mindset that embraces advertunity will set you in motion toward learning, growth, and resilience wisdom, all of which will ultimately help your brain and body cope with future adversities.

- Recognizing there are brain distortions and building awareness of them enables you to continue to make a plan and act accordingly when facing obstacles and building resilience.

CHAPTER 4

THE MODEL: ENERGY

SO FAR, 2019 HAD BEEN THE WORST YEAR OF MY LIFE. January started with the death of my beloved Aunt Jo. After a four-and-a-half-year battle with cancer, she passed away. Our family saw it coming and we were fortunate to get to say our goodbyes but that didn't make losing her any easier.

Two weeks after her death, the mother of my best friend, Steve, died. Then my elderly Great Aunt Bea died in March. That same month, my dad lost another sibling, my uncle Mike. They say that people die in threes, but for me it was four people I called family all in the first three months of the year.

Before that, while I was undergoing so much personal tragedy, the community around me was reeling from another death: that of the "one country, two systems" philosophy that had been cracking since the handover agreement between Hong Kong and Beijing in 1997. The introduction of new fugitive and extradition laws born from a high-profile murder case led to protests in March 2019. By early summer, protests comprised of *millions* of people became a mainstay. The scale of the events alone brought international media coverage; then there were the fires, the violence, the tear gas, the bombings, and the riot police.

Normal life came to a halt and was replaced with this Battle Royale on the streets of Hong Kong. It became dangerous to go anywhere in the city, leading to the shutdown of public transportation and many businesses.

Still, the fleet of retail stores I helped support and operate were trying to stay open, so my workdays were filled with the stresses of handling cases of employees who may or may not have been involved with the protests or who had been arrested. Not to mention dealing with the social media policies that were causing fear and internal fighting among employees who sat on different sides of the political issue.

Work. Social media. The streets of the city at large. In no part of the environment around me could I escape the external adversity. On top of that, I was dealing with yet another personal adversity: being in an unfulfilling job with a thankless and unsupportive micromanaging leader who was impossible to please.

And it just kept coming.

In June, upon my return from vacation, I learned my elder dog Vivi—a white toy poodle weighing about four kilograms—was attacked by a sixty-five-kilogram dog at the dog sitter's. Instead of waiting for me at home, Vivi was at the vet's office forty minutes away.

The dog that attacked her had put her in a "death shake" (whipped her back and forth in its jaws) and caused a severe spinal injury. She was nearly killed, but I guess my dog had her own sense of resilience, because she survived—though it left her paralyzed in all four legs due to a massive blood clot on her spinal cord. The clot eventually broke up on its own, and she ultimately did learn to walk and play again after three months of therapy, acupuncture, and rehabilitation.

By September, all of my well-being buckets were empty. I had no physical energy, emotional energy, mental energy, or spiritual energy left—making it not a great time for me to then be hospitalized for five days with an acute inter-ureter kidney stone that failed to drop on its own.

All of the deaths, the near dying of my dog, the daily conflicts of Hong Kong, the conflict of my daily work duties, and the stress of my health issues brought me to my breaking point. As much as I tried to use previous experiences and learning to persevere, regrettably, I took on a learned helplessness. As a result, nothing I tried to do to problem-solve or think differently was working. I tried to chalk it up merely to having no playbook for protests and war zone experiences, but there was something more going on.

I became increasingly numb to taking on more challenges. I had no empowerment. My decisions at work were always trumped, so why bother? I felt like I had no control over any of the work or life decisions I was trying to make because no one ever listened to my input. It was not just stress; it was beyond burnout. I didn't realize that the weight of all of the adversities was stacking up. They were piling on and depleting me slowly.

None of my usual tactics for self-care and recovering (yoga, listening to music, and journaling) were working for me. They weren't helping me hijack that hopelessness spiral or cope with all the death. I felt stuck in crisis. I lost hope that I'd ever get to the place where I wanted to be professionally at that company—or in my life. That hopelessness fed my helplessness, creating a feedback loop known as "the spiral of despair."[32] Psychologist Dr. Paul Stoltz clarifies it this way, "Helplessness validates the loss of hope. Hopelessness becomes a self-fulfilling prophecy, proving how helpless one truly is." Ultimately, he adds, "hopelessness is the cancer of the soul. It sucks the life and energy from its host."[33] As someone who has had skin cancer twice, I can confirm that it truly *felt* like a cancer. My soul felt empty and I realized I was falling deeper into not just a funk, but a full-on depression.

There was one thing that briefly picked me up. It was a decision that I'd made to try to go for one last hijack in a big way, which was to join the relay triathlon that the company leadership team did annually. I signed up for the running portion, knowing I could handle it because I've run full marathons before. When the event came, I ran the race and the team finished. We all had a hurrah. Everyone felt great...but I still felt very flat.

We had achieved our purpose, but it didn't hijack anything. In fact, I felt worse. I realized the real reason I had signed up was to try to please the team and the boss. But no one cared. No meaning was derived from the event other than "to have a good time." When we got back to the office, nothing had changed between my boss and me.

I, on the other hand, was different. It was in that moment that I started to see my therapist and realize the importance of having a good network outside of work. I realized I needed to make some different choices and refocus, take control of my energy, and do some things differently.

Case in point: in December, during yet another unearned lecture about my performance from my self-righteous boss, something in me snapped and I bluntly announced that I didn't actually believe he prioritized psychological safety or its people, the way he preached. Moments later, I was asked to consider leaving the organization. At the time, I was devastated: *was this the end of my career?* But in retrospect, after a year of helplessness and hopelessness, it was actually one of the best things that could have happened.

That's what I want to share in this chapter. In the worst year of my life, I able to start shaking off the helplessness. I started to rebuild hope, because I was able to remember who I was and what my energy needed to be. I was finally in a place to take control, breathe life into my plan, and make better choices. Even better, this time would lead me to a place where I could use the learning of all of that year to ensure that nothing would ever break me again.

BREAKING FROM LEARNED HELPLESSNESS: THE CORE TENETS OF ENERGY

Once I'd accepted reality and built a plan for how I was going to get back to myself, I was ready to rebuild hope and refocus all of the energy that had previously been draining out of me.

In Chapter 3, you learned how to get to this point by acknowledging and accepting reality and embracing the advertunity mindset. When you've got a plan, you need to breathe life into it. Let's talk about how to harness the Energy portion of the REAL model to bounce beyond.

Becoming aware of your energy management is crucial to the process of building and using authentic resilience because energy gives you the most control to *respond* to adversity (with intention, mindfulness, and a recollection of resilience) rather than just react (instinctively and without jurisdiction of your own lived experiences). Controlling your energy enables you to manage your time and your emotions more effectively as you work to rise above the adversities you face. There are three core tenets to the Energy anchor: Understand Your Energy Regulation, Recover Your Energy, and Use Your Energy.

CORE TENET 1: UNDERSTAND YOUR ENERGY REGULATION

Think of energetic domains like an electric battery. You have to be charged up in these main aspects of your well-being to operate at your best. But like electric batteries, your energy can't run 24/7 without any time for recharging. We're not built to "keep going and going" like the Energizer Bunny (who ironically is the mascot for a product that does eventually die).

The key to optimal performance in everything you do is the *oscillation of energies*. Authors and performance and engagement experts Jim Loehr and Tony Schwartz describe oscillation as the controlled fluctuation between engagement and recovery time. In their research, they exemplify this concept through observations of athletes. When athletes are at peak performance, they are fully engaging all energetic domains. But between competitions or events, there needs to be a lot of recovery time for them to be able to perform at their best in the next round.[34]

According to Loehr and Schwartz, there are four domains of energy: physical, emotional, mental, and spiritual. (Their book *The Power of Full Engagement* offers a game-changing way to think, and I have adapted many of its techniques in my own life and coaching practice.) Let's get started.

Physical energy is self-explanatory; it's energy in your body. The power that you use to move, eat, and breathe all draw from this domain. On a biological level, physical energy is connected to the hormones in your brain (cortisol or adrenaline, for example) that activate physiological responses—such as fight/flight/freeze, hunger, or exhaustion—in your body. Taking these responses as signals and cues is fundamental to your physical well-being. Physical energy entails the "essential" stuff: sleep, hydration, exercise, and nutrition. It's blood pressure and cholesterol, diabetes and menstruation; it's all those things you talk about with your doctor.

It's here in our physical energy that humor emerges from our lips in laughter or when we spit out water in hysteria. Physical energy is what wires us as humans—literally during sexual intercourse—and keeps us continuing to evolve as a species. The physical energy among us keeps us connected and it's why we love eating together, hanging out together, connecting and sharing life's moments together.

Emotional energy is the accessing of your feelings and experiences. Those positive emotions that feel empowering and the negative ones that feel disengaging draw from this domain. The biological aspect of this energetic domain deals with mood-affecting hormones such as oxytocin, serotonin, dopamine, and endorphins. You build your "emotional muscles" of self-confidence, self-control, social skills, and empathy through flexing and tearing your emotional energy. This usually occurs by going through challenging emotional experiences. These can include difficult changes such as divorce or the death of a loved one; daily experiences such as a bus being late; or more subtle, long-term experiences like growing irritation and resentment at the workplace. All of these experiences are small "tears" that we can use to build our "muscles" for emotional capacity. Even positive emotional experiences help build capacity. Our emotional energy encompasses the fundamentals of the human condition: relationships with others and our own experiences with joy, sorrow, pain, triumph. The old American television show Wide World of Sports had a catchphrase—"the thrill of victory and the agony of defeat"—that provides both a melodramatic and humorous way to remember emotional energy.

Mental energy is the stimulation of your brain. Learning, making plans, thinking through visualizations, mental preparation, and focusing your attention all draw from this domain—as does your creativity. Mental energy is our focus and ability to sustain concentration and thinking over time. We bounce between rational thought and intuitive thought and often contain several points of view about many topics. The mental energy domain powers many important functions in your daily life. This can get overwhelming some days, especially when the calendar is full of work, family, and social appointments.

Spiritual energy relates to your calling. Any work you do toward defining your goals, inner beliefs, and values draws from this domain. Spiritual energy comes from understanding who you are, your authentic self. It's the wind in your sail as you chase your north star, the direction you take in living your life with purpose. It is within this domain that we hold purpose and generally empower ourselves to make meaning of our lives. For religious people, this is also the space where faith in a higher power, deity, or the universe is anchored. Purpose and spiritual energy are often connected.

Angela Duckworth writes in her book, *Grit*, that spiritual purpose is likened to her "ultimate aim, my life philosophy... My compass, once I found all the parts and put it together, keeps pointing me in the same direction."[35] Her book is rooted in the notion of perseverance and the desire to drive life with purpose. To be "gritty" is to know what drives your life force. To this end, purpose and spiritual energy are often connected. Duckworth opens a chapter in her book by declaring, "purpose—the intention to contribute to the well-being of others."[36] I love that. We will talk more about this connection in the next chapter on Authenticity in the context of purpose building.

Energy Is Interconnected

The nature of the four energetic domains is deeply connected. They tend to deplete and replenish in tandem because your physical state heavily influences your mental and emotional state (and vice versa), which all contribute to the state of your spiritual energy.

An excellent illustration of this for physical and emotional energy is in the energy matrix by Loehr and Schwartz.[37] In a matrix of four quadrants where high and low physical energy intersect with positive and negative emotional energy, each quadrant represents the moods that result from the interconnected influence the domains have on each other.

If you have high physical energy and positive emotional energy, that's when you feel invigorated, confident, and up to any challenges that come your way.

When high physical energy is influenced by negative emotional energy, you end up feeling angry, fearful, anxious, defensive, or resentful.

When you have low physical energy and positive emotional energy, you tend to feel relaxed and peaceful.

If your physical energy is low and your emotional energy is negative, you experience depression, exhaustion, burnout, hopelessness, and defeat.

A matrix can be made for each combination of the energetic domains, because they all impact you in a similar way. Understanding how your mind is organized and how it uses mental energy is also very important to understanding self-regulation of your energy. If our mental energy is down and our batteries are drained, we make poor decisions. It's why we misspeak or say things we normally know we shouldn't. The filters that control our emotions and how we process language—and therefore, what we say "in the moment"—come from this space.

ENERGY MATRIX

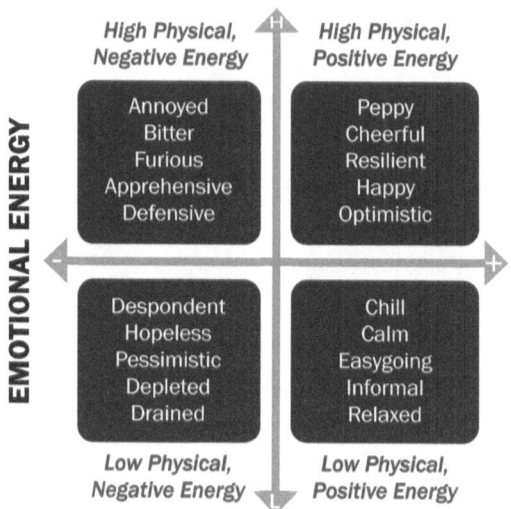

Adapted from *The Power of Full Engagement*, Loehr and Schwartz, 2003

All of your energies influence each other, and therefore your mindset. Think about how physical stimulation is shown to improve mental performance. Ever go jogging and get your million-dollar idea? Or as you're in the shower feeling the hot water fall over you, you have a moment of clarity? Perhaps you've been at synagogue or in temple and experienced overwhelming feelings of love and calm as you feel connected to a faith and your spiritual and emotional energies become connected. These are just a few examples of the deeply interconnected nature of your energetic domains.

The interconnectedness of these energies affects your well-being and, notably, how you develop authentic resilience. Without the right balance and the "charge up" of those batteries, it's nearly impossible to do anything. I have said in my well-being work with clients and employees that "if you don't fill up the well-being tank, you will never make it to the bank." It's true. Without the interplay of these energies working inside you in the right balance, it is extremely challenging to have high-quality output for the important (and maybe not-so-important) things you do in your life.

Just as bodybuilders lift increasingly heavier weights to grow their muscle capacity, we also need to grow the capacity of our well-being energies. That is, we need to learn as much as we can from adversities each time they happen, use the right energies to solve those adversities, and then use that learning to fuel our growth toward resilience. Loehr and Schwartz sum this up perfectly in their work: "Stress is not the enemy in our lives. Paradoxically, it is the key to growth."[38]

It's not a coincidence that our well-being energies are closely connected to the hierarchy of needs developed by Abraham Maslow. (It should be noted that Maslow's construct isn't perfect and has been criticized in academia for good reason. But for the purposes of this core tenet, the generalized model is sufficient.) You can see the connection easily between how we use energy to fuel our motivations in life. Each one of the energy domains builds on the other and, as stated before, are interconnected.

If we look at the energetic domains and the hierarchy of needs side by side, you can see that physical energy and physiological needs align and form the bottom of the pyramid. As energy connects to the emotional level, the correlation to safety, security, love, and relationships is in parallel. Similarly, mental energy and cognitive needs form the next level of energy to perform work and be satiated to learn. Finally, the connection between spiritual and self-actualization.

ENERGY/MASLOW STACKS

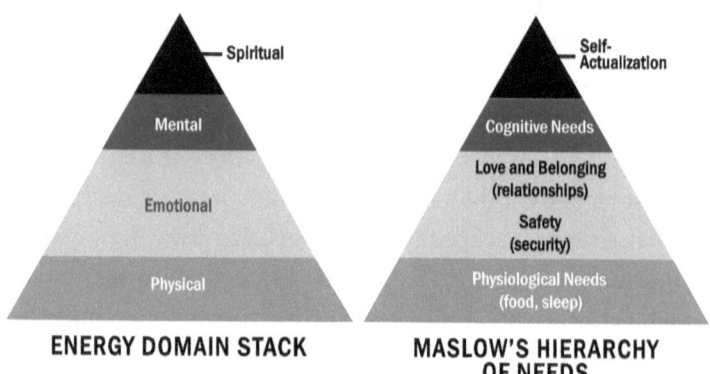

ENERGY DOMAIN STACK **MASLOW'S HIERARCHY OF NEEDS**

Maintaining and regulating your energetic domains is vital to building authentic resilience and overcoming adversity because they are the power source of everything you do. It's where you can find the drive to take control back from the stressors in your life. If you want to do more in your life, a key factor is to continue to build that capacity in your well-being batteries. Think of it like increasing the size of your tank. More capacity in the well-being tank is what builds resilience, giving you more energy to learn and grow.

CORE TENET 2: RECOVER YOUR ENERGY

While recovering from the multiple heart surgeries he's had throughout his life, my father would always say, "You have to spend energy to get energy." He's right. But I would add to that, you have to make your energy *count*.

As alluded to earlier, think of your energy like a muscle. People build muscle by putting their bodies under strain to break down that muscle so that afterward, when they're in recovery, the muscle can grow stronger than it was before. This builds the body's capacity to handle even more strain.

Energy works the exact same way. Growing your capacity to handle the strain of adversity is vital to building your authentic resilience. And just like your ideal workout routine should be unique to your individual needs, your methods for building your energetic capacity should also be unique to you. Different activities work for different people, so this is the part of the process where you really need to know yourself.

If your basic needs aren't met, you can't build your capacity for strain (energetic or physical). The nature of the energetic domains is interwoven. You can't have the mental clarity you need to think problems through if you're not taking care of your body's need for food and water. You have to meet the pyramid of needs to properly build your capacity in each energetic domain.

A famous study of elite chess players in the 1970s discovered that playing at the highest level around the world could burn more than 6,000 calories a day and lose up to twenty pounds over the course of a chess tournament.[39] This is due to physiological responses to the mental stress of playing the game. Today, chess players train similarly to professional athletes in order to sustain their energy during long tournaments.

Robert Sapolsky, a Stanford biology professor and neuroendocrinology expert, references the study in his own investigation into the connections between mental and physical energy. I am especially interested in Sapolsky's findings on stress recovery and his insights into the costs of energy. He explains that a failure to recover energy can lead to a host of health problems.[40] Recovering energy is just as important as spending it. We cannot function at an energy deficit. In the same way, recharging and recovering energy is key to building resilience.

Audit Your Energy

There's not much point in diving into all the good things you can do to recover your energy if it's all just going to get spent on things that don't serve you. So before you start figuring out what recharges you, take the time to think about what's draining you, and why. I like to think of it as energy-positive activities and energy-negative activities.

My therapist, Dr. Kaili Chen, once pointed out that I was spending a lot of time and energy on things that didn't fulfill me. In fact, often I was in pursuit of goals that did not bring me any personal satisfaction and frequently left me depleted. In this session, we talked about how to evaluate the things that were draining me.

We created a list of the biggest energy-negative aspects of my life. This included my job, lack of control in my work and personal life, confidence depletion about both my body/appearance and performance in my roles, and lack of time to do work I enjoyed (among a number of other things).

Creating the list was super helpful. In addition to seeing the energy drains, I was also able to tie a few of them together. Like the helpless-hopeless spiral, many of my stressors were linked in ways I hadn't realized. On top of that, many of the pressures robbing me of energy were entirely self-imposed! Pema Chödrön's famous words made more sense to me: "The most difficult times for many of us are the ones we give ourselves."[41] Over time, I came to realize much of my own pain and suffering was from things I was consciously choosing, like my job. I was constantly spending energy on this energy-negative aspect of my life and failing to recharge, resulting in constantly running on "low battery" mode and ignoring the prompts my body and mind were giving me to fuel up.

So how could I fuel up? I couldn't just quit my job and stop working. Dr. Chen helped me answer this question by doing an energy audit. We systematically reviewed each energy domain, evaluating what fills up the battery and what depletes it.

We identified factors like sleep and diet choices that were impacting different energy domains and exacerbating problems that previously seemed unrelated. The list was long and messy, because nearly everything was connected. Ultimately, the energy audit process revealed that I was not working in my purpose. Looking at my spiritual energy sources and drains made me realize my purpose was far from the center of my day-to-day life.

This energy audit had a strong impact on me. Exploring the things that light me up and recharge me—and those that didn't—gave me the clarity I was seeking. It helped me understand that goals are very different from purpose. This distinction is important because often we chase goals at the cost of being truly in the higher purpose of our lives.

Letting go of the things that don't serve you is not an easy venture. Sometimes it's work; other times it's people or relationships that you have to let go. A few signs that indicate your energy is in the wrong place include prolonged lack of fulfillment in the activities in which you're engaging, continued frustration with outcomes from energy inputs, and overall tendency to skew toward negativity in your life. These signals can help you understand what might be worthy of letting go.

For example, a colleague once told me she had decided to stop going out with some girlfriends she'd had for many years after realizing the only thing they still had in common was getting drunk together. She realized she no longer derived fulfillment or joy from drinking with them and she often regretted losing time that could have been spent doing something else. The activity had evolved into an energy-negative experience.

Similarly, many of us have experienced when a friendship emerges as one-sided and we realize we're the one doing all the work to make the friendship work with no reciprocation on the other person's part. These are simple but powerful examples of when the signals that something's not serving you speak loudly—and letting go of those things can help you to return to energy-positive activities.

Now that you have an idea of what falls under energy-positive and energy-negative for you, you can better regulate your energy spending by looking for ways to "invite in" energy-positive activities. If the energy-negative activities are draining your needs, look for things that can be energy-positive contributions to help fulfill those needs. Enjoyable activities stimulate the happy hormones in the body and can help you shift energy.

Charge Your Batteries

Now let's talk about how to charge up your batteries. The short answer is this: you need to build good routines, habits, and boundaries that are authentic to you to help create consistent outcomes of recovering your energy at each level of the pyramid, starting from the bottom (that is, first physical, then emotional, mental, and finally spiritual).

As we discussed in the previous chapters, building resilience is taking back control from an adversity. When you charge your batteries, you enable yourself to be in control of what you do through energy-positive activities with your physical body, your emotional self, your mind, and your connection to purpose. These are going to help build resilience. Gaining this control back and banking the energy enables you to then take action in combatting the adversities you find in life.

There is no one-size-fits-all formula for building these. Activities that make me feel refreshed and charged up might be draining to you. Boundaries that bring me comfort may be unnecessary for you. We all have different preferences. I can't give you a step-by-step guide to follow to the letter to get your energy back.

What I *can* do is tell you two key concepts. First, charging up your batteries is a practice. It's a discipline, something you have to do regularly, if not every day. Like charging your phone, it's not a one-and-done thing. Second, you need to explore your feelings to find charging methods that are authentic to you. Tapping into your feelings and emotions will help you get to your core values, which will help lead you to the activities that bring you positive energy and help you recharge. When we tap into the things closest to our core, we are more committed to following through with those activities.

Understanding these two concepts enables you to create a continued rhythm of balance, empowering you to breathe energy into your plans for tackling adversity or stressors when they come.

Here are some of the things to look for as you explore your feelings surrounding each energy domain.

For **physical energy,** charging your batteries is all about how you look after your body. Taking control of your diet, sleep routine, and exercise routine will make a difference both in how you regulate your physical energy and in how you *feel* about regulating your energy.[42] Figure out what foods and drinks you should have more of (or less of) in your routines, depending on your needs. In my well-being work, I always encourage people to "eat the rainbow" of foods. Looking for foods and drinks of all colors will help you find a better nutritional baseline. A good tip is to shop the outer ring of a grocery store, where all the fresh foods are located, and try to avoid the middle aisles, where more processed, less-nutritious foods are located.

Find what forms of exercise you like the most. Even if you hate exercise, there's likely some kind of activity you can tolerate. Consider hiking, yoga, aerial dancing, or swimming...or maybe just walking or secretly singing and dancing in your living room. During the COVID pandemic, I often "had lunch" with Lady Gaga—that is, a lunchtime karaoke and dance hour—with me, my sandwich, and a playlist. It did so much to light up my afternoon energy. My endorphin-high from the dance party lunch helped me be more creative, more productive, and happier every afternoon. The possibilities for finding exercise you enjoy are endless.

Sleep is the key recharge here. Experts stress the importance of circadian rhythms and having a solid sleep routine.[43] Avoid napping so you can consolidate rest at night. Try to use your sleeping room only for sleep, and avoid screen time and blue light from mobile devices at night.

This sounds so basic, but you'd be surprised how many of us forget to nourish our bodies with food, sleep, and exercise. Often, we say, "I will start tomorrow." A big part of taking care of ourselves and our energy is paying ourselves first. Dedicate your physical energy-positive activities to yourself. This is how we take back control, learn about ourselves, and build our physical authentic resilience.

Once you find the routines that bring you fun and enjoyment, you'll easily be able to keep your physical batteries charged.

To recover your **emotional energy,** think about what helps you keep up meaningful and appreciative relationships. Maybe you enjoy one-on-one time with your friends individually. Or perhaps you're more extroverted and feel refreshed after a good dinner party with a group of your favorite people. Engaging in social activities that bring you joy will charge your emotional battery. We are social creatures. We evolved to be. Humans would not have survived or reproduced without social contracts. When we connect to others, we can see ourselves more clearly. Creating rituals around how we connect with others helps replenish emotional energy. Some of these rituals may include the practices of kindness and gratitude; both have scientific evidence to support higher emotional regulation and happiness.[44]

A fast way to take back control of your emotional energy is to name your feelings. This is applicable whether the feelings are positive or negative. Then, when experiencing energy-positive feelings, bank them! Savor them so you can recognize what energy-positive emotions feel like.[45] Similarly, when there are energy-negative emotions getting in the way, call them to attention and work through the thoughts and feelings. Mindfulness in this moment—that is, pausing to consciously move that emotion to the prefrontal cortex of your brain—will enable you to regain control of emotional energy.

Many people also use physical energy to help replenish emotional energy. For example, I know a boxer who loves to clear his emotions while in the ring. Find the way that helps you recapture a sense of control over your emotional energy, whether it's an activity you find soothing or cathartic.

Recovering **mental energy** happens when you engage your mind in positive ways. This can be as simple as stopping to take breaks. Try a mindful practice, such as guided meditations (which have been proven to greatly benefit people's brains and mental well-being), or stretching, yoga, or a light walk (remember that our energy domains are connected, so sometimes combining mental with physical recoveries can help the brain relax). Sometimes I can rebuild mental energy simply by pausing to gaze out of a window or to hydrate, as long as I'm being mindful about it. The idea is to shut off your brain and allow your senses to take over and just "be."

If you're a lifelong learner like I am, you may find studying topics that interest you to be the most effective method for this. If you're more introspective, you might prefer things like listening to music. Mental energy-positive activities come in a variety of packages. I always recommend free-flow writing of some kind, but I've had clients who prefer doing crossword and Sudoku puzzles or practicing brief escapism through reading or binge-watching TV. Whatever makes your state of mind feel refreshed is what charges your mental battery. Finally, and as you find out later in Chapter 6 about the Love anchor, sometimes mental recharge comes in the form of speaking with your network, family, and friends, or in the form of giving back by volunteering your time and energy to others.

Spiritual energy is the fuel that sets the rocket to your authenticity on fire. Activities that charge this battery are going to involve investing time in getting to know yourself, uncovering who you are and what you want to do in your lifetime. Tapping into your purpose and sense of calling can charge up your spiritual energy. When I am working in my purpose—writing this book, coaching a client, or talking generally about resilience building and authenticity with people—I both tap into my spiritual energy and recharge it simultaneously. When I am not engaged in my purpose, I find my spiritual energy depleted. Other ways to recharge your spiritual energy include connecting with a higher power or with the community built around your faith-based practices, venturing out into nature, seeking perspective of your life in the bigger picture of the cosmos, and writing and engaging in reflection. Find what works best for you.

When you get **all four of these batteries** charged up and overflowing, that's when you're living in your purpose and achieving a state of flow in which everything moves seamlessly. This is why understanding yourself (and your realms of adversity) is so powerful; you can do so much when you know what's costing you energy and how to recover it. Building good routines to recover energy helps you make better choices in life. And those better choices help you get to a space where you can purposefully focus your energy.

Advertunity Mindset and Energy

In the Reality chapter, you learned about how reframing your mindset empowers you to build resilience. Adversity is an opportunity because it allows you to build the *capacity* for adversity—this is what makes it possible for you to bounce beyond next time. If we go back to our exercise analogy, adversity is the heavy weight you lift to break down (and strengthen) your muscles. Building your "resilience muscles" through managing stressors, and then *resting*, is how you do that.

The resting is just as important as the workout. The same idea applies to energy regulation. When you are in control of regulation and really understand what you need in order to perform—which in our case is using energy to get over an adversity or stressor—you will also understand how much time and effort need to be placed on energy recovery. That's how we grow and build the capacity to take on more.

I once counseled a manager who worked with a junior professional struggling to get her work done each week. It was starting to create a performance issue. The employee was headed toward burnout but didn't know it. What she did know was that her job was in jeopardy. Her manager sat down and asked what the employee found challenging in her daily tasks. It turned out, it wasn't the work itself, but getting to work and home on time. It came to light that the employee was the sole caregiver for her elderly and disabled mother. She was not getting enough recovery time at home for herself because she went home every night and continued to work caring for her family member. While this was a delicate situation, the suggestion to job share and split the role with another part-time worker enabled this employee to have more sleep and self-care time, care for her elder family member, and ultimately improve her work performance. It was a semi-complex action to a simple resolution: more physical energy recovery.

Experiencing adversity isn't the only problem that drains energy. Undervaluing the recovery time needed to recharge your batteries can create more problems. This is common in today's "hustle culture," when people boast about "rise and grind" and the proverbial eight-hour day isn't really eight hours anymore (it's more like ten to twelve).

Think about how much time you have in a day. If you're lucky, you get eight hours of sleep. Which means if you work twelve of those remaining sixteen waking hours, you only have four hours every day to do other things. And because we all have responsibilities and obligations outside of our jobs, you won't spend that entire four hours recharging your batteries. Sure, there's the weekend to rest, but if that were enough, we wouldn't all dread Mondays.

We don't spend enough time recovering after burning so much energy on work. Two days can't fully restore the energy we all push ourselves into spending during the week. And yet we all expect ourselves to just keep going at peak performance despite the lack of recovery time.

The solution isn't to avoid adversity, but to take more opportunities to recover so you're ready for the next advertunity that comes your way. There are a lot of ways you can go about doing this. In addition to building the routines, habits, and boundaries discussed above, you can also work with your brain and your environment to recover energy. Things like scheduling your work and sleep cycle around natural daylight, scheduling time to practice gratitude or go outside, and paying attention to your natural circadian rhythms can contribute to optimizing your energy recovery.

When you understand what depletes you, you can turn it around right there. That's the opportunity in the adversity that weighs on you.

Of course, you can't understand what depletes you until you have a better sense of your authenticity. This is because engaging and aligning with your purpose is one of the most powerful battery chargers available to us. After you've read Chapters 5 and 6, on the Authenticity and Love anchors of the model, come back to this chapter and apply what you've learned to continue focusing your energy and making it count.

CORE TENET 3: USE YOUR ENERGY

Now that you have a good understanding of how to charge

your batteries, you're ready to learn to use energy more effectively. After all, you only have so much to spend between charges; you should be spending it where it does the most good in service of yourself. Many experts emphasize the effectiveness of routine and positive rituals for managing energy. Over time, these rituals become automatic behaviors and help us harness the power of using our energy most productively and efficiently. Here are three guidelines to help you create rituals for making energy count wisely.

The Ritual of Choices

Every single day is full of countless choices in your life. Coffee or tea, black or blue pen, answer or ignore. All of these things are choices you actively make. They all require energy and you are in charge.

Choice is all about control, which you've already learned is something you need to take to start overcoming adversity. Every choice you make has consequences, to which we consciously and unconsciously adapt, leading to more choices.

For example, if you decided to try a new flavor of coffee but found it too bitter, you may then adapt to that choice by either adding sugar or giving it to your friend who prefers bitter coffee. If you give it to your friend, you then unconsciously adapt the rest of your choices for the day because you chose to forego your morning caffeine fix.

But then, in addition to whether or not the results of a choice drain or replenish us, the choice itself costs energy. Further, adapting to those choices also costs energy. But these adaptations are *also* forms of resilience. To better understand your level of control over your choices and adaptations, I suggest embracing what I call the open-arms technique.

If the *act* of making choices and the *results* of those choices both require energy, then it follows that you will want to make beneficial choices. However, we don't always consider all of the options available. Have you ever heard yourself say, "I had to do it—I didn't have another choice"? I call bull on statements like that. You almost always have another choice. You just might not be aware of it.

So, if you're comfortable doing so, take a moment to spread your arms wide so that you feel your shoulder blades touching. Look at your reach. When your arms are that wide open, you can reach way more in front of you than you can with your arms closed off. I believe that when your arms are wide open, your energy is open and you're therefore more able to receive all the things that come to you. When you receive all that energy, you become aware of all the choices available to you. By opening our arms to more energy and advertunity (or opportunity), there is more choice. When our energy is abundant and open, we are able to see those choices and decide what to choose. We are in control. Remember that.

If you live your life with closed-off arms, you're significantly shrinking the window for energy to come into you. Your choices become limited—and if that's the way you want it, great. It's valid to know what you want, stick to that path, and block out distractions.

But if you haven't been happy with how things are going, maybe it's time to consider more choices. Open your arms wide and embrace your growing capacity for energy and resilience in the face of adversity. Try to physically enable as many choices to come in as possible so that you can process and weigh them all, then spend your energy on the choices that will be in the best service of yourself so that you can create new routines that serve your highest good.

Now, let's acknowledge that adding additional options to your decision-making process will require more energy. However, when you're building your authentic resilience, you're pulling on prior learning—developed from prior choices and experiences—to use in future decision-making endeavors, which will simultaneously diminish your tendency to return to choices that deplete. And if you ever get overwhelmed by an abundance of options, hit the pause button. Instead of trying to make the perfect choice, invest a bit of energy and time into determining what you're *not* going to do. Then return to the decision once your energy is topped up.

Making choices that are authentic to you gives you control over your life. When you have control, you're less susceptible to feeling like a victim and falling into learned helplessness. That is the power of choice, and practicing it is one of the best ways to build your resilience.

The Ritual of Learning

The human brain is built to learn. There is research suggesting that 20 percent of the calories we ingest each day go solely to fueling and controlling our brains.[46] Calories are fuel, so essentially that means 20 percent of your daily energy is reserved for your brain to operate and learn.

Every day, through conditioning and neuroplasticity, your brain learns how to respond to the stimuli of different circumstances. Whether you're doing great or making mistakes, actively reinforcing habits or consciously hijacking your mind to break them, or just doing the daily things you need to do to get by, you're spending energy on learning all the time.

It even takes energy to fail. The energy you put into a project or relationship that ultimately doesn't work out is spent.

And while that "failure" has an energy cost, it's not wasted energy. It's energy that was spent on learning. Now you can go forward with that learning and adapt accordingly, which builds your resilience.

Learning is a suggested place to spend energy because, at the same time you're learning whatever you're learning, you can also rewire your brain to become more in line with your purpose *and* to become more resilient. Resilience can be learned. That's been proven by scientific studies.[47]

The Ritual of Making It All Count

When Angela Duckworth talks about grit, she talks about using your practice of learning to build endurance. This is the power of perseverance: spending your energy and then, after recharging, taking what you learned from that cycle and applying it to your next round of spending. Figure out how to use those moments that drain you, recharge your energy, and reconnect to your purpose—so you can make your energy (and time) count.

For example, going back to the events from the worst year of my life, 2019, I realized that spending so much energy on a boss who didn't care for anything I did was a huge waste of time. I was getting nothing out of it. It was time for me to move on and figure out how to get back to doing work that aligned with my purpose of helping people—the thing that drew me to working in HR in the first place.

To make your energy count, you need to spend it with purpose and intention. This is important, so I'm going to say it again: *do things with purpose*. Whenever you're using a substantial amount of your energy, it should be spent working toward a purpose-driven goal.

To achieve that, you need to get good at doing multiple things at once. I don't mean multitasking—that's just performing tasks. In the REAL model, doing multiple things at once means pursuing and balancing the different tracks of your pyramid of needs.

For example, one track that fulfills your basic needs is having a job to pay bills. So, follow the track to get a job. But if that job isn't your dream job, you should also be spending time and energy on another track pursuing a dream job that contributes to your purpose. That can mean doing research, getting an education, finding a mentor, or hiring a coach—which introduces a third track. Track three is accomplishing those steps to make progress on track two, which will ultimately improve (and help you minimize energy spent on) track one.

Think of it like a role-playing video game. There's the main quest for the story, and then there are side quests. Some of those side quests are optional and can be skipped. But others are necessary to the game's main plot, so before you can progress on the main quest, you need to accomplish the steps of the required side quest.

To make energy count, make sure your "side quests" or tracks are contributing to your main quest of living in your purpose. (To a certain degree, I'm also talking about making *time* count. Not always, but often, time and energy line up in a one-to-one relationship. Being intentional and deliberate about how you spend your energy will also help you manage your time. Time is a finite resource, so we always want to spend it in the best way possible before it runs out.)

Chevy Rough, a well-being and energy coach from Britain who has worked with HRH William, Prince of Wales, and other British royals, discusses energy as a resource that compounds on itself. The choices you make today build into how you handle tomorrow, which feeds into how you take care of your well-being for the week, and so on. Think of a compound interest savings account, but with energy instead of money. How you spend that energy now is going to affect what you can do with your energy in the short- and long-term future.

Making energy count in this way will help you live in your authentic self and develop resilience to adversity. You have to build endurance and persevere through adversity to make it to the end of those tracks you're laying down on your path toward your authentic self.

ALIGNING YOUR ENERGY WITH YOUR PURPOSE

After 2019, the year of death, chaos, and the most exhausting daily drains I've ever experienced, I came to a point where none of my favorite activities were helping. Not the small ones like yoga and journaling, and not the big ones like traveling. I even tried taking another vacation. I remember being in Europe with my husband and sister, who were out having a good time while I sat in the car, miserable and in my own choice. I spent more than two weeks on a vacation that did nothing to ease the emptiness I felt as soon as I got back to Hong Kong.

Then I snapped at my boss and was left facing the potential death of my career. What I needed to realize was *that* death had long passed; I hadn't been working in my purpose for a long time. What was I even so hurt for? By that point, I didn't want to be there any more than that company wanted me there.

This moment of reaching my breaking point led me to realize that I needed to go to therapy, grieve the deaths of my family members, grieve the death and loss in my Hong Kong community, and acknowledge that what happened with that company wasn't all on me—but falling out of my purpose was. Dealing with this reality and taking control back was a rebirth of sorts that I needed to initiate.

So I did. I clawed my way out of the spiral of despair and took control of my choices to break from the learned helplessness. I left the company and took these steps to get back to a place where I could recover my energy. Only then was I able to figure out where I needed to go to realign with my purpose and move forward from that awful year.

In this chapter, you've learned how to take control of your energy and think about what depletes you and charges you up. This chapter is all about absorbing, adapting, and recovering. When you make good choices, learn from your mistakes, focus your energy, and push through, you're able to build a capacity to take on different kinds of adversity. You are able to build resilience. Because this process is unique to every individual, it's no surprise that this ties heavily into the next anchor of the REAL model, Authenticity. The next chapter is about aligning your choices with your purpose so that you can build your resilience. Once you find your purpose, *nothing* can stop you from charging your batteries as much as you need.

KEY TAKEAWAYS

- The Core Tenets of the Energy anchor are Understand Your Energy, Recover Your Energy, and Use Your Energy.

- There are four key energetic domains: physical, emotional, mental, and spiritual. Together these make up the batteries that power everything you do. They are also interconnected and heavily influence each other and the overall state of your well-being.

- You can draw parallels between the energetic domains and your generalized hierarchy of needs. Ensuring your needs are met at every level is just as vital as maintaining and regulating your energetic domains when you're building authentic resilience or facing adversity.

- It's important to audit your energy and identify aspects of your life that charge you up (energy-positive) and that drain you (energy-negative). This includes things like activities, relationships, and your environment. Identifying which category everything in your life falls into is helpful because it empowers you to better regulate your energy and make it count.

- Recharging our batteries in all our energy domains is important to help us find balance and achieve resilience at an authentic level. When we do this in ways that are unique to ourselves, we build authentic resilience.

- The key to energy management is creating routines and positive rituals to encourage better habits. Building good routines, habits, and boundaries that are authentic to you helps create consistent outcomes in recovering your energy in each domain.

- You are in control. You can use the Rituals of Choices, Learning, and Making It All Count to build better routines and habits for yourself. These contribute to your ability to learn and be resilient. Taking an open-arms approach will help prepare you for adversity.

CHAPTER 5

THE MODEL: AUTHENTICITY

I LED A DOUBLE LIFE FOR SIX YEARS. NO ONE SAID I HAD to go back into the closet at work. But I did.

When the elevator doors opened on the thirty-first floor at 245 Park Avenue to reveal the beechwood walls and marble floors in the shape of a baseball diamond, I felt *I had* to work for Major League Baseball (MLB). Though I walked in applying for a job in international broadcasting, after a long process and many interviews, I wound up with a job in Human Resources.

I had never heard of it. *Human Resources? What is that?* I had pinned the first six years of my career on being an all-things-Japan know-it-all; what in the world would I know about Human Resources? Eventually I would come to realize that I had actually been doing that work for many years, including in Japan. I would simply take my experiences in people management, relationship building, and recruiting and bring them to a formal department. But at the time, I took the job out of curiosity—and to get back to work and cobble a life together again in the adversity jungle of New York City post-September 11.

It was also a chance to convert my wardrobe to business attire, to be considered serious and credible, to try my hand at building trust in corporate America, and to work in one of the most Americana of work environments: professional baseball. Plus, the man who took a chance on me, Ray Scott, was a decent, logical, and loving man whom I could work hard for, learn from, and make proud. With that pressure to be a "super professional," somehow all the free thinking and liberating feelings I had from twenty-plus years of figuring out who I was as a gay person went out the window. I decided it was best to shield myself from exposure to ridicule in such an environment.

While MLB at that time was growing its diversity programs, hiring more people of color, and taking on more diverse business partners, its representation of gay people was quiet, seemingly absent, or closeted. There I was, another white guy in Baseball, but homosexual with flamboyant tendencies (I'd just come from the fashion industry for god's sake!), and I had to tame my authentic self because I didn't see any other people like me. My boss took a chance on me as a young guy because he saw my potential in HR; he didn't select me for my sexual "diversity." I didn't want to disappoint him.

It didn't help matters that some of my chosen family—both gay and straight—advised "don't ask, don't tell" as the way to go, especially at MLB. Not coming out at work was a better plan than coming out and risking losing one of the best jobs in America. Or so I thought.

Let's not forget that in those days—only twenty short years ago—gays in baseball were still a taboo. The closest I got to knowing other gays in baseball was when former San Diego Padre player Billy Bean had to quit his career in 1995 on the stress of hiding his sexual orientation. He publicly came out in 1999—one of only two openly gay former MLB players out of the 20,000 players who have played the sport at the highest level.[48] The game of America—arguably the thing that sews American culture together along with apple pie—contained a quiet culture where no one dared to be openly gay.

Neither did I. I put myself back into the closet. No one asked me to, certainly not my new employer. It was a choice. For me, the stakes were too high to live with the fear of being outed, losing my job, and having to start over again. Those were the (decidedly untrue) things I told myself, at least.

I wanted to control my career. I think I was worried that if I ever had to interact with players where homophobia was rampant in clubhouses, it would diminish my credibility as representing the office of Human Resources/Player Relations. This was particularly true for me when I was promoted and moved to Los Angeles to work with the Angels.

It was ironic. After twenty-five years of self-discovery and living my values of truth and authenticity, there I was so readily and easily sending myself back to a place of shame, guilt, and hiding. The mental health mantle of living a double life is complex and heavy. Yet so many of us have been willing to do that for our careers. Despite living my best and most open life just before working at MLB, like Billy Bean, I also decided it was not worth coming out.

YOUR RESILIENCE IS UNIQUE TO YOU

In hindsight, choosing to go back into the closet was not a mistake—but neither was it a good choice. In the end, it turned out to be a choice that had an accidental consequence. I got to know myself even better and had an additional chance to identify and nurture my authentic self. I realized the two lives

I was leading—one as the closeted professional and one as the young, urban gay and proud former fashionista with Hollywood connections—were in direct opposition to one another. That tension forced me to have a good look at myself; the tension between my lives was an adversity I had to face.

Knowing yourself and staying true to your inner core is one of the greatest gifts you can give yourself in order to live free and with joy. Authenticity is a key ingredient in the magic formula of resilience, which enables you to overcome any obstacle.

I've always said that my first ten years of adulting in the real world gave me the baseline tools I needed to know myself. But it was the experience of going back in the closet at MLB that truly enabled me to come back out again better for it. In living my double life, I got to know what I truly value about myself and what my core values really are. While I was professionally happy at work—learning about HR, going to school, having a kickass boss and workmates, having my development invested in by my employer—I was still trying to make sense of what it meant to be successful at work while sacrificing part of who I was. Especially in an area where I was spending and investing so much of my time.

Going back into the closet forced me to clearly understand the difference between *knowing* things about myself and *being* myself. It forced me to take a key look at my life's purpose. This path also led me to face self-sabotage, imposter syndrome, and my fears and vulnerabilities while also dealing with my demons. It helped me to release myself and ultimately taught me how to love myself.

When your authenticity is clear in your life, you are acting in service of yourself. This enables you to live true to yourself and build your resilience. Knowing who you are and being in love with and proud of who you are will fuel your ability to move confidently toward your north star and confidently fulfill your purpose. When you're doing that, nothing gets in your way.

CORE TENET 1: KNOW YOURSELF

Getting to know your inner self is vital to defining your authenticity. This stems from understanding your core values, beliefs about yourself, and personal strengths. You need to figure out what makes you *you* so that you can use that information to define your purpose in life.

Mike Robbins said it well in the title of his book on authenticity: *Be Yourself, Everyone Else Is Already Taken*. There is a significant difference between knowing yourself and *being* yourself. To get to that point of your authentic self, you need to understand what blocks you, what fuels you, and what unique experiences led you to those things.

Identifying Your Values

Your core values are the guardrails between which you steer through life. They are the principles that determine your behavior. Your values are uniquely yours, and they are behind all of your day-to-day decisions. They drive your motivation and fuel your understanding of your intrinsic worth to yourself.

Core values are what you hold dear about who you are and how you choose to engage with the world and with yourself. Values are the things that you consider important to your self-worth, self-motivation, and understanding of how you want to live your life.

Finding your values involves visiting important moments and beliefs in your life and evaluating how they affect you now. Investigate what has become important to you. Ask yourself questions and be honest with yourself about the answers. Self-reflection is the key to this step, which is why it's a good idea to do this with a trusted friend or to hire a coach. Having someone to listen and make observations can help you talk through and identify the key information you need to reflect on.

If you prefer to do this work alone, I suggest writing your answers in extensive lists with copious notes. Once you've made a list for each question, read through all of them, look for commonalities, and see how they fit together.

Together, these musings you've created should form patterns that point to stronger themes. These are what you will use to define your purpose in life. Consider them while asking yourself: What moves you? What drives you? What makes you angry? What are things that you love?

You can see your values in the way that you engage with yourself and engage in the world. For example, imagine you're standing in line waiting to check out at a grocery store, and the people in front of you are carrying on a long conversation with the cashier. If speed and efficiency are important values to you, you're probably going to be annoyed at the situation (and act accordingly). In that case, self-checkout is probably the best option for you, because you can control the speed of scanning the items and paying for them. However, if you're a person who values connection or entertainment more than speed, you might not mind the conversation taking place and enjoy eavesdropping or even joining the exchange. This is just one of the many daily occurrences that illustrate how your values influence the energy you put out in a given situation.

CORE VALUES QUESTIONNAIRE

Prompt your inquiry with the following questions:

- What do you see at the end of your life?

- What are the important lessons that you've learned as you look at the earlier part of your life?

- What stands out to you about values you've witnessed or learned along the way?

- Think about people you admire. What values do you see in them? Chances are you hold those same values for yourself too.

- How do you engage with yourself?

- When you're at your best, with your batteries topped up in all of your energetic domains, what feelings are related to that? Uncovering the feelings around the energy might help you uncover values specific to you.

- What guidelines do you use to make decisions? What rules determine your choices in various situations?

- What insights can you draw from major choices you've made in the past?

When I went back into the closet, every day became a fight to be my true self. It was in that fight that I eventually came to understand that authenticity is part of who I am. I don't believe in covering up certain parts of myself for any reason. I had authenticity as a value before I started working at MLB, but I didn't understand its importance or even know what to call it before I experienced what life was like without it. When I came back out, it hit me that *this* is what it means to live as my authentic self. And I'm never going to sacrifice that again. It's a core guiding mechanism for how I live my life.

You don't necessarily have to sacrifice a value to discover what it means to you. As I mentioned above, the main process involves revisiting key moments in your life and extracting insights from those moments. One client and I spent eight sessions going over her childhood, professional life, experience of motherhood, a divorce, and other key aspects of her life. It took all that talking for her to realize that one of her core values is equality. She recognized that in each part of her life there were inequities that separated her from others in her life. She connected the dots between not being an equal sibling in her family to not being treated equally in the workplace as a woman and, later, as an unequal partner in her marriage. She grew up in Japan, where the idea that women should only bear children and be homemakers is still very prevalent. During our sessions, she realized that she'd spent her whole life battling that value both internally and in the people around her, and it affected every aspect of her personal and professional life. In the purpose work we explored together, she crafted a value-based purpose statement and now lives as a "pioneer for equity, taking action and standing up for women and other marginalized people in Japan." It's powerful when we see values come front and center and fuel individual purpose.

Values hold us accountable for our own behavior and conduct. On a deeper level, values also serve as a source of energy. They often lead us to engage in energy-positive activities that help supercharge our well-being batteries.

Below are some commonly held values that show up for many people in my sessions with them. Note that these are all positive values. Some of the values that surface for you may not be in this list; and some may be negative values, such as greed, overindulgence, dishonesty, or jealousy. Although negative values may lead us to certain behaviors, we needn't choose to focus on them. Rather, we can acknowledge them with self-compassion and try to let them go.

Identifying Your Beliefs

Beliefs are easily influenced. It's possible—common, in fact—for people to hold false beliefs about themselves fueled by negative experiences and feedback. For the purposes of the REAL model, I define belief as a process of evidence-searching in your reflections about yourself. What do you believe about yourself as a person, and why? "Evidence" in this context refers to the memories that support your beliefs. For instance, if you believe you're a smart person, you can probably point to achievements in school and work as evidence that supports this belief.

It should be noted that beliefs are not necessarily based in values. For example, you can believe you're a funny person without humor being a strong value you hold. Values are what you think is important when engaging with the world; beliefs are evidence of some of your core strengths (and weaknesses) at play. When you see your core strengths working, they show up as beliefs about yourself.

Identifying Your Strengths

Core strengths are your skills and abilities, conceptualizations of what you are good at in your engagement with the world. They indicate the things that you like to do and how you prefer to engage in the world.

LIST OF COMMON VALUES

Accuracy	Achievement	Authenticity
Autonomy	Balance	Beauty
Belonging	Bravery	Candor
Change	Collaboration	Commitment
Compassion	Community	Connection
Control	Creativity	Daring
Discipline	Efficiency	Empathy
Excellence	Fairness	Faith
Family	Freedom	Friendship
Fun	Generosity	Genuineness
Gratitude	Happiness	Hard Work
Health	Honesty	Humor
Innovation	Integrity	Intelligence
Justice	Kindness	Knowledge
Leadership	Learning	Loyalty
Openness	Perseverance	Positivity
Professionalism	Reliability	Responsibility
Security	Service	Spirituality
Teaching	Teamwork	Trust
Truth	Understanding	Variety
Warmth	Wealth	Wisdom

Several great industry-standard resources already exist to help you identify your core strengths. Via quick online assessments, they ask dozens of scientifically designed questions and immediately collate your responses. It will be a far more efficient use of your time to visit one of these sites than to answer in print a list of questions I provide. Anyway, that's what I do with my clients! Here are my favorites:

- VIA Character Strength Assessment (viacharacter.org)
- Gallup StrengthsFinder—CliftonStrengths (gallup.com/cliftonstrengths)[49]
- High5 Strengths Finder (high5test.com/strengthsfinder-free)

There are a ton of other options out there as well. If you want to dive deep, I recommend using a few different ones and looking for common patterns in the results.

Identifying Your Purpose

Now that you've looked for themes within each of these three areas of exploration, it's time to look at how they can be stitched together to form a picture of what your authentic self looks like and wants to be doing.

It's important to find the connections between your core values, beliefs, and strengths because those are what you use to craft your purpose, which is vital to living your most authentic life. You have to define your purpose with the best of yourself.

For some, this is easier said than done. Occasionally, someone's personal strengths will align directly with their values in name. For example, a person who values curiosity and learning might find that learning is one of their main strengths. But oftentimes, the connection is not so direct. You have to do the work to connect your values and beliefs to your strengths by seeing both the black and white core values that drive you and the evidence about yourself.

Purpose is a unique source of spiritual energy and power. It can be the north star that helps you focus and find direction in this life. Your purpose fuels your passion and perseverance. When your purpose is clear, it puts you in what psychologist Mihaly Csikszentmihalyi calls a state of flow.

Flow refers to those moments when you're completely absorbed in a challenging but doable task. It's often described as "being in the zone," where time passes quickly, personal performance or productivity is at optimal levels, and your state of happiness increases. In Csikszentmihalyi's words, flow is "the state in which people are so involved in an activity that nothing else seems to matter; the experience itself is so enjoyable that people will do it even at great cost, for the sheer sake of doing it."[50] It is often when we connect with the deepest part of ourselves—through our spiritual energy, values, beliefs, and strengths—that we can tap into our flow, a state that can help propel our purpose.

Part of why we may enjoy flow states so much? Studies have shown that they silence our inner critics. Without getting too technical in the neuroscience, flow essentially causes a temporary inactivation of the prefrontal cortex, where our inner critics live in our brains. This inactivation is what leads to feelings of time distortion (like when you've been "in the zone" on a project for hours at a time without realizing the sun went down or you missed a meal) and loss of self-consciousness in the moment.

BELIEFS QUESTIONNAIRE

To uncover what you believe about yourself, here are some questions to ask yourself:

- What...

    - adjectives would you use to describe yourself? Some places to start are *smart, funny, pessimistic, optimistic, oblivious, observant, studious, carefree*, etc.

- Why...

    - would you describe yourself that way? What evidence do you have to support each of the adjectives you listed?

- Do...

    - you believe yourself to be a good person? Why or why not?

    - you believe yourself to be a positive or negative person? Why?

    - you believe that you have what you need to achieve your goals in life? Why or why not?

You don't need to look through your answers to these questions for patterns like you did during the values questions. Just hold on to them, because later you'll use them to examine whether or not each of those beliefs is true.

Consider this connection: if being in a state of flow is often a secret to happiness, and if living in your purpose is a path to a fulfilled life, imagine what happens when you enter flow states *by* living in your purpose. These are connected in my experience. When I am coaching and in my purpose of bringing authenticity and resilience-building skills to others, I am often in a flow state. And by consequence, I often get a massive recharge of spiritual energy from this energy-positive activity.

That energy you use when you're in flow is aligned with who you are. In that state, everything becomes easier—including overcoming adverse events, obstacles, and stressors—because you know exactly who you are, and you can stay true to that by acting in service of yourself.

So how do you define your purpose? A good place to start is by crafting a purpose statement. A few of the companies I've worked for in the past have had employees do this, and there is a lot of great thinking around different ways to approach purpose statements (see bibliography).

I like to start with the big questions: Why are you here? Why do you do what you do? What do you want to do with your time on Earth? The answers to these are the foundation of building your purpose statement.

Based on this, I've created a visualization to help you build that foundation.

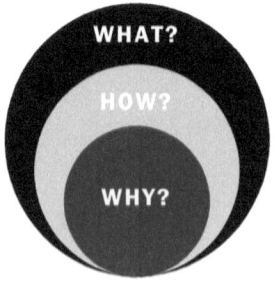

In the first ring, ask yourself the heavy "why" questions.

In the second ring, ask "how" questions. How do you leverage your core strengths? Now that you've identified them, what are you going to do with them to make a difference to yourself, your family, your community, and the world?

In the third ring, ask "what" questions. What impact are you going to make using your strengths?

Using the answers to these questions, construct a statement that starts with "I am" or "My purpose is" and fill in the blanks using the why, the how, and the what answers. I am [the what]. I do it by [the how], in order to [the why].

For inspiration, I'll share my purpose statement with you:

I am a light to help people see their authenticity and an architect to help them design the building of their resilience. I do that through coaching, impacting one person at a time, in order to relieve human suffering by helping people respond to adversity.

Think back to my client in Japan. Her purpose statement was "to be a pioneer for equity, taking action and standing up for women and other marginalized people in Japan." Another client of mine described her purpose as a writer as "being a bridge to understanding and thereby compassion and calm."

Hopefully, when we craft powerful purpose statements for ourselves using our strengths, values, and beliefs about ourselves, we see the pathway we can step on toward a life that is purposeful and built with meaning.

The Price of Living Inauthentically

Living a double life by going back into the closet at MLB was not an act in service of myself; it was an act in service of my career. Living that double life caused me to judge myself. On top of that, I was also in a bad relationship at the time. Both of these ongoing choices I made against my higher purpose were shifting me away from my core values.

When I was in fashion, there was less judgment and worry about my dating life because I felt good about myself when I was being open and authentic. After coming out in Japan and going through all of my intellectual and social pursuits prior to returning to New York, I felt like I was on my way in life. Putting myself back in the closet to fit in at MLB undid a lot of that. As a result, I turned to alcohol and battled self-judgment because my inner critic grew increasingly loud each day.

Here's a sad truth: not much has changed since the aughts years. Sure, *I've* moved on and come back out and improved my life, but there's still so much suffering for LGBTQ+ people in the professional-sports space. As recently as 2021, an Australian soccer player (there they call it football) came out on social media. Josh Cavallo is only the second person in the Australian Football League to come out as gay—and, at the time of this book's printing, the only active gay male professional soccer player in the world. It was a huge deal. It was really bold and courageous—but it's sad that we have to see it that way, that coming out is still scary for people in so many spaces.

That needs to change, because the best thing you can do for yourself—LGBTQ+ or otherwise—is live authentically. Being openly true to yourself *is* in service of yourself. It gives you the power to use your energy management and resilience to overcome anything and rise to levels beyond what you believed possible.

CORE TENET 2: RELEASE YOURSELF

Authenticity is *the* core pillar of authentic resilience. All the experiences that live in your body and mind build your core beliefs. By utilizing the REAL model and living in service of yourself, you can overcome the beliefs that no longer serve you.

Getting clear on your purpose is a good start to defining your authenticity. It enables you to let go of things that denigrate your authenticity and get in your way, such as self-judgment, imposter syndrome, and your inner critic (to name just a few). At this stage of the REAL model, you're going to hone the tools you need to examine and manage the inner turmoil we all experience.

Negativity, as adverse as its effects are to us, is hardwired into our brains, just like memories and fight/flight/freeze responses. That's why it takes so much hard work to let it go. Just as getting to know yourself involves identifying strengths and unique tendencies (as we did in Core Tenet 1), you also have to acknowledge your weaknesses to be able to combat the negative beliefs you hold about yourself and the self-sabotaging behaviors that manifest as a result. This is a vital step because releasing negativity about yourself makes space for energy to be spent on living in your authenticity and serving yourself instead.

Combating Negativity

I explained in Chapter 1 that our brains are hardwired to scan for danger; this innate survival instinct in humans creates what's called a negativity bias. Neuroscience research suggests that negative thoughts have more powerful lingering effects in our minds than positive thoughts. In other words, negative experiences large and small stick to our brains and somatic (body) memory like Velcro while positive experiences stick like Teflon.[51] That is, we are more apt to remember that we missed the bus and were late to work (and then feel guilty for it) rather than remembering how delicious and buttery the Danish roll and cup of coffee tasted once we got to work.

While this survival instinct served our ancient ancestors very well, it's more problematic for us in modern society. We tend to dwell on mistakes, beat ourselves up over little things, and fixate on insults and inadequacies in ourselves rather than our gifts and positive aspects. In work and social settings, this skew toward negativity causes us to take criticism harshly and reject compliments.

Negativity bias can get in the way of building resilience. My friend Janelle Aaker (a fellow HR executive; diversity, inclusion, and belonging expert; and former colleague) once said it best by calling this negativity bias "an internalized oppression." It's this same bias and oppression that fuels self-sabotaging behaviors, so it's important to build habits that help you combat negativity. However, in your efforts to combat negativity, it's important to ensure you don't take it to the extreme and end up too far on the other end of the spectrum—in a state of toxic positivity.

Toxic positivity is often described as the overgeneralization of a happy, optimistic state that results in denial, minimization, and invalidating behavior toward authentic human experiences. This can often be seen in blanket statements like "just get over it," "everything happens for a reason," or any supposedly sympathetic statement that starts with the words "at least." These kinds of responses are toxic because they diminish the true essence of the human emotion behind the adverse event for the person who experienced it.

While it's important to combat your brain's natural inclination to dwell on negativity, you *don't* want to force positivity to the point of neutralizing your ability to feel the full spectrum of your emotions. You shouldn't feel guilty for experiencing negative thoughts or emotions. Fostering positivity in daily practices is completely different from obsessively dwelling on positive feelings and refusing to acknowledge the negative at all costs.

Feelings, whether positive or negative, let us know what we're thinking (because our thoughts cause our feelings). In the words of the famous American Tibetan Buddhist Pema Chödrön: "Feel the feelings. Drop the story." Leaning into feelings and dropping the story behind them (or the story that is associated with causing the feelings) helps us feel those emotions even deeper (and thereby release them, which we'll get to shortly).[52] It's often in the story that negativity lingers, so when you drop the story, you have the ability to drop some of the negativity. In other words, experiencing the feelings and emotions without giving any narrative about them enables us to truly be present with ourselves. The practice is to learn to interrupt the negative storyline. In doing so, you learn not to follow the thought. Releasing the story (and its negativity bias) enables you to truly feel what you feel.

When you sort out the negativity and actively release it, you are unburdening yourself of that negativity bias so that you can move on more easily. Repeating this behavior helps your brain learn to become more resilient to negative energy and thoughts, enabling you to master your thoughts and free yourself from beliefs that are not serving you in a genuine and authentic way.

In the spectrum of negativity to toxic positivity, you want to balance in the center. There, you are actively working to avoid negativity (in people, media, your own thoughts, etc.) and reprogram any negativity you do encounter to a more positive response (just not at all costs). This balance enables you to experience situations as they really are and helps build your resilience. It also enables you to connect more deeply with who you are.

The key is to release negativity in a heathy way. You can do this by naming the emotion and acknowledging it. Doing so helps you move the processing of that emotion in your brain from the amygdala (where your fight/flight/freeze reaction is stored) to the upper brain. Now you can enact some top-down self-control. Drop the story, sort out where the negativity is, name it, talk about it, lean into it, and start to release that energy to combat the negativity it's causing in your life.

Some people find it helpful to say aloud to themselves, "I'm releasing the feeling of [negative emotion]."

Self-Sabotage

It's stating the obvious to say that most of us don't consciously work to sabotage ourselves in our daily lives. Nevertheless, it *is* worth stating because self-sabotage is common when we're experiencing things that take away from our sense of worth.

What does that look like? Self-sabotage happens whenever you don't put yourself first, which can look a lot of different ways depending on if you're actively or passively taking steps to prevent yourself from living a fulfilling life in your purpose. For example, self-sabotage can show up in the form of battles with bosses, colleagues, loved ones, your ego, and even your relationship with yourself. This sabotage can lead to the downward spiral of learned helplessness, which contributes to a low sense of self-worth. When you rob yourself of value in your mind, these feelings drain your batteries, remove your ability to recharge, and lead to lack of confidence in your purpose. Straying from your purpose and authenticity can leave you feeling constantly depleted.

Self-sabotage often has a compound effect. In her book *Option B*, author Sheryl Sandberg describes a phenomenon called second derivative feelings, which is when you experience a feeling followed by a second wave of feelings in response to the initial feeling.[53] For example, if a relative you didn't know well dies, you might feel unaffected when you hear the news of their death, and then feel guilt over feeling unaffected by the loss.

During my time in baseball, I felt like a fraud for not being myself and not talking about my "closet." I took pride in being a certified HR professional and was very self-assured as a professional. But I often felt conflicted about bringing my whole self to work. That internal struggle of being my whole self vs. just my professional self then made me feel ashamed that I couldn't completely share the details of my life with close workmates, as they often did with me. I also suffered resentment because I couldn't fully participate in conversations from my perspective.

I kept having thoughts like, *I'm a professional, why am I feeling like this? I shouldn't feel this bad. I'm as human as everyone else. Why can't I share my story?* This led to guilt, which led to doubt in my professional abilities, which seeped into my personal life, and on and on in the downward spiral. At a certain point, I was unconsciously sabotaging my own energy and authenticity at every turn.

It's easy for self-sabotage (and other negative behaviors that result from living inauthentically) to lead to a negative spiral of learned helplessness and hopelessness without you consciously noticing. It can start small; things that didn't bother you before suddenly eat at you, then you make what seem like isolated choices (such as choosing to cope with a bad day by drinking), then your behavior changes (such as drinking daily), and things escalate until you've fallen down a spiral and feel you've lost all control. As mentioned above, internalized oppression leads to negative self-talk and internal statements that spiral downward, such as "I'm not worthy" or "I'm not smart," and then later, "I'm not good enough," and ultimately, "I'm a bad person." This is what the REAL model is designed to help you combat and recover from.

Knowing yourself really well is the key to preventing some of that spiraling from occurring in the first place. I know it's easier said than done. *But* if you face reality, rechannel your energy, and shift your focus to living in your purpose and core values, you'll have a better chance of preventing spiraling even further down, enabling you to let go of the negativity pushing you in that direction. When you release beliefs and behaviors that no longer serve you, you gain invaluable space that you can then use to create love for yourself.

Resilience is built by letting go of the negative beliefs you hold about yourself. Doing so allows your inner authentic self to shine because your values speak loudly to you—so loudly that it can overpower the inner critic compelling you to act in ways that don't serve you. This enables you to jump out of moments of self-sabotage and overcome the obstacles, adversities, or stressors in your life.

Inner Critic/Negative Self-Talk

Negative self-talk is another common behavior that sabotages authentic living. Quieting your inner critic is important because in addition to releasing the negativity it causes, you create space for yourself to do more listening and exploring within yourself. Negative self-talk muddles your values, so removing that noise from your inner world allows your values to ring clear and shine through. You need to be connected to your values to be able to define them and use them to release negative habits and behavior.

For the purposes of this book, I'm going to stick to the bird's-eye view. A surface-level understanding of the inner critic is enough to empower you in applying the methods of the REAL model's core tenets to make strides in overcoming this negative behavior on your journey to build your authentic resilience.

The simplest explanation of the inner critic is the figurative "devil on your shoulder." You can think of its counterpart, the "angel on your shoulder," as your inner nurturer.[54] That's the voice in your mind responsible for keeping you focused on self-compassion and encouragement. The inner critic is the opposite. You're probably much more familiar with this voice; it's the one that has something harsh to say about your every thought, feeling, and decision. I'm sure you can guess which one is naturally louder and stronger for most of us.

Don't get me wrong; the inner critic has its place. That negative instinct in your mind is there to help you recognize when you've made a mistake and think about how you might remedy it. It's an important part of learning and growth. It's sometimes there to protect you. However, the negativity bias in your brain gives that shoulder devil a tendency to take its criticism overboard. This is why most people speak more harshly about themselves than they would about someone else in the same situation (and conversely, speak more positively to praise someone else than they would about themselves in the same situation). Self-criticism is the archenemy of self-compassion. You need to reduce the noise of the inner critic living in your subconscious mind; this will help you gain control and release the negativity that's preventing your self-compassion and perpetuating habits and behaviors that aren't serving you.

Often, the words your inner critic speaks don't reflect the truth of your reality, especially in adverse situations. The negative thoughts that arise as your brain processes information between the left and right hemispheres rarely reflect the full story.

To combat this negative bias, you first need to sharpen your awareness of it. See the critical thoughts for what they are: the words of an inner voice that typically does not speak the truth. You have to be aware of this because the list of things your inner critic can pick at is infinite. My whole life I've had my inner critic put me down over my sports abilities, coming out as gay, running with certain social crowds, my physical fitness, and a million other things. If I wasn't the literal best at something, I was inadequate. There was no middle ground. Sound familiar?

Because your inner critic comments on so many things every day, it's easy to get swept up in those words and take the criticisms as truth. But I cannot stress enough how detrimental it can be to do so. Taking that voice's words at face value can lead to crippling mental, emotional, and psychological patterns, for example, **imposter syndrome.** Feeling like a fraud in any aspect of your life gives you even more to work through on your journey to release negativity and build authentic resilience.

This form of self-sabotage is a strong belief that you don't deserve the success you have achieved and is accompanied by feelings of fraudulence about that success and dread that you will be found out.[55] It is estimated 70 percent of people will experience this imposter syndrome at least once.[56] There are many resources available to combat this inner-saboteur technique, but the best ones are those we have discussed: reframing negative thoughts to something positive and dropping the story behind them. Recognizing that not every thought is true and not engaging in the false ones will help you release the imposter. No amount of success makes us immune to imposter syndrome caused by our inner critic.

INDICATORS OF SELF-SABOTAGE

- Losing confidence

- Doubting yourself and your decisions

- Telling false stories about yourself in your mind (e.g., "I used to be a good leader, but I'm not anymore.")

- Slowly declining productivity in your home, social, and professional life

- Experiencing choice paralysis or workload paralysis, i.e., the inability to "do" or "think"

- Believing you're not worth it or don't deserve good things

- Rising feelings of insecurity

- Sinking interests in relationships and hobbies

- Failing to articulate yourself and express your needs

- Ultimate failure (giving up doing anything, complete loss of desire to try)

- Changing the way you receive love from others or yourself

Another common symptom of an overzealous inner critic is **shame.** Shame over who you are or shame over *feeling* ashamed (remember those second derivative feelings I talked about) is a vicious cycle that creates more obstacles for you to overcome in your efforts to quiet your inner critic. We are all, sadly, quite familiar with shame, so I won't spend too much time belaboring this definition.

Yet another common result of excessive negative self-talk and shame is **process addiction,** which is a behavioral dependency (rather than the substance dependency that comes to mind for most people with the word "addiction"). Behavioral dependency happens when people regulate their moods through compulsive behavior, despite knowing the negative impact that behavior may have on their life. Some common examples of process addiction are dependencies on shopping, gambling, excessive exercise, social media, or excessive sex.

Process addiction is different from simple overindulgence in that it feels like a compulsive need to indulge in excess—even knowing that the behavior is not good for you—in order to activate the "happy hormones" in your brain and improve your mood.

Negative self-talk can lead to process addiction because this dependency often evolves from feelings of shame, a connection explained by clinical psychologist Alan Downs in his book *The Velvet Rage.* Getting a hit of those hormones in your brain by acting on a certain behavior can become addictive because it gives you a (false) sense of combating the negativity going on in your mind and body.

The problem is that the hormone release triggered by acting on the dependency is temporary. Engaging in that behavior only further feeds the inner critic making you feel so bad—either indirectly, by providing ineffective, short-term solutions, or directly, by causing you to feel shame from having indulged in that negative behavior. It will never silence the inner critic in the long run.

Negative self-talk and the behaviors that result from it diminish your ability to live an authentic life. While they serve the inner critic's natural purpose of regulating your behavior, letting it do so to this extent is regulating in the wrong way. To get to a place of strong authentic resilience, you have to work to beat this tendency. The REAL model can *help* with that, but if you have severe struggles with imposter syndrome, process addiction, or feelings of shame, please seek professional help from a licensed therapist and/or a medical professional. As a general guideline, if your inner self-talk is overpowering your life and taking control of your behavior in ways that you believe are self-destructive or harmful to yourself, these are good signs that you may need to seek further advice.

Embracing Vulnerability: Dismantling the Radar

Now that we've talked about behaviors that get in the way of authentic living, let's discuss one that boosts it. Vulnerability is the state of being exposed to possible attacks (physical or emotional). I'd like to build on that definition further with a quote from author Brené Brown: "Vulnerability is not winning or losing; it's having the courage to show up and be seen when we have no control over the outcome."[57]

Getting comfortable with being vulnerable is key to the core tenet of releasing yourself because it allows you to let go of the walls that you've built around yourself (and the negative beliefs trapped within them). This fortress can take many forms, including general defensiveness, a facade or even a false identity, and toxic positivity/denial of emotions.

When you break down your armor and allow people to experience you as the real, unique human that you are, you build your authentic resilience. Showing up as yourself and being open to the possibility of adversity enhances your authenticity and empowers you to build resilience to adversity instead of hiding from it.

Brown describes vulnerability as "the birthplace of love, belonging, joy, courage, empathy, and creativity. It is the source of hope, empathy, accountability, and authenticity."[58] Let that sink in for a moment. That's a *lot* of good coming from one state of being. So, let's talk about how to embrace vulnerability.

The opposite of vulnerability is defensiveness. While you've spent a lifetime enduring adversity big and small, your brain has built defense mechanisms and habits in response to these attacks on your well-being. As a result, you've likely got natural defenses that are second nature to you. Think of it like a radar system you've constructed that is on high alert for any indication of a threat headed your way. To embrace vulnerability, you need to dismantle that radar.

The first time I heard the phrase "dismantle the radar" was when I was working with my mentor coach, Craig McKenzie. While training to become a coach myself, I decided to hire him to coach me (outside of my training) because I was dealing with a work situation that I felt was in conflict with who I was. At that time, I was a new member of the executive leadership team at an organization. I was still fairly new to the executive-level stage of my career, and as a result of this (among other things), I was always showing up to board meetings super defensive of my right to be in that position.

I wasn't aware of that. It wasn't until a few sessions in that my coach, Craig, recognized and pointed out to me that I had a highly sophisticated emotional defense radar system that was always at a heightened state of alert when I was at work. It wasn't necessarily a conscious choice, so I wasn't aware of where it was coming from until I talked about it in that coaching session.

Together we identified the source of that defense system I'd built: years of being relentlessly bullied. Growing up, I learned to overcome teasing and bullying by working to always be the smartest person in the room, always have a quip ready to retort, and always turn the situation into humor. That became my way of fighting the bullying.

This radar system became so second nature to me that I carried it into all situations, especially professional ones; the last place I ever want to be bullied is in the workplace. So I kept showing up in this heightened state of awareness that translated into self-righteous behavior at work. Looking back, I was kind of an asshole. I knew I was right more often than I was wrong, and I felt I needed to be armed with multiple ways to defend that (even though I wasn't being attacked). I wanted to show up as a good leader, but I was getting feedback saying I'm too defensive, opinionated, and explosive. That's not who I am. It was completely in conflict with my inner self and my value of being a caring and nurturing person who is there to help people.

I needed to remove that tension by dismantling the radar and showing more vulnerability to my colleagues. Instead of operating in a self-righteous and defensive state, I needed to draw on my strengths of empathy and authenticity to create a more calming work environment. Craig and I crafted a plan for me to dismantle my radar system, and it was magical. Vulnerability enables leaders to be great, and I saw that in my changing interactions with my team at work.

You can't dismantle your radar system overnight. It's a long process that involves revisiting your values, drawing on your empathy and strengths, and coming to terms with the possibility of exposure to the very thing you're defending yourself from. You have to identify the causes of your defense systems and reframe them so that you can use a new mindset to embrace vulnerability and show up as your authentic self in your daily life.

It's not sustainable to live with your energy on red alert all the time. Instead, refocus your energy into a state of vulnerability that will serve you. This is why I recommend getting the help of a coach (whether that's me or someone else). I did it, and now I can be on the other side of that for others.

CORE TENET 3: LOVE YOURSELF

In letting go of the negativity that was holding you back, you've created space to build your sense of self-love. Loving yourself is liberating yourself. It allows you to truly live your best life so that you can do what you need to fill your tank of well-being and breathe life into your purpose.

Loving yourself means putting yourself first. You don't want to be selfish, but you can be self-ish. What's the difference? Selfish is lacking consideration for others in favor of your own benefit. I define *self-ish* as being concerned with and involved in managing your own thoughts, feelings, and beliefs in order to unlock the best version of yourself. Who is better qualified to do that than you? No one.

Being self-ish isn't an *act* of self-love; it's a *journey*. Self-love is an ongoing, disciplined state of mind. The practices and beliefs associated with self-love take time to develop because you can't outsource them. It must come from within you, and it's not optional. Self-love is an essential part of living authentically. No one else is going to do it for you—and no one else *can*—so you have to make time to practice self-compassion, self-care, and self-advocacy to move toward loving yourself in an authentic way.

Self-Compassion

In Core Tenet 2, you worked to quiet your inner critic, the devil on your shoulder. Now it's time to turn your attention to that angel on your other shoulder, the voice I referred to earlier as your inner nurturer.

In her book *Self-Compassion: The Proven Power of Being Kind to Yourself*, psychology researcher Kristin Neff defines self-compassion as being able to relate to yourself in a way that is forgiving, accepting, and loving—especially when situations are tough.

Treating yourself with compassion is not only one of the best things you can do for yourself, but also one of the most important things you can do for others. When you take care of yourself, you remove the burden of your care from the people who love you. Practicing self-compassion is doing a great service for yourself *and* the people you care about. So, let's dive into what that looks like.

The first step on your journey to self-love is building the self-awareness I talked about in Core Tenet 1: Know Yourself. Recognizing and connecting to your values allows you to exist as your authentic self in the world because when you *know* your values, you see them every day. For instance, if generosity is a value that you live by, you'll notice yourself acting on it in the choices you make. Maybe you throw some extra bills into the charity bucket at the grocery store. Or maybe you pay it forward at a drive-thru. If generosity is a value for you, it will speak to you, and there is a validating warmth that comes from seeing yourself act in alignment with your values. That validation lifts you up when you're experiencing suffering and pain and allows your self-compassion to come through.

Spending time getting to know yourself in this way improves your relationship with yourself, which enables you to find compassion for yourself in those adverse or stressful times when you need it most.

One way to show yourself compassion is to be kind to yourself. Think about how you would talk to a new friend in various situations. If they made a mistake, the behaviors and words you use in response would be kind, right? You probably wouldn't use negative harsh words or beat them up over a simple mistake. You have to treat yourself with the same care you would give to that new friend.

In her book, Neff writes about being kind to yourself as a practice of goodwill, not good feelings. Showing self-compassion is a mindful choice to embrace yourself with kindness in moments that might otherwise be painful. It's important to remember that imperfection is part of the shared human experience, so you shouldn't treat yourself (or anyone else) poorly for being human. If you can honestly say you treat yourself the same way you treat others, then you're on the right path of building love for yourself.

Being kind to yourself doesn't mean you have to shower yourself with compliments or positive affirmations like the comedy-sketch character Stuart Smalley did on *Saturday Night Live* (though you absolutely can and should if you want to). If you're not into that, try focusing instead on flipping the negative self-talk. If you find yourself thinking negatively about yourself, stop and tell yourself something like, "That's not true. I'm human. It's fine." Actively stop yourself from any name-calling, harsh criticizing, or otherwise negative thoughts directed at yourself and instead say something you would say to a friend (e.g., "It's just a mistake. You're not stupid. Things are going to be okay.").

The thoughts you have while ruminating create pathways in your brain (as I said in Chapter 1, this is what makes humans so unique as a species). The more often you flip negative self-talk into positive or understanding self-talk, the more you train your brain to be kind to yourself. It takes practice, but after a while you will strengthen that inner nurturer and be able to hear its voice more clearly than ever.

Another form of self-compassion is practicing forgiveness toward yourself. When you forgive yourself and embrace your own perceived shortcomings, it leads you to recognize that you are actually stronger. It also allows you to let go of the past and release any feelings of guilt and shame you carry. Freeing yourself from these burdens is one of the most compassionate things you can do.

You can take that even further and show yourself more compassion by trusting yourself. Believe in your values and strengths and trust in yourself to put them to good use, especially when you're up against adversity.

Self-Care

These days, "self-care" is a buzzword that's often used to sell people items and services such as beauty products and spa packages. While those can be *acts* of self-care, they are not the definition. Self-care is not going to the Maldives or the Mexican Riviera for a beach week. That's called a vacation. Self-care is more than that.

Just like self-compassion, self-care is an ongoing state. It's a practice. It lives in the daily reinforcement of choices that serve you. Good nutrition, regular exercise, and regular sleep are all examples of self-care.

Self-care is about taking care of yourself so that you can provide better care for others. Also, if we connect back to Chapter 4 on Energy, often self-care is the explicit management of your physical, emotional, mental, and spiritual energies. It's good to look after your immune system and brain function so that you can connect to your energies and ensure you're making time to charge your batteries.

Activities such as taking a vacation or getting a massage can help jump-start a cycle of self-care, but they should not be taken as a one-and-done activity that allows you to check self-care off your to-do list. Self-care is about how you manage yourself in the long term; doing so enables you to generate love for yourself over time.

In addition to taking care of your physical needs, self-care also happens when you act in service of yourself. Being aware of your emotional energy and setting emotional boundaries is self-care. Keeping promises to yourself about breaks, plans, and commitments is self-care. We often stand ourselves up when we promise ourselves to make time for an activity or event we've been wanting to do. You wouldn't want to stand up a friend and break your promise to them, so you shouldn't do it to yourself either. Holding yourself to those promises is a way of showing yourself love. Mindfulness and meditation practices are good ways to practice self-care around your mental and spiritual energy.

Below are just a few examples of simple practices in self-care that relate to your energy and well-being batteries. For these suggestions to be effective, you have to stick to them. Develop them into an energy-positive ritual or routine to help you love yourself.

SELF-CARE PRACTICES

Energy Domain	Self-Care Practice Suggestion
Physical	• Practice a regular bedtime and eating time • Hydrate throughout the day • Step outside for a walk and serotonin top-up • Stretch, even at the desk at work
Emotional	• Put on your favorite music • Skip a whole day of social media • Reflect or write about the favorite part of your day • Make time to forgive yourself for the day's shortcomings
Mental	• Read your favorite poems or books • Take a TV break and escape • Learn a second language • Meditate and clear your mind
Spiritual	• Journal or write about your feelings or connection to a higher power • Dedicate specific hours of the week to working in your purpose • Connect with an elderly neighbor or friend or relative • Practice gratitude by recording three things you're grateful for

Self-Advocacy

Self-advocacy is the third component rounding out what I call the trifecta of self-love. It starts with getting connected to your energy and understanding where you are in each area of your well-being. Self-advocacy is pushing back against that inner critic and outwardly fighting for yourself. It's also being super clear about the times you need help or support—and then asking for it! We often are afraid to ask for support or help. Or to have hard truthful conversations about our suffering. But vulnerability is powerful; it builds your authentic resilience. If you can't ask for help, you won't be able to push through adversity either. Building resilience isn't something you're meant to do alone.

In his book *Resilient: How to Grow an Unshakable Core of Calm, Strength, and Happiness*, psychologist Rick Hanson reminds readers that their inner critic is usually wrong and fighting against it is a way to lead yourself further into the journey of self-love. Trusting your own credibility over that inner critic is key to being able to advocate for yourself.

Advocating for your authentic self and your values by standing up for what you believe in (including yourself) is the driving force behind your self-love and your authentic resilience. I've seen it, and there is research that shows it.

Ingrid Handlovsky, a scientist in Vancouver, conducted an investigation into how middle-aged gay men developed resilience over the course of their lives after facing systemic discrimination, homophobia, and living in a heteronormative healthcare system that couldn't handle HIV and other illnesses related to gay men. Her research found that support, both from a community and on an individual level, is a key factor in boosting resilience and wellness.[59] Asking for help and connecting with others for support are proven ways to build resilience. Advocating for yourself in the way that people in the LGBTQ+ community have done for decades will boost your self-love, and your resilience.

Here are a few simple ways to practice self-advocacy. There are so many more; my goal here is to point you in the right direction. Don't be afraid to inquire. Curiosity killed the cat; it didn't kill hope of improving your life.

SELF-ADVOCACY PROMPTS

If a moment of mental uncertainty arises...	Ask for clarity, double-check to ensure you understand what you need.
If you have a physical ache or pain...	Talk about it with someone.
If you're overwhelmed by a stressor...	Seek guidance from a friend or mentor, teacher, or leader and ask how they solved a similar stressor.
If you feel lost in your life's purpose...	Check in with family or seek counsel from a coach.

NO MATTER THE CLOSET, OPEN THE DOOR

I'd be lying if I claimed to believe my colleagues didn't know about my sexuality. I'm certain they did. LGBTQ+ people have gay-radar ("gay-dar" as we sometimes say) senses that are often hyper-tuned to know who else is gay, who is not gay, and when others are talking about us behind our backs about our gayness. In baseball, however, I never felt that people talked behind my back about me; after all, I was small potatoes in the front office compared to the talent on the field.

We just never talked about me or my life while I worked in professional baseball. I kept many things about my personal life private at work. I had two serious relationships in the time I worked in professional baseball. But not once did I ever carry on or chat about it; definitely not the same way that others used to go on about who was getting engaged, the wedding plans, and all the traditional hoopla that comes with office gossip. I never shared my personal affairs or conquests, either, when engaged in clubhouse banter. It was my inner critic who silenced me from being myself.

In Los Angeles, the camaraderie and fun created a sense of having a chosen family of colleagues that I have come to love and respect. I cherish my memories of all the jokes, the long baseball season, the offseason, the pranks, the salsa-tasting parties, and being lovingly teased about my choices in clothing or the car I drove. In our humor it was clear that they all knew. But even after bringing my "special friend" (aka boyfriend) to a game one evening, none of us ever talked about it. I think at the time, I still tried to pretend they didn't know about my secret double life.

Baseball banter is familial and loving; often in sports it's also a rite of passage to "earn your stripes" by taking a good ribbing from the fellas. While that may be hard to understand for an outsider, handling the "banter" is something many LGBTQ+ people have to navigate their entire lives. Living in fear and going to great lengths to keep our sexuality a secret can take a massive toll on our mental health and how we think of ourselves. It certainly messed with my mental health on and off during my time in baseball. But it also played a part of how I wanted to love myself and remain true to my authentic self. In some ways, the banter was a resilience builder. I had to get over some of the slurs and epithets I heard my whole life, but hearing them in a passive banter helped me tune them out. Only later did I discover that the combination of authenticity and resilience is a superpower—but baseball certainly helped me check back in to defining my sense of authenticity.

Don't get me wrong; my baseball days contain some of the best highlights of my career. I feel blessed to have gotten a formal start in HR through that organization.

I built a massively successful career inside MLB; America's pastime was very good to me. I am in a debt of gratitude for the chances and opportunities Ray Scott and (now) Commissioner Rob Manfred gave me as a professional. I treasure my many colleagues in baseball for the gift they gave me in forcing me to reexamine and define my authentic self; after I left professional baseball, I never again returned to the closet.

If I had only known then what I feel and know today about authenticity, I would have been bolder, more courageous, open, and truer to myself. I would have found a deeper love for myself to stay the course and not allow my ambition to outweigh my self-love. This is what I want for you. I was true to my career, but I put myself—my whole self—in the back seat. It should be the other way around. We should put our whole selves first in the driver's seat and enable our authentic selves and sense of purpose to light the way for us in our jobs, careers, and passions, and use our authentic selves to lead a purposeful and meaningful life filled with well-being and joy.

Gay people have to come out more than once in life. In fact, we are constantly coming out—at first to ourselves, then to our loved ones, and then later to our friends, associates, and workmates. Part of my aim is to share the tools of authentic-resilience building so that you, dear reader, never doubt yourself. Whether you're part of the LGBTQ+ community or not, whatever the closet represents for you—because we've *all* got one to hide in—I want to empower you to always keep the doors open and *never* go back inside.

This book and my work's focus on authenticity is my contribution to that. I want to help all of my LGBTQ+ friends openly live their best queer lives with compassion and conviction. And if your life isn't queer, I hope this message still resonates with you, because I want you to live your best life too.

KEY TAKEAWAYS

- First of all, **you matter.** Your life as a human being counts, period.

- The Core Tenets of the Authenticity anchor are Know Yourself, Release Yourself, and Love Yourself.

- Build your authenticity and resilience by learning who you are and knowing your core values, strengths, and beliefs.

- Stay vigilant and recognize blockers that lead to self-sabotage and harmful behaviors that get in the way of your authentic living. Work to release negative self-talk, imposter syndrome, learned helplessness, and any other habits or behaviors that don't serve you.

- Know when you are suffering and call on self-love and self-compassion to interrupt the cycle of negative blockers. This will help you build both your authentic voice and your resilience.

- Putting yourself first *is not selfish*. It's okay to be selfish and concerned with the self first. Doing so enables you to remain authentic and develop an authentic response to adversity.

- You can't fake it till you make it with adversity—it never works to simply pretend like everything is okay because your brain and body always know better. The faster and more efficient way to bounce beyond adversity is to get to know yourself and be authentic. Then, your authentic self, brain, and body can move forward together.

- The path of these core tenets isn't linear. They're interconnected. Releasing negativity creates space for you to get to know yourself, which you can then fill with love for yourself. You're going to be moving among these three tenets throughout the process, so don't worry if the order of your journey varies from the order I'm suggesting in this chapter.

CHAPTER 6

THE MODEL: LOVE

THE AMYGDALA IN MY PREHISTORIC BRAIN WENT FULL red alert. "Flight! Flight! Leave this place *now*," my inner voice shouted.

The terrifying threat that had me full of adrenaline and ready to bolt? My high school reunion.

In February 2016, it intrigued me that after twenty-five years, I still had reservations about going back to my high school alma mater. When I graduated, I vowed never to look back at that school (and some of the horrible memories that occurred there) or return for any reunions, despite being class treasurer. I had kept that promise. But, twenty-five years later, I couldn't deny the curiosity I had for what became of my former classmates. With the encouragement and support of my good friend Jen, I finally decided to go. I felt I was emotionally ready to face those demons and actually be humorous with myself about the real reasons I hesitated to go back.

About five years after graduating from high school, I accepted my sexuality. One of the driving forces that underpinned my hesitation to attend was the fear of being bullied by the old boys who marred my high school experience. That, and having to confront some form of validation that they were "right" about me being the homo/gay boy/f*ggot they so often called me. (How in the hell did they have better gay-dar than I had in those days?!)

Truth was, I'd never been ready for that level of emotional confrontation (self-imposed or otherwise), and I never wanted to have to deal with those feelings, especially in public at a reunion. But much of those raw vulnerabilities changed during the course of twenty-five years of accepting, healing, and loving myself.

I met Jen about ninety minutes prior to the start of the reunion. She confessed that she was also nervous to revisit the past. Her nerves were rattling similarly to mine at the idea of having to confront some demons of her own. We both knew this reunion would be well attended. The social media invite and conversations among alumni on the social platform had developed into a wide and deep web of memories, conversations, and anticipations.

Jen and I crossed the street, held hands, and took a deep breath before opening the door to the pub/bar. The name badges "Hello, my name is ___" that people were wearing were funny at first, and then surprisingly helpful. My own tension was released upon seeing a group of old music, band, and theatre kids I ran around with who all applauded my entrance and rapidly gave me hugs, kisses, and laughs. It was immediately comfortable. Any remaining nerves were quickly eradicated by a glass of red wine and the comfort of twenty-five years of distance from old familiar faces. The evening was capped at a high point for me early in the night when I was able to thank a very special teacher, Mrs. Sue Bauer, for helping me become me.

This highlight was quickly eclipsed, though, by the sight that sent me straight into fight/flight/freeze mode, that made my inner voice scream, *Run*.

Alan Ward, the face next to the "bully" entry in my mental dictionary, walked toward me. My heart sank and my mind raced back to tenth-grade locker-room horror. The potential for this confrontation is why I avoided earlier reunions. And now, it was right in front of me.

Alan made eye contact and gave me that same overconfident grin I loathed and feared. Suddenly, I was called over to a private corner for a chat. I ignored my panicking brain's voice and quickly coached myself back to the confidence and comfort I'd felt during the earlier part of the evening. Maybe the encounter wouldn't be negative or, if it was, maybe there'd be something positive in it too. It was a quick shift to the advertunity mindset.

I took a very high road by opening the conversation with, "Alan, how good it is to see you. How have you been?" and agreed to participate in the forthcoming conversation—and I'm glad I did. What came out of his mouth was extraordinary. So much sorrow and apology, words heavy with remorse for the pain he inflicted on me. It was evident that his mean behavior had stuck with him for many years, and he needed to get it out. It was somewhat creepy and distressing to hear the sound of his voice again, but also strangely calming. The mere resonance of his tone was surreal. And it felt genuine. The shock nearly pushed me back on my heels.

I'm a generally loving and forgiving person. And this is largely because of the bullying I took as a young person. In a weird way, I never needed to acknowledge what happened. I grew tough, found my authentic self, and built more resilience as a result of it. Throughout all that work, though, I never expected one of my bullies to want to make peace with me, or that *he* would make the peace offering—and in a genuine way.

It turns out karma does come around. I think all those years finally caught up to Alan. He said, "Nate, I'm sorry. I've been carrying this stuff around with me for many, many years. What I did was wrong."

There were lots of instances he referenced—specific ones that I had long forgotten—that stuck clearly in his mind. The "roughhousing" in the locker room after tennis practice. The antics designed to sabotage my game. The snide looks in our Catholic church. The snickers and name calling in the hallways. The chanting of "Nay-nay is gay-gay." And the F-word. The dreaded F-word. An '80s epithet from which any young closeted or naively ignorant gay boy would forever try to disassociate himself. The list of Alan's transgressions against me was long. But these were so many of the things that made me stronger, more resilient, and more authentic in my life. However, those transgressions that developed me into a stronger person instead tormented Alan.

What appeared in front of me was truly a beautiful thing. The poster child of "bully" that lived in my head emerged from the wall like a pop-up book illustration and became a compassionate human.

LOVE WINS

The power of love is more than just a Huey Lewis song.[60] It's healing.

We have the power to forgive and love. I forgave those mean boys from high school many years ago. In an ironic way, they knew I was gay before I did (I will never know how they figured it out before I did)! But to actively forgive and adjust in life—and to do so in the very face and eyes of the other? Well, that's just something altogether tied to love and the universe. It's also a fundamental and critical part of bouncing beyond adversity. When we do this in an authentic way that is true to ourselves, we can build our resilience.

I'd hesitated to go to this reunion for fear I might run into those "clowns." What possibly could I, a global citizen, share with them? Would it be the satisfaction of them being "right" about my sexuality? Would they sense my fear of being shamed again for sharing my life and marriage with another man? I was never prepared for the result: People were more interested in who I was and how I became me than reliving the old days. It was humbling. And so many people I truly loved then (and now) were there to reconnect.

I'll never forget that interaction. Alan Ward came of age.

The rest of the evening was lovely. He bought me several drinks and kept lingering around to hear some of us talk about our lives. He kept apologizing. As if another glass of wine might help. Perhaps the closure that results from an act of forgiveness was most important for him. I'm certain it was hard for him to say those words, "I'm sorry." But say them, he did. In a powerful, genuine, and seemingly non-self-serving way. It was almost as if he had surprised himself by saying them and was even more surprised that I forgave him and championed his evolution as a man.

This is the power of forgiveness. This is what it looks like to heal relationships (with yourself and others). And this, my friendly reader, is what authentic resilience looks like, too.

GETTING REAL ABOUT LOVE

Humans are hardwired to connect through all things that we

do with others: eating, laughing, caring for each other, and healing each other (to name a few). This is our special gift as a species: the ability to love in many different forms.

All iterations of love help you build resilience. Meaningful connections make you stronger and healthier and help you build an authentic community rooted in your core values. Having a support system of people who love and believe in you will help you build your own sense of resilience.

Love enables you to develop the capacity to respond in different, more positive ways to adversity. When you foster love for yourself and others, all the anchors of the REAL model and their various steps (taking control of your reality, redirecting energy, practicing self-compassion, etc.) become much easier to coach yourself through. Rather than as the fourth anchor of the REAL model, I tend to think of love as the outcome of the first three. Love is how you grow and part of that process involves using what you've learned from adversity. It's what builds your resilience and creates connections.

In the last chapter, Authenticity, you learned some great starting tools in Core Tenet 3 to begin growing love for yourself. Now we're going to build on that and talk about how you can bring more love into everything you do and everyone you meet. Surrounding yourself with loving systems built on forgiveness, communication, and humor is key to thriving and growing in your authentic resilience after working through adversity.

When you use the REAL model, you connect to your values and to people who share those values, even if that wasn't always the case. For example, Alan Ward clearly came to value compassion in the twenty-five years since I'd been his schoolmate. It's a value we share, which enabled me to connect with him in a new, authentic way at the reunion. What started feeling like an adverse event became a fond and meaningful memory for me because of that ability to connect and reconcile.

In this chapter, you're going to learn how to use love to further develop the skills you need for authenticity building and resiliency. Love empowers you to support yourself when adversity comes your way. That's the difference between before and after "getting REAL." When you've taken the time to get to know yourself, redirect your energy, and nurture your authentic self, people pick up on it. Knowing and loving who you are fills you with a confidence that radiates outward, and people can't help but notice you shine. That's why the ultimate by-product of authentic resilience is joy and peace. When your inner self is aligned with what you present to the world, everything comes together beautifully.

CORE TENET 1: FORGIVE YOURSELF AND OTHERS

The story I shared with you in the beginning of this chapter isn't only a moment of forgiveness; it's a moment of reconciliation. I wasn't the only one who had to forgive Alan for the things he'd inflicted on me during our school years—he had to forgive himself. In our mutual forgiveness for his actions, we were able to reconcile with each other.

You can't have reconciliation without forgiveness, which is why forgiveness is an important core tenet of this anchor. Reconciliation helps you release negativity, build relationships that strengthen your community, and ultimately serve your purpose by strengthening your authentic resilience. As you go through life facing adversity with your loved ones and your community, you won't always agree with the people around you about how to tackle adversities that you face. It better serves everyone involved to reconcile those differences so that together you can bounce beyond the adversity.

The goal of forgiveness is to use the past to learn and grow in a loving way. Psychologists who study forgiveness have found that in the aftermath of incidents that resulted in being wronged or hurt, people's first natural response is to seek vengeance.[61] This isn't surprising given our brains' negativity bias. The power of forgiveness comes from flipping that vengeful inclination on its head and choosing to instead respond with empathy and compassion.

Choosing to forgive enables you to live more fully in your own authenticity by acting on the value of generosity, because forgiveness comes from generosity. There is power in being generous with love and forgiveness—even if you choose not to reconcile.

Vinita Hampton Wright, an Ignatian spirituality writer, believes that people often hesitate to forgive others because we tend to automatically associate that with reconciliation. But the two are not inherently inclusive. It takes two (or more) to reconcile, but forgiveness is inner work that you can do by and for yourself. Forgiveness is an intentional and voluntary process wherein a person who feels victimized undergoes a change in feelings toward the offense that led to the sense of victimization. This allows that person to overcome the negative emotions (resentment, vengeance, etc.) associated with the events and people involved. Reconciliation, on the other hand, is the coming together of people to restore a broken or damaged relationship. You can't have reconciliation without forgiveness, but you *can* have forgiveness without reconciliation.

The Power of Forgiveness

In her book *The How of Happiness,* psychology researcher Sonja Lyubomirsky talks about forgiveness as something that you do for yourself, not for the person who has wronged you. She explains, "forgiving does not mean that you should necessarily restore the relationship with the transgressor, nor does it mean excusing or condoning. Some acts may indeed be inexcusable."[62] I agree. However, whenever reconciliation is imaginable, I encourage it, since both forgiveness and reconciliation play a part in building resilience. When you're working to reconcile with someone, you're doing the inner work of forgiveness *and* the larger work of addressing the needs and feelings of someone else. Both of these are powerful muscles to exercise in your efforts to strengthen your authentic resilience, because there's a connection between forgiveness, happiness, and resilience.

When we ask ourselves why we forgive, evidence demonstrates that keeping hostility, resentment, or preoccupation with ill feelings only serves to hurt us emotionally and physically. There is also evidence that forgiveness is regarded well in our communities and helps deepen the shared sense of humanity we all feel with suffering.[63] To me, this is proof enough that forgiveness is a key to moving on, growing, and learning from adversity—and ultimately gaining resilience.

I once worked with a CEO who came to me for guidance on a difficult decision he needed to make to remove one of his executives from their position with the company. While he was listing off different "what if" scenarios for the affected employee, I asked him, "Is there any forgiveness in this for *you*?" After a long pause, he told me that he needed to forgive himself for not making the decision sooner. So he did, then and there, and was able to move forward with the lesson gained from the situation. There is a clarity that can come from forgiveness of yourself and others so that you don't repeat your mistakes.

Remember the client of mine I discussed earlier, who came to realize through coaching that many of her struggles stemmed from her life's lack of gender equality, which she further discovered is one of her most important values? To overcome her struggles, she not only had to seek equality but also forgiveness. She had to forgive her family for raising her with certain mindsets and herself for internalizing and conforming to those mindsets. It was only after she'd done this work to practice forgiveness that she was able to determine her life purpose: to be a trailblazer for girls and women in her country, so they don't feel the need to conform like she had for so long. The power of forgiveness unlocked that for her.

Learning and self-insight can be found in the acts of forgiveness and reconciliation. This important stage of the REAL model leads to growth. In Chapter 1, you learned that the brain learns by creating neural pathways in the part of itself that processes events (the prefrontal cortex). Learning also happens when you change that pathway and structure (neuroplasticity). When you forgive someone, you actually learn how to feel differently about the transgressor. There is a before-and-after effect in your brain that shifts your thinking, decreasing your desire to take revenge against your transgressor and increasing the desire to make peace with them.[64]

Psychologist Donald Hebb coined the phrase "neurons that fire together, wire together." You develop your psychological resources by repeating and sustaining experiences in your life, like when practicing driving or playing an instrument, so that the actions become almost automatic for you. To become a more forgiving person, you need to continue to build and install experiences of forgiveness in the brain—in other words, practice. The more you practice forgiving yourself and others, the better you get at it. It becomes easier to generate love for yourself and the people around you.

Practicing forgiveness has been correlated with better health, happiness, and a sense of serenity.[65] Research also suggests that people who practice forgiveness are better at empathizing with others, connecting with their spiritual energy and higher purpose, and developing close connections with others. Further, it's been demonstrated that those who find it hard to forgive are often stuck in the part of their brain that ruminates on the past.[66] Dwelling on hostile or vengeful thoughts is an energy vacuum that sucks out all your power, which then contributes to self-sabotaging behaviors (discussed in the previous chapter). People who practice forgiveness are more able to move on from past hurts, including self-inflicted ones.

I've had two different clients who had to forgive themselves for being what they considered poor mothers after incidents of forgetting to pick their kids up from daycare. In both cases, it was an honest mistake due to overdoing it at work, but that mistake caused them a lot of guilt. To release that guilt, these ladies had to realize that their priorities between work and motherhood were out of balance, and they had to forgive themselves for this imbalance before they were free to realign themselves with their purpose of being moms that make a difference and putting their kids first. Once they did, they were able to forgive themselves for being neither the mothers nor professionals they wanted to be. Then they could move forward. That ability to move on helps you grow and build your resilience, the ability to bounce beyond and move on from adversity.

EXERCISE BOX

Here are some starter questions to prompt you in the journey of forgiveness within yourself. I suggest getting comfortable first by sitting or lying down. Breathing gently will also help your body relax. These are some exercise questions I have adapted from my coaching practice and from other experts.

Ask yourself first, **Is the time right to seek forgiveness from myself?** Forgiveness is a journey that takes time. Unless you're already ready to give yourself the full absolved all-in-one-fell-swoop pardon, you will need to create time to consider the forgiveness journey based on where you are in the Reality Curve. If you're not willing to give yourself absolution, go back to the previous chapters and evaluate where you stand with each anchor and its core tenets. Which of these needs to be addressed before you're ready to forgive yourself for all your past self-harms?

Next, ask yourself, **What is that truth?** While working to feel the feelings and drop the story, it helps to first understand that story. What's true and what's just fabricated by your inner critic in an attempt to fill a void of missing context? Seek facts and accurate observations about the event(s) you need to forgive. You're looking to tell yourself the truth about what it is you seek to forgive. If you're trying to forgive something that isn't true, you're not really doing the work of forgiveness; you're just further fabricating stories.

Follow this by asking, **How do I feel about this truth?** Name and explore these feelings further and examine why you have them. For example, are these emotions connected to feeling you've done wrongdoing or harm? Does this cause shame or guilt? Whatever you're feeling, try to see if you're able to be objective about it.

Then, **What is the opportunity or cost if I forgive this harmful act? What is the opportunity or cost if I don't?** When we don't weigh the risks and costs of forgiving or not forgiving ourselves, we miss the bigger picture of how that forgiveness fits in with the rest of our lives. This understanding is important to gain perspective about what we are seeking to forgive in the first place.

Last, look for responsibility by asking, **What is my responsibility in this? Can I feel remorse? Have I made any amends for my actions?** If you feel remorse, or even just a sense that you did something wrong, close this practice by asking yourself for forgiveness.

A good closure to this practice is to write a letter to yourself or to otherwise document you've moved on from the event. Keeping a gratitude and/or a forgiveness journal is a convenient and fast way to practice self-forgiveness on a regular (ideally daily) basis.

Growing the durability of forgiveness in your brain allows you to build a deeper sense of connection through the shared human experience. There is research that suggests remembering you forgave someone helps to rewire your brain from a "me" to a "we" mindset that focuses more on community and relationships.[67] This shift helps bring people closer together and also inspires in those around you a willingness to help others. Forgiving yourself not only helps you heal from negative events but do so in a way that enables you to move forward in a positive manner that will allow you to forgive others more easily.

To help you gain a better understanding of this exercise, I want to share a deeply personal story about a time I had to practice forgiving myself in the midst of traumatizing adversity. Warning: the following story includes substance abuse, an eating disorder, and suicide.

When I lived in Tokyo, one of my colleagues took his own life while on assignment in Singapore. He was only in his mid-twenties. For weeks this person had been battling extreme substance abuse on top of mental health issues, including a potential eating disorder. And in one coaching conversation I had with him, he told me in confidence that on top of all this, he was struggling with his sexuality and the matters that surround coming out.

His death devastated me; I felt like my counsel as his coach, his colleague, and a fellow LGBTQ+ person had failed him. He trusted me with his secret, but I hadn't been able to do enough for him to prevent this decision. He was a kid who so desperately needed love in his life, but I hadn't realized how much until it was too late.

The choice was his alone, and I understand that, but I still felt like I came up short. That shortcoming was something I had to forgive myself for in the midst of one nightmare after another. His family lived in another country, so I had to call to notify them of their son's death. I also had to identify his body, clean out his apartment (under the watch of a landlady more concerned with the future rentability of an apartment someone had died in than in showing compassion to those grieving her tenant), and deal with the collective grief that came with the death of an employee at the company—all on top of being the only person who knew one of the biggest demons he had battled.

The thing that got me through it all was love. I hadn't been able to give him enough love when he was alive, but I could damn sure show him the love he deserved in death. I spoke with his family and made all the preparations to ensure his body arrived home safely and with meaningful items his family wanted with him. He went home in style. I also made sure to treat his parents with love and compassion, even while disagreeing with some of their methods for dealing with the death of their son. I gave him and everyone involved as much love as I could in that situation, including myself.

I forgave myself for making his death about me in my thoughts, however brief it was. I forgave myself for blaming myself for failing to get through to him. And I forgave myself for the judgment I felt toward the people who had made this kid feel like it was better to die than to show them his authentic self.

I am in Singapore from time to time and this person crosses my mind when I walk by the place where we had that sensitive conversation or by the general hospital where I identified his body in the morgue. And while they're not happy memories, I'm grateful for this experience because thinking about my approach to this situation forced me to grow my capacity for empathy and compassion, which has served me well in the years since his passing.

CORE TENET 2: DEVELOP AUTHENTIC COMMUNITY

In the self-advocacy section of Chapter 5, I wrote about Handlovsky's research with gay men's battles with healthcare-system failures. It suggests the importance of support—on both the community and individual levels—in building resilience. While it's important to practice advocating for yourself, no lone person can handle everything life throws at them. That's why you need to surround yourself with people you can rely on to support you when you're going through adversity.

Having a support system based on mutual love and respect—rather than money, career, or reputation—helps you stay on the path to authentic resilience when things get hard and you're tempted to succumb to learned helplessness (as we all are at some point). Think about the activism the gay community organized to support their peers suffering from AIDS and HIV. We can learn everything we need to know about developing authentic community from queer people.

Handlovsky found that resilience comes from not just individuals (through practices such as optimism and reframing, as we discussed earlier). It's also developed by protective processes—that is, strategies that build resilience development through social and relational dynamics such as family, peers, mentors, or community-based organizations. She was able to prove that community makes a difference in the development of coping mechanisms, and these processes validate the notion of what I call "community connection" in the REAL model.

Even in the twenty-first century, gay people fight systemic homophobia while living in a heteronormative society that discriminates on a macro and structural level. Many queer people are constantly under threat of discrimination in every facet of life, including housing, employment, immigration status, and healthcare. We are also more at risk of living with HIV/sexually transmitted infections, identity issues, and a myriad of mental disorders caused by trauma, including some we discussed earlier, such as imposter syndrome and process addiction.[68] This list barely scratches the surface of the adversities this community must combat on a regular basis. *Of course* we would turn to the power of numbers in our efforts to survive all of this.

Additionally, LGBTQ+ people often find themselves migrating from small places to urban areas. This can cause a sense of isolation and drive them to seek community, connection, and support. It's often how and why gay community centers popped up all around the world—in order to support people.

Community and connection building starts with taking action. When a group of people acts and forms grassroots initiatives, it alleviates the sense of helplessness that exists among individual community members. This can contribute to the healing process and further spur continuation and advocacy. As this collective energy-positive action continues, a stronger sense of community resilience can grow. Individuals benefit from this by building self-confidence and esteem for themselves and others. Support groups, counseling, peer groups, and community centers all play a critical role in the development of personal resilience.

When you lean on community, you can create change for the collective *and* build both individual and community resilience. That's exactly what Handlovsky found; the gay men who had survived the AIDS epidemic and all the associated issues related to the stigma in the community had done so as a result of building a community, fighting together for better healthcare, visitation rights, and a higher standard for duty of care by medical professionals.

When I say you need to build an authentic community, I mean people you choose to be part of a support system. That can include relatives, chosen family, professional and social connections, and (perhaps most important) a network of health and wellness professionals. Community can come in countless other ways: sports-team fandom, political connection, and workplace identity, to name a few social examples. It can also take shape in ways connected to our biological identities such as gender, race, and ethnicity. Further, churches, synagogues, temples, and mosques are often bedrock community support systems for their members. So are parent-teacher associations, twelve-step programs, and neighborhood and community groups. Think of alumni groups, women's clubs, and civic service organizations. People naturally seek connection with other people. Tapping into the community that is right for you will help build a support system and network that, if invested in and fostered over time, will pay dividends to your resilience building and overall well-being.

Blood family can be some of the best support you have, but there's also the risk of conflict if they're too close to the struggles you experience while developing your sense of authenticity. Chosen family and close friends are important because those people are usually connected to the same core values and life choices that resonate with you. They can become critical to helping you stay true to yourself on the path to authentic resilience. And of course, I absolutely advocate for a strong system of doctors, psychologists, counselors, and professional coaches to help you maintain your health and well-being, and unlock your best life.

Building an authentic community is vital because it's going to deliver time and time again when you need to support yourself with love. Surrounding ourselves with other people who "get it" fosters that connection and deepens understanding, often beginning with care and compassion. This is the foundation for love in the community. Investing in and fostering deep relationships in your community will help keep you on the path of living an authentically resilient life, with happiness and well-being as a happy by-product.[69]

This core tenet is simple, but crucial. So many people choose relationships based on artificial aspects of life, such as proximity or social media. I'm not here to criticize social media, but Instagram followers and Facebook groups don't hit the mark when it comes to building an authentic support system to help you grow on your journey. Social media relationships just aren't capable of providing deep enough connections to fulfill that need. For your support system, you should nurture real connections with real people because connection is part of the human condition.

The Power of Connection

You might be wondering what makes connecting with others and building a community so important. The answer is happiness. Current research suggests that human connection drives happiness. There are even studies that show connecting with strangers can lead to happiness. Still other research connects close social ties to lower risks of premature death, such as from fatal illness.[70]

Human connection empowers you to create resiliency to bounce beyond adversity more easily than you otherwise would on your own. Just as there is evidence that connections make us happy, there is also evidence that isolation causes pain.[71] Dealing with stress and adverse events alone will be a larger drain on your energy resources than if you did so with the support of your chosen community behind you. We often underestimate the importance of connection and how painful isolation can be. Our minds are not always so considerate of how important social connection is to our overall well-being. While some things can and should be handled alone, it's important to think of how you can turn to your network to help ease your burden.

Connecting with others over shared experiences is a key component of fostering more resilience, authenticity, and happiness in your life. Bringing the lived experiences of others to light in a safe way also stimulates and promotes understanding and deeper support among the community. This exercise also helps educate others outside the community too, tapping into the empathy wells of those who seek to learn and understand the suffering of a certain group. My goal is always to strengthen the learning of others while building resilience at the same time.

CORE TENET 3: COMMUNICATE WITH LOVE

The goal of communicating with love is to continually build loving, authentic relationships and to be intentional about the language used in relationships (not love languages; I'm talking about literal language here). Using positive language to communicate with yourself and others makes a significant difference in the outcomes of your communication and energy usage.

Think about the section on negative self-talk in the previous chapter. This goes a step further than breaking that habit with yourself; now you're breaking that habit with others and replacing it with the habit of using positive, supportive language. Doing so will make a world of difference for all four of your energetic domains (physical, emotional, mental, spiritual).

If this sounds like censoring yourself, don't worry, it's not. You don't have to express only positive opinions or agree with everything someone says in order to avoid negative language. It's just a matter of reconsidering *how* you present what you want to say. For example, if someone mentions that they want to do an activity you don't enjoy, consider the different impact of responding with "I *hate* that!" vs. "I'm not into that, myself." The same idea is communicated, but the language of the second statement is indisputably a more positive form of communication.

You control the energy in a conversation with the energy you put into it and with the words you choose. That's why you should practice being intentional with the questions you ask and the answers you give. To intentionally communicate with love, it's important to ensure you keep your mental energy batteries charged, because your prefrontal cortex (where a lot of the mental energy activity happens) is where you process and choose words when communicating.

Further, the words you choose can help or hinder your (and others') ability to learn and bounce beyond situations where you have to say something you (or they) don't want to hear. How you say something influences how the listener reacts.

Commonsense as it sounds, I had to learn this lesson the hard way (and I'm sure I'm not the only one). In an argument

I once had with a former company director over HR policies, I said to him, "Don't you even care about these people?" He tore me a new one in response! The insinuation that he was apathetic to his employees was a huge insult to him, and I'll never forget his outrage. Looking back, I know what drove me to say that, but it wasn't a good way to communicate my frustrations. I made the situation worse for both of us and much more difficult to bounce beyond. If I were in that situation again, I would speak my mind from a more loving place, perhaps saying, "I have concerns about the policy implications we are discussing. What are your thoughts? How might we partner to see this more evenly?"

This is especially important in the context of delivering bad news. I once worked with an executive who had received negative press and, as a consequence, negative sentiment from a few internal colleagues. It was feedback that he needed to hear because his team wasn't happy and wanted him to do things differently. This person didn't have a great sense of self-awareness, so I delivered the feedback as gently as possible without undermining its serious nature. I started the conversation with "Listen, I have to tell you something awkward that's not easy to share, but I want you to know that this is coming from a place of good intention. The team is upset with you."

Sure, it's wordier than saying, "The team is pissed at you." The message is the same, but again think about the impact of the words. Which one would *you* rather hear?

Sometimes you're delivering news that's so bad, you're basically dropping major adversity into the receiver's lap. Speaking with love is even *more* important in those times.

The Power of Words

Language is a trait unique to human beings (at least in the capacity we use it). The words we vocalize and the words we hear in our heads are all part of how we live in the world. The words we use, consciously or unconsciously, are connected to our actions and the behaviors we form. When we respond to adversity and build resilience, we need to be in control (remember the Reality anchor). Language is a tool to exert that control. We have the chance to ask, *Am I telling my story, or is my story telling me?*

I was introduced to the concept of controlling and owning your story (or being controlled by it) in the work of Chalmers Brothers.[72] He wrote that adverse events usually arrive without explanation—yet we often make one up anyway. We then hold our story to be the truth and forget that our own mind made it up.

For example, think about the scenes in popular courtroom TV shows where there are differing explanations presented as "truth" in a he-said, she-said situation. Oftentimes, the characters telling opposite stories in these fictional cases *both* believe they're telling the truth. This is because people are often poor observers of our own actions.[73] Consequently, we forget that events are not equal to explanation—and when we believe so much that *our* explanation is truth, we stop listening. Our narratives are powerful influences.

I touched on this a little in Chapter 3 when I wrote about identifying adversities affecting you. Using words to name what you're experiencing helps you come to terms with reality faster. I also discussed it in the last chapter's section on self-talk. Words are powerful, whether positive or negative. The words you use for those stories (of denying reality or acknowledging it) bring you to action. Think about the Reality Curve in

Chapter 3. If you're facing adversity and telling yourself, "I'm never going to get through this," then it's likely your mindset and ability to reframe advertunity will be limited. The word "never" is a red flag. However, if you say, "I'm strong and I see the silver lining in this; it might be hard, but I know I can do this," then there is a higher likelihood you will take action and move through and up the Reality Curve to gain control over the adversity and learn through it. A great deal of what you do in the world (and your reactions to stressors or adverse events) is actually accomplished through what you say. This is best summarized by the famous Henry Ford quote (which I've seen quoted a bunch of different ways, so consider this paraphrasing): Whether you think you can, or think you can't, either way you're right.

Language is critical for your well-being as it enables you to act, speak, be heard, connect, forgive, and love. You are the author of your own explanations, interpretations, and events, especially around an adverse situation. You control sharing the story. You are the authority on how to generate, create, and innovate the language with which you communicate your truth as you build loving relationships with yourself and others and as you build your authentic resilience.

During his life's work of asking his patients about their illnesses, physician Matthew Budd discovered that the words we choose when discussing illness can unlock memories, secrets, anger, and fears that play into illness.[74] He found that when patients were encouraged to reflect on their lives, behaviors, and words, they were able to shift from being trapped in suffering from life's adversities to carving out a sense of their own well-being.

How we talk about things can affect the outcomes of how we get through an event and, ultimately, build our resilience.

Budd and Rothstein make the case that the words you say and use in your own health and well-being play a major role in determining the outcomes of adversity. Consciously or unconsciously, the body learns how to "react" through language. Changing the script for yourself can help you bounce beyond more easily while also combatting the stress, anger, and depression that adversity so often brings. The power of our own narrative can do so much for our resilience and well-being.

For example, if you get sick and say, "Oh not again, my life blows," there is a sudden internal inference in the body that is going to cause your neuropathways to light up as negative stimuli. Saying instead, "Oh, I've been here before, I know what to do" will more likely lead you to a better bounce beyond. (This is why I was able to navigate the blackout effectively, as a result of having experienced September 11.) This is as true for a common cold or flu as it is for cancer diagnoses. "I've got cancer and I am going to die" vs. "I can beat this thing and I am going to live"—such a choice makes all the difference in how we wire our brain language for healing. In the end, this rewiring technique can help us *survive* and build resilience.

One last note about communication and the words we choose. I'm an advocate for speaking openly and using positive words when talking about mental health treatments such as therapy, counseling, and psychiatry. Speaking out helps remove the stigma around this important topic and encourages people to consider therapy as a way to heal themselves, which is always a good thing. If you want to be proactive about wielding the power of your words, start with the ones you identify with mental health and well-being so that we can make it as normal as telling someone with a broken bone that they should see a doctor.

The Weight of Silence

Understanding the power of words does not mean refusing to speak negative or difficult things for fear of creating negative realities. Sometimes, responding to adversity with authentic resilience will require you to say hard things (e.g., "I don't love you anymore" or "I don't want to work here anymore"). Speaking difficult truths is part of acknowledging and accepting the reality of adversity. Adversity is hard, and if we don't say how hard it is, the bounce beyond becomes more challenging.

Some things are harder to say than others. Painful truths can be difficult to speak to yourself, much less out loud. But you must, because saying them—when speaking from an authentic place—is another way to foster learning and personal growth, as well as maybe a little courage. People say hard things all the time to help define their inner authentic selves, and also to help push through adversity with resiliency. Some examples include:

- No. (It's a complete sentence.)
- I am going to beat cancer.
- I am gay.
- I think getting a divorce is best for us.
- I've selected the other person because it's best for the business.
- I'm sorry.
- I forgive you.
- You're no longer needed in this position/role.
- It's just not a match.

In her book *Radical Candor: Be a Kick-Ass Boss without Losing Your Humanity*, author Kim Scott provides great advice for saying hard things. She explains that when you are radically candid with someone, you'll be able to avoid some of the pitfalls of saying hard things. Stumbling through your words, not being clear enough, and not getting the message through to the people you're talking to are all pitfalls that make communication hard.

Scott suggests getting through these difficulties by caring personally and challenging directly.[75] When you do these two things, you give guidance to others. Radical candor is not a personality trait or way of being, but a method of communicating better and more honestly.

I mentioned earlier that saying hard things can sometimes be an adversity for those hearing it. Saying hard things can also be an adversity for the speaker. For example, plenty of gay people can tell you that it's hard to say "I'm gay" out loud, especially at first. But doing so is powerful because knowing you're able to say the words enables you to recognize your own sense of resilience in overcoming the adversity of being unable to voice it. This also applies to saying "I'm sorry" or "I forgive you," which can at times be really difficult to say.

It's important to learn to communicate with love because words matter; responding with love always leads to better outcomes, not least of which is the cultivation of more love. When you tell people you love them, you grow more love and make it easier to bounce beyond adversity together (and provide support for each other). And that love builds on itself over time as you continue to communicate from a loving place.

It's also important to recognize the moments when your words fail you. When you stall and don't have the right words or actions in the moment, it's sometimes better to say *something*—even if it's not the right thing—to acknowledge the difficulty and adversity than to say nothing at all. Saying nothing can cost you...another lesson I learned the hard way.

In 2004, I was in Los Angeles with my former college roommate, Gabe. I hadn't seen him since our last year in university, in the first half of which he flew off to NYC to be an intern for one of the late-night TV talk shows. He was working on trying to be a "somebody" in the entertainment industry. Everyone in our friend group perceived this to be an act of one-upmanship as he got a head start before the rest of us during our senior year. Many of us were perturbed or annoyed at Gabe's return to our Midwestern Catholic university; he had an air of confidence and flamboyance about him. He'd changed.

Gabe's time in NYC was everything it was supposed to be; he gained priceless life experience while pursuing exploration and ambition. We didn't recognize him in many ways, as he had grown up. So, we ostracized him from our friend group. Right up to graduation day, we held grudges toward him and barely noticed how much school he had missed. He lived off campus, drove his car around and did his thing. None of us really cared to take notice. The adversity, so we thought, was our own ambition and jealousy.

I wouldn't learn anything different until I met up with him in LA to try to rekindle our friendship ten years later. After all, I had lived my dream job in Japan and did my own growing up, so I felt maybe I could connect with him again. After meeting up in West Hollywood for dinner, Gabe invited me back to his house for drinks. We proceeded to reconnect about family, work experiences, and other happenings in LA. And then, we had a powerful and difficult conversation about our last days at university.

It was another coming out story, only this time, he wanted to tell me he was HIV-positive. As it is for so many people discussing something as personal as illness, speaking the words was hard for him. But it was also liberating. It prompted us to face our ill will from the past and share the bounce beyonds of old adversities. And yet, the tension was palpable because it seemed neither of us had the nerve to initiate the conversation (or the right words for it) until it was time to have it.

I learned that in the last semester of university, just as we were all preparing to start new chapters of our lives, we had all turned our backs on Gabe while he was dealing with a devastating diagnosis—right off the heels of such an exciting preview to his future in television production. Just when he needed his community of friends the most, he had to go it alone. I was horrified to learn of this massive turning point in his life. The news was painful to hear, and it was sobering to acknowledge my immaturity in how I treated him all those years before. How cruel we had all been to turn our backs because he had "come back different."

In those moments of adversity (both at university *and* that night in LA) were opportunities for reconciliation. Just as Gabe had struggled to tell me how it all had happened, how he felt at the time, and how he bounced back, I was struggling to bring myself to say words of sorrow, empathy, and understanding. Apologizing is hard. But it is freeing, when it's real. And inside a genuine apology, there is love. So, I swallowed more humility and shakily said, "Gabe, I am so sorry. Had I known then, I'm certain I would not have known what to say. Even now, I don't have the right words to acknowledge your experiences, your health status, or your journey. But I'm glad you told me." Gabe hugged me, we both cried a little, and we began to heal. There were no more words because the embrace of friendship said it all.

They may not have been the *right* words, but inside this statement was curiosity, introspection, respect, and love. It came from an authentic place inside of me. I will never forget the profundity of how hard that conversation was for both of us, but also how healing it was to move forward and build capacity not only to be friends again, but to love each other as humans in shared experience. It's sometimes hard to find the words for reconciliation, but when you do, the words and the act of forgiveness can be a powerful tool to build both authenticity and resilience.[76] Gabe and I went forward to have adventures in LA and share our cares of life again. We continue to be friends today and swap stories and travel notes.

Words matter because they prompt the brain to create the behaviors we want to exhibit. Saying words with love, from an authentic point of view, enables you to be real and true to yourself. In many cases, it enables you to show respect and love for the person to whom you say them. Humility is part of the experience. Choosing humble and compassionate words enables others to be heard and seen. Creating spaces where the walls can come down removes the protective armor that many people wear as they face adversity. Building resilience from a place of authenticity reduces judgment of yourself and in others. There is real power in that. There is power in being REAL.

My friend and author Mike Robbins says that people often choose not to express their true feelings because they are afraid that if they do, they will be misunderstood, perceived wrongly, or let down by the response.[77] This withholding is a pity and a missed opportunity to connect with others in an authentic way. It also robs you of the opportunity to include more empathy, learning, growth, and love in your resilience equation.

Gratitude

I would be remiss if I didn't mention the importance of communicating gratitude in the Love anchor. There is a reason so many books have been written about gratitude—it works! Ask any psychologist, guru, coach, or anyone else in the wellness space. Science has even proven that when people show gratitude to others, the happiness by-product of this act actually has a longer-lasting effect than receiving it! Showing gratitude is a *really* important practice for building resilience, but I don't want to dig into it too much when there are already so many great resources available to help you start.[78]

CORE TENET 4: HAVE FUN!

Looking for ways to have a little fun can make tough moments easier and help prevent spiraling into negative self-talk. I often laugh at my own ridiculous complaints, such as when I get mad at myself at the gym for a lack of patience, and take it out on the equipment. I remind myself, "It's a dumbbell, you dumbbell! Why are you getting mad at a dumbbell that *you* struggled to lift!" Laughing at ourselves helps keep things from getting too serious. I often advocate people laughing at themselves first, because when you get the first laugh, you're not the last laugh. This always helps me keep balanced, especially in challenging situations. Laughter leads to resilience and further enables your authentic self to emerge. With that said, keep in mind there is a difference between poking fun at yourself and engaging in negative self-talk. I don't really believe I'm a dumbbell (literally or figuratively), so it's okay for me to call myself that in jest. If you actually believe an insult you're saying, you should stop and investigate.

I've always loved the globally famous Drag Queen RuPaul,

especially for one of her quirky mottos: "If you can't love yourself, how in the hell are you going to love someone else?" For many years before RuPaul became known for her phrase, and especially during my time in HR, I've said my own version of this in every workplace I was a leader: "If you're not having a little bit of fun, why in the hell are you here?" Work should have elements of fun, at least in my opinion. When I worked for a popular apparel company and people got too serious about an HR policy, I would always remind people with a little jibe that our business was not life or death—just jeans and flip-flops.

I strongly believe that having some fun and laughing at yourself (and others) enables you to get over the hard stuff in life a little more easily. Even in moments of hard stressors and major adversity, if you're missing the moment of humor, you may be missing an opportunity.

Humor helps soften the hard things. If you don't believe me, just look at how many comedians come from backgrounds of major hardship. If you can laugh at yourself, you have a better chance of quieting the negative self-talk and remaining positive as you get through hard times. It works in groups too. If you work in the corporate world, you've surely experienced the relief that occurs when your group is stuck on a stressful project and everyone is exhausted...until someone does something silly or says something funny and rejuvenates spirits.

Interestingly, science backs this up, too. In the face of stressful events, smiling and laughter can help eliminate negative emotions, distract, and bring about more peaceful emotions. Other research has shown that laughter can lower stress hormones and even the expectation of laughter can elevate beneficial hormones. When we smile, laugh, positively interact, and give hugs, we improve our ability to manage adversity, create connection with others, and make friends.[79]

Ultimately, humor helps make your life count. It's in this space of humor and love that we can rise to the occasion with stressors and hardship. Laugh and laugh often. It's good for you.

Even in times of severe tragedy, moments of humor can be found. When I was in Japan during the three-peat earthquake-tsunami-nuclear meltdown, there were moments of humor in the panic that was happening. People really thought we were all going to turn into green nuclear popsicles, or that the main island of Honshū was going to sink into the ocean. The ignorance was simultaneously funny and not funny, but you have to take what you can get in situations like that.

Talking about the moments of humor in times of adversity helps you build capacity to love yourself and the people around you. Sharing joy, kindness, and laughter enables your authentic self to emerge and your resilience to grow.

NO ASSEMBLY REQUIRED

Usually at the end of these chapters, I go back to the story I shared in the beginning and reveal some new information that sheds light on the lessons described in the core tenets. However, with this one about my reconciliation with Alan Ward, there is no new information. It's all already there (it had to be for me to tell you what happened). I think that's a good metaphor for this anchor's lessons in general: everything you need to practice forgiveness, build a community, and communicate with love is already with you. These actions are inherently natural to human beings, so you didn't need to be taught what they were. You always had the tools, now I've just given you new ways to use them.

So instead I'll end the chapter with this: I always hoped

that Alan would someday turn out to be a good person. Even when he tormented me as a teenager, I saw the potential for good in him. I learned at a very early age that you can forgive people; if you believe in the capacity of people to grow, it can help bring out the best in them. Even though I'd started off the interaction afraid, I'm glad he came to the reunion. It was a privilege to see him all those years later and be proven right.

KEY TAKEAWAYS

- The Core Tenets of the Love anchor are Forgive Yourself and Others, Develop Authentic Community, Communicate with Love, and Have Fun.

- Forgiveness is inner work that is done for yourself, while reconciliation is work that's done to mend the relationship with someone you feel has harmed you (or that you've harmed).

- You need forgiveness for reconciliation, but you can forgive without reconciling.

- Authentic community starts with connection with others, usually in a common cause to seek understanding about the human condition.

- How we talk about ourselves and the words we use can affect how we get through an event—and ultimately how we build our resilience.

- It's hard to say some things, but when you do and they come from an authentic place, it leads to learning, personal growth, and courage. This is also a way to build resilience while staying true to your authentic self.

- Sometimes it's more important to acknowledge the difficulty of an adversity than it is to have the right words to say.

- Words matter! Even the hard ones, because they will affect the outcomes!

- Laugh, hug, connect with humor because it's often a secret antidote to help battle off stressors and move faster to authentic resilience.

CHAPTER 7

SELF-COACHING THE MODEL

"I FEEL LIKE MY ENERGY IS BEING SUCKED AWAY FROM me," Amy said.

This client came to me in the summer of 2020 because she felt blocked at work. She was an architect of infrastructure technologies, developing software for companies through her own consulting company. Even after acknowledging the effects of the COVID pandemic on her life, Amy still felt something else was "off." She wasn't making the breakthrough relationships she wanted at work, and it was affecting her motivation and interactions with colleagues and clients.

As soon as she said "energy," I knew that was the anchor through which she needed to enter the REAL model. Amy had already moved through the Reality Curve and was ready to Plan It & Take Action, which started with identifying where her energy was going and how it needed to be redirected. The REAL model is dynamic. It's not necessary for Reality to be the starting point for the active self-coaching process if it feels more natural to start elsewhere.

Amy's first session with me focused on how work was

impacting her energy domains and her ability to recharge her batteries in her (steadily decreasing) off time. During that discussion, she realized very little of her energy was actually going into things that mattered to her. I gave her homework to figure out why that was the case, and we started the second session by digging right into the disconnect between where she was putting her energy and where she instead wanted to put her energy.

To do that, she needed to revisit and refine her purpose. Our next session and its homework dug into the Authenticity anchor, identifying her core values, beliefs, and strengths and connecting them to her purpose. She felt the exercises really helped her check back in to who she is. Luckily, Amy already had a strong sense of purpose as an entrepreneur and mother.

It didn't take her long after that to reassert her purpose and identify the depletion of her energy as the result of not operating in her purpose. Rather, she felt she was a slave to someone else's domain. Once we had that, we were able to spend the next session oscillating between the Reality and Love anchors in the context that these discoveries provided.

Amy was having problems at work because she was butting heads with a colleague on a project. To get past her blocks, deeper down, she needed to forgive herself for failing to recognize what was happening sooner, forgive her colleague for their actions that contributed to the conflict, and work with that person to reframe how they were going to approach the project together. In this process, Amy was able to reconcile with this person through honest and open communication and felt like herself again. She reconnected with how she wants to deliver herself as a consultant (both to colleagues and clients) and acknowledged that moving away from her purpose in her work takes her away from that goal.

After having that hard conversation with her colleague, Amy's energy for work returned in full force. With a better understanding of her core values and how much she needed them present in her daily life, she resolved to complete the project and then move on to a new gig or client that would allow her to work more in her purpose. She finished the project with glowing remarks from everyone involved. In an interesting turn of events, that colleague she'd initially clashed with became one of her biggest advocates to encourage Amy to stay with the company, but move to a new department and work on a different project that was more aligned with her purpose.

THE COACHING PROCESS

The purpose of these coaching sessions is to lead you through your adversity via the model. We do this by asking important questions and exploring their answers. The approach is really that simple, even if the work itself is much more complicated. This chapter will teach you how to act as your own coach and how to work through the model at any time under any circumstances. Now that you understand each of the anchors through which to coach yourself, let's talk about the tools you need to execute the process.

It's time to get proactive. Start listening to yourself and taking note of how you currently react to things that come your way. Self-awareness is the key to self-coaching, so pay attention to yourself and use the language you've learned from this book to categorize and understand your current behaviors. Once you do that, you're ready to start reprogramming the neuroplasticity in your brain. This is done using the four stages of self-coaching: reflect, record, analyze, and act. To reach authentic resilience, you reflect, record, analyze, and act your way through each anchor of the REAL model.

THE FOUR STAGES OF SELF-COACHING

When you get in the habit of reflecting, recording, analyzing, and acting every time you encounter adverse moments, you'll get better at not only recognizing adversity but also overcoming it more quickly. And you'll do it in a way that works for you because it's authentic to your unique self. Later in the chapter you'll see some charts with prompting questions to help you apply these tools to each individual REAL anchor and tenet—but first let's break down each stage through an example scenario.

Imagine you've stubbed your toe while getting dressed for the day. I'm not suggesting that stubbing your toe is a major adversity that will require self-coaching to get through, but this example is a simple way to show how a universal experience prompts different reactions in different people. (That said, if stubbing a toe sends you into a tizzy, then it *may* be worth applying the REAL model to that experience. Use your discretion to decide when an adversity is important enough for self-coaching.)

Reflect

A good place to start is to ask yourself: *What just happened?* What are you thinking in response to this adversity, and what can you start to process about this event? Putting names to your immediate emotions and the thoughts connected to them in that moment is helpful because it prompts your brain into activating your prefrontal cortex (where you process things).

This is an important step because if you don't consciously move your thoughts toward processing, you could get stuck in the instinctive fight/flight/freeze response that comes from the amygdala in your lower brain. The point of resilience is to get past that quicker, so you want to prompt your upper brain to take over as quickly as you can in a given moment. Reflection is the best way to do that on command.

In this context, "reflect" doesn't mean looking back so much as being present with the information you're processing—like how a mirror reflects what's happening in real time. Identify and reflect what you're thinking and feeling in this moment, and what triggered those thoughts and feelings.

So in our example scenario, you've stubbed your toe. Now your foot hurts like hell, and you're processing this as you try to catch your balance and avoid worsening the pain. This is the moment when you process things such as what you stubbed your toe on and what choices led to it occurring.

Record

Once you've identified what you're experiencing, the next step in processing that is to really *feel* it. I always suggest recording (typically through journaling) because it gives you a record upon which to build your understanding of yourself and your patterns.

This stage is where you make your deepest connections to your thoughts and your emotions. You've identified *what* you're feeling by reflecting, now you're identifying and recording *how* you're experiencing those feelings. We all experience emotions in different ways. Some people sweat when they're anxious while others get itchy. Some people experience both simultaneously. Do you hold your breath or start breathing quickly when you're afraid?

When you stub your toe, do you get angry and start thinking about how the pain is going to affect the rest of your day? Or do you get mad at yourself and feel stupid for not watching where you're walking?

Your reactions to your stressors are valid, and it's fine if they're contradictory. You're not doing this to judge how well or poorly you react in the moment; the important part here is just to acknowledge and record those experiences. After stubbing your toe, acknowledge to yourself how you reacted in the moment. Consider jotting it in a note on your phone, then including that in a larger journal entry about your day. Or at least make a mental note so the reaction is recorded in your mind.

The (typically) physical record you create in this stage is an important resource. It becomes evidence for laying down new neuropathways for future encounters with that adversity. If you want to repeat a reaction or avoid a pattern of yours in the future, writing it down is a great way to wire what you did (and what you want to do next time) into your memory so that you can more easily recall the desired reaction in the future as you build and use your resilience. This will help you build a mind-body map of the experience because the memory lives in your body and on paper (or screen if you prefer digital notes). This stage is where the learning that occurs through resilience and taking control happens.

Analyze

This is the evaluative stage of the self-coaching process, and it involves three main factors to analyze: the reasons for your feelings, the potential actions you can take, and the potential outcomes of those different actions. In this stage, you explore the reasons behind your reactions to adversity.

Start by asking yourself *why* you feel the way you do. What's causing the emotions and thoughts you identified in the Reflect stage?

Let's say you're more inclined to get mad about how stubbing your toe is going to affect the rest of your day. Perhaps your thoughts spiral into the domino effect caused by this incident, such as not being able to wear the shoes you planned today and having to choose a new outfit and running late because it took longer to get ready, etc. Imagine this incident makes you feel stressed and angry. Why did you react this way? Where does this tendency come from? Why is it affecting you this way?

Once you've answered that, take a moment to see if this information can help you ascertain the potential behavior outcomes that would occur following the potential steps you intend to take. That is, think about your options for what to do next, and what result each option might entail. How do *those* make you feel?

In our example adversity of stubbing your toe, perhaps you realize it's the lack of things going to plan that is causing the thought spiral that's stressing you out. So you could decide to stick to the plan as closely as you can and wear your intended shoes anyway. But how will the pain affect you for the day? Is it worth it? Maybe you could spend a minute or two icing it. Or maybe you could decide to breathe through the stress and let go of your attachment to the plan you had set for yourself and choose to pick a new outfit instead. Consider what neuropathways you want to reinforce or replace and think about which option would best contribute to that scenario.

When I go through this stage with clients, I ask them if they can predict behavior outcomes based on past choices and results, and if there's anything they can learn from those examples. If we determine that a certain behavior has worked in the past, I encourage them to take that action. However, if we determine their past choices haven't been working, we co-create new behavior options. Either outcome—strengthening an existing method or learning a new method—will lead to resilience building.

The questions for this stage in the charts that follow next tend to be behavior based. This is because understanding your behavior patterns leads to a much more insightful view of yourself, which helps you make more informed decisions about the action you want to take in the next stage.

Act

The title of this stage is self-explanatory. It's time to decide what you want to do about the event causing those thoughts and feelings. You laid out your options in the Analyze stage, so choose one. Use what you have learned in the previous stages to make an informed decision.

You want the action you take to be in service of building your authentic resilience. Make a decision that is true to your unique style and way of doing things, then go do it. This enables you to learn and grow while taking back control from an adverse situation, which is the whole point of this process—so after you've acted on your choice, don't forget to spend time thinking about how you're learning from this experience.

In our example scenario, imagine you decided to go with the pain-reducers and ice before sticking to the intended outfit. You lost a couple minutes, but you're not running far behind, so you're confident you'll catch up. This is you taking control back from that fateful toe stubbing!

Consider what you learned about your ability to endure discomfort in favor of executing a plan and what that means to you going forward. This is you learning and growing your resilience!

JUST SO YOU KNOW

I want to acknowledge here that it may seem pedantic to go through the framework schema that follows next question by question. When I'm coaching a client, we move through these questions fluidly and the conversations we have act as the process stages prescribed above. But since I can't be there with you while you read this book, the questions have to be presented all at once in this one-sided interaction between us. Though it doesn't flow as naturally as a live conversation with a coach, I want to stress that it is still helpful for you to do this work (and it's fine if you go out of order). It's important to actually write things down as you have this conversation with yourself because you don't have a coach there to listen and observe patterns or ask follow-up questions. When it's all you, it's even more important to have that record for reference in your work to pay attention to your mind and body, identify existing pathways, think of new pathways you want to build, and plan the actions that will get you there.

With that said, I also want to put a disclaimer here. Doing this work is challenging, especially alone. If processing these difficult feelings triggers you and you experience a spike in your negativity bias—or access a traumatic memory—please reach out for professional help. If something is re-traumatizing you, seek a coach (whether myself or someone else), counselor, psychologist, or other medical professional. Do whatever you need to get back to a safe space (and make sure you *start* this work from a safe place, too). Make sure you have access to your resources and community while you're going through self-coaching so that you can fall back on them if you need to.

THE PATHWAY FRAMEWORK

Congratulations! You have the tools you need to propel yourself through the REAL model. Now it's time to *do the work*. You need to make time and space to sit with the questions below and coach yourself through the model for the first time.

This is the process that's going to create those new pathways to resilience for you. However, I hesitate just to call it "*the* Pathway" because that implies there is a correct linear order/direction to take, which isn't necessarily true. So, I'm calling it the Pathway Framework.

I structured the REAL model the way I did because moving in that order is a good approach to general situations—at least, it's what makes the most sense to me. But as I mentioned at the beginning of the chapter, this model is dynamic. You can bounce between any of the anchors as you need to process the adversity you're experiencing.

This begs the question, then, how do you know where to start?

Well, if Reality Core Tenet 1 doesn't feel like the best place to start, then consider what needs to be addressed. With my client Amy, her energy was suffering the most, so we started there. Someone who is dealing with a lot of self-sabotage and learned helplessness may do better if they start with Authenticity.

There is a valid argument to be made for any of these anchors being a good starting point. Off the top of my head:

- If you're facing a specific adversity, then start with Reality.
- If you're feeling drained all the time, start with Energy, then go back to Reality.
- If you're not facing a specific adversity right now, but you want more introspection and to build authentic resilience for future adversities, start with Authenticity.
- If you just want to learn how to love your life, then start with Love.

The best use of the model is going to vary with every situation, so don't worry too much about the order you go through it. In fact, consider this an oversimplified version of the Pathway Framework, because I couldn't possibly include every question that could ever apply to every adversity you could ever face. And I *definitely* couldn't include them in the perfect order for every scenario!

Go over the chart. Add questions that come to mind. Skip questions that don't apply. Skip a stage or tenet if you really can't think of how it applies. There is no right or wrong way.

This is a foundational framework for you to make sure you process what you need to. Start with the questions that feel most pressing and go from there. If that's at the beginning, great. If not, then come back to that box when it feels most appropriate. The important thing is not to rush through it or take shortcuts. You want to dive deep into this to make sure you have all the information you can to build your self-awareness and your authentic resilience.

THE FRAMEWORK PATHWAYS

Reality

R.CT1 – Face It

REFLECT	RECORD	ANALYZE	ACT
What has just happened? What is the adversity/challenge I am facing? What evidence is available to me to acknowledge this adversity just happened?	What is the feeling I have about this adversity? What part of this adversity am I accepting? Not accepting?	What is the suffering I am experiencing? Is this internal or external adversity? Is this intersectional adversity? What part of the suffering prevents me from fully acknowledging or accepting I can take control of the situation?	What action can I take to begin to accept this adversity is real?

R.CT2 – Control It

REFLECT	RECORD	ANALYZE	ACT
What is it about this situation that I don't want? What have I done in the past to take control of similar circumstances? Do I have experience in this area or not?	Where is my current mindset? Am I open/closed to taking control/learning/growing? If I don't want "x" to continue to happen, what is it that I do want to happen? How will that feel?	What am I going to do about this? What is in the way of getting through the adversity? What is the "advertuity" in this circumstance? Are there any distortions in the way causing additional stressors or adversity to fight the primary adversity?	What can I take control of? Right now? Later?

R.CT3 – Plan It and Take Action

REFLECT	RECORD	ANALYZE	ACT
What are the hard parts of this situation that I have to overcome to move forward? What is my inner critic telling me?	What limiting belief do I have about my situation that might be in the way? What is the feeling I associate with this? What reframing can I do to reevaluate addressing the circumstance?	What are my options? What is feasible? How can I change my perspective? What is the outcome if I do "x"? If I say yes to "x," what will I say no to?	What am I learning from this? What am I gaining? Am I able to rewire or learn new wiring from what I am doing? Am I getting through the hard part of this adversity? What else can I do?

THE FRAMEWORK PATHWAYS

Energy

E.CT1 – Understand Your Energy Regulation

REFLECT	RECORD	ANALYZE	ACT
What is my current balance of energy? What is my go-to mechanism to recover energy? What energy do I recognize as my go-to energy for spending (e.g. stamina, endurance, physical)?	How do I feel/behave when I have a full battery charge on my four energy domains? How do I feel/behave when I do not have a full battery charge on my four energy domains?	What impact does my energy (high/low, all stages) have on my life? On my work? Where is my optimum engagement with myself? With others? What energies are involved?	What can I do right now to begin to get better awareness and understanding of my balance of energies?

E.CT2 – Recover Your Energy Action

REFLECT	RECORD	ANALYZE	ACT
Which energy do I consume the most? Which energy do I lack? Crave? What energy gets depleted easily? Why?	What is getting in the way of recovering my energy? Which one? How do I feel about that? What can I stop doing to prevent spending energy on the wrong things? How can I spend more of the right energy on the right things? How will that help me get through this adversity?	How will I address depleted energy? What energy habits can I change? What can I do to charge up my batteries? Do I need to sleep more? Better nutrition? Exercise?	What can I do right now to take better care of my energy? What can I do right now to charge my batteries? What will I release (not do anymore)? What will I start doing? What will I continue to do to ensure I stay topped up?

E.CT3 – Use Your Energy

REFLECT	RECORD	ANALYZE	ACT
What energy do I rely on to welcome choice? What am I learning when I spend energy? Am I making energy count for myself?	Am I connected to my bigger purpose? If so, how? What activities can I do to help stay charged in my purpose? When I use my four energies at optimum levels, what do I notice about myself?	How does energy play in the choices I make? What would the outcome of my choices be if I had better energy in my batteries?	What can I be doing right now to make my energy count? Is my energy in the right place on the right things?

THE FRAMEWORK PATHWAYS

Authenticity

A.CT1 – Know Yourself

REFLECT	RECORD	ANALYZE	ACT
Do I know my core values? What are my core beliefs? What are my strengths? What is the shadow of my strengths?	What are my core values? What is my signature strength? What is my purpose in life? How do I feel about these elements of myself?	How can my core values, strengths, beliefs, and purpose help me in the world? With adversities? What consequences do I pay if I don't live authentically to my core values, strengths, beliefs, and purpose?	What can I do right now to check in with myself, my core values, and my purpose?

A.CT2 – Release Yourself

REFLECT	RECORD	ANALYZE	ACT
What does it look like when I am living in my core values, strengths, beliefs, and purpose? What is in the way of allowing myself to live authentically, aligned to my core values, strengths, beliefs, and purpose? What belief about myself can I let go of?	What negative thoughts can I release? How do I feel when I let go of thoughts/behaviors that are no longer serving me? How do I feel when I let go of things not aligned to my core values, strengths, beliefs, and purpose? How do I feel I am living aligned to my core values, strengths, beliefs, and purpose?	What self-sabotaging behaviors am I potentially demonstrating? Am I missing opportunities to release other things not serving me? What is my inner critic saying? How do I quiet my inner critic and bring out my inner nurturer?	What can I do right now to dismantle my radar of self-destructive behavior? What can I do right now to live authentically?

A.CT3 – Love Yourself

REFLECT	RECORD	ANALYZE	ACT
Am I putting myself first? What do I do to love myself and show self-love components (self-compassion, self-care, and self-advocacy)?	When I demonstrate self-compassion, self-care, and self-advocacy, how do I feel? How do I feel when I don't?	What do I notice about myself when I am not true to my core and not taking care of myself (with self-love components)?	By auditing my own sense of self-love, what do I learn about myself and my current level of authenticity?

THE FRAMEWORK PATHWAYS

Love

L.CT1 – Forgive Yourself and Others

REFLECT	RECORD	ANALYZE	ACT
What, if anything, is forgivable in the situation I'm facing?	Are there things in the past or present that I can forgive to move through/beyond the circumstances I'm facing? What feelings do I experience when I forgive myself? Others? What feelings do I experience when I hold grudges?	What can I learn about myself when I forgive myself? Others? What does reconciliation mean to me?	How can I consider facing circumstances with forgiveness of the other side?

L.CT2 – Develop Authentic Community

REFLECT	RECORD	ANALYZE	ACT
What network do I currently have in my circle of friends, family, and chosen family? What core beliefs or shared experiences do we have in common?	How do I feel when I'm with my community? What feelings do I have toward my friends? Why? How do I feel when I'm not with my community?	Who is in my network today? What system of friends, family, doctors, workmates, professionals, and coaches do I employ? How frequently do we connect? How can I strengthen this community? What can I do to activate this community when I need support during an adversity?	What can I do right now to pull my community together? What action can I take to ensure I have support and a network to consult when facing adversity?

L.CT3 – Communicate with Love

REFLECT	RECORD	ANALYZE	ACT
What filters do I apply when speaking to myself? To others? What does my inner critic say? What trigger words put me in a state of disruption?	What words/phrases make me feel good? Feel bad? How do I feel when I get critical or harsh feedback? How do I feel when I give critical or harsh feedback to myself? To others?	What can I do to control the intention/tone of messages I communicate to myself? To others?	What can I say right now that will help me communicate with love to myself (in this adversity)? To others?

L.CT4 – Have Fun!

REFLECT	RECORD	ANALYZE	ACT
What in this circumstance/adversity is fun? Where is the opportunity to have a laugh? Is there humor in this situation?	How do I feel when I laugh at myself? How do I feel when I am overly serious?	What could I do to soften the circumstance with some humor? How would this change the circumstances?	"If I'm not having a little fun in this moment, why the hell am I here?" Audit this.

ADVERSITY COMES IN ALL SIZES: CASE STUDIES

Adversity is all around us. From day-to-day inconveniences such as losing our keys, rescheduling a flight, or missing an elevator when we are already late for a meeting to life-altering events such as losing a loved one, getting divorced, or facing discrimination. Adversity of any size can help you build resilience and get to know yourself intimately—sometimes at the same time.

The focus of this section is *not* to compare the impact of major or minor adversities. If you read through these scenarios and wonder why anyone would need to coach themselves through the model for some of them, remember that the purpose of this whole book is to teach you everything you need to know to coach yourself into building authentic resilience in the face of adversity. Be careful not to discount the small ones. They can be the most insidious because we tend to ignore them. Then their unacknowledged ill effects fester inside us until they can no longer be contained. Have you ever spilled your drink and inexplicably fallen apart? That's why!

My client Carrie came to me beaming one day with a tale of airport drama behind her smile. Yes, you read that right.

While sitting in the airport after a long work week away from her home in Boston, Carrie's red-eye flight from San Francisco was cancelled due to bad weather. Unable to get any other flight until the next day at the earliest, she started to spin out about not getting home to her daughter, but quickly stopped herself. She shifted her focus to her core values of family and curiosity (which she'd recently uncovered in a session with me). Then she accepted the reality of the cancellation, put her energy into problem-solving her daughter's needs, and then looked for the advertunity. First she called her mom (who was very understanding about watching Carrie's daughter a couple more days even though the call to the east coast was late at night) and then her local friend Janet, who was delighted to take her to some of San Francisco's hot spots. Feeling her energy coming back and reinvigorated at the prospects of getting to explore the city as a tourist over the weekend, Carrie rebooked her flight to Boston for Sunday morning.

She beamed when she told me this story because this is the kind of adversity that would previously have crumpled her into tears. Instead, that day at the airport, she bounced beyond it in five minutes.

The model works irrespective of the degree of adversity in events because its goal is to develop your authentic resilience, which carries you through life no matter the circumstance.

Additionally, adversity has a way of snowballing into a cascade of other related adversities that are often intersectional and cause us to question our values, reevaluate our energy, and lean on family and friends to work through the situation along the Reality Curve. In short, you can benefit from using the REAL model anytime, because doing this work helps you avoid losing energy or authenticity and ignoring reality. The more you practice, the faster you'll be able to do it in the future.

SOME ILLUSTRATIVE CASE STUDIES

To help you better understand how to coach yourself through the model, I've included some scenarios as examples of different pathways clients of mine have used with me (or sometimes after working with me).

In these case studies, you'll see the REAL model guiding people to discover and develop their authentic resilience. This will help you use the model to discover and develop your *own* authentic resilience. With practice, you will work the muscle of authentic resilience until it becomes second nature and you are quickly and easily bouncing beyond adversities large and small.

In time, you'll reach a point where you can take a pause and ask, "How do I get REAL?" to help yourself adjust. As you adjust, you'll tap into that magic power of authentic resilience that leads you through any obstacle—and does so in a way that makes you proud of having built up the resilience because it's been done with integrity to yourself.

Core Value Conflict: The Empathetic Engineer

Starting Point: Reality
Pathway: Reality → Energy → Authenticity → Love

Andy was a product development engineer at the toy manufacturing division of a major toy brand. He was also a self-proclaimed "guy with a heart." Andy came to me after his company announced reorganization. His superiors informed him that he would need to make changes to department procedures (an advertunity) and the staff he managed—including firing James, the group's weakest link (Reality).

Andy was struggling to face reality. He acknowledged that the business dynamics had changed, but he was in denial about having to let go of someone who'd been a loyal member of his team for 15 years. Andy didn't have much experience in terminating employees *or* in having hard conversations. His fear, frustration, dread, and disappointment were all draining his energy. His performance at work, sleeping habits, diet, and even his streak of days without smoking all suffered because of it. He was physically, emotionally, and mentally exhausted (Energy).

In our sessions, we explored the connection between the adversity he was facing and his (lack of) energy. At first, he viewed the connection as "I'm just a nice guy and don't want to ruin James's life," despite knowing he needed to recalibrate the division to help the business and his team.

It became clear in our conversation that we needed to tap into his spiritual energy (Energy) and core values (Authenticity). Through this exploration, Andy realized he was penalizing himself because the situation put his core values of empathy and loyalty at odds with his core value of commitment to excellence. But the decision was out of his control, and this self-inflicted penalization was taking a toll on his own health.

Andy had to choose to put his commitment to excellence above those other values in that moment because that's what the situation called for. He was responsible for producing toys at a high standard to ensure children's safety when using them—which made him realize he also felt empathy for and loyalty to his customers. He couldn't, *wouldn't* place his loyalty to a friend and colleague above the quality of his company's products and loyalty to his customers (Authenticity).

Andy's moment of triumph over this adversity came when he faced the music and had the hard conversation with James. In doing so, he further realized that if he really cared for James, the best thing he could do for him was to be honest. So Andy gave his old friend candid feedback and explained to James *why* he was the weakest member, rather than just shifting the blame entirely to the company's restructuring (Love). In that way, he was able to reconcile the tension between his core values of empathy and excellence and finally get back in alignment with his spiritual energy.

Protecting Your Needs: Chen Speaks Up

Starting Point: Energy

Pathway: Energy → Authenticity → Reality → Love

Chen came to me because he was struggling to enforce his boundaries at work. Known for being a reliable leader able to take on large-scope projects, Chen's workload for the upcoming year was strategically planned out. His team was known for producing great results, but many of his star performers struggled with work-life balance and were starting to burn out. Chen could feel work taking over his life and the lives of his team, so he planned project schedules accordingly to avoid exacerbating the situation.

One day Chen's boss requested his involvement in a big project at the last minute—with a 48-hour window to reply and begin work on the project.

He wanted to say no; the project had no place in the rest of his business year. It would be a major disruption to the ecosystem Chen had built for his team's already-large workload. But he was afraid that if he declined the request, it would hurt his reputation and his team's standing in the company. He also worried that refusing would just result in angering his boss and being told to do it anyway. Feeling like he'd lost all control of his time management, Chen's energy was abruptly drained.

Our sessions had initially revolved around getting clear on his purpose; we'd already uncovered some of his core values when the situation arose. In light of the circumstances, we shifted our conversations to focus on the energetic issues that were plaguing him. His stress and anxiety over the request were interfering with his performance, his sleep, and his emotional energy, leaving him drained and exhausted (Energy).

In one of our conversations, I pointed out the self-sabotaging nature of Chen's outlook. "If you say yes to this, what are you going to say no to?" I asked. He couldn't answer. We then recalled some of Chen's values we'd revealed in previous sessions: fairness, balance, and honesty (Authenticity). Accepting the request would require him to compromise on all of these fronts, which is what was causing all the emotional distress stealing his energy.

But saying no would put him at odds with his priority to protect his team and his core value of commitment. So I asked next, "If all your time and energy is going into protecting the team, who is protecting *you*?"

That was the lightbulb moment for him. Chen had all these boundaries set up to protect his work and the people he managed, but he didn't have any for himself personally. He'd never even considered that was part of the deal—and realizing it in that moment unblocked him to do what had to be done: set some boundaries for himself (Reality). He forgave himself for neglecting to prioritize himself before (Love) and formed a plan to take control of the situation. In doing so, Chen found the confidence to assert himself and initiate a conversation with his boss about work-life balance.

Combating Negative Self-Talk: Tarik Comes Out

Starting Point: Authenticity
Pathway: Authenticity → Energy → Love → Reality

Tarik was a younger internal client of mine still discovering themselves as a nonbinary person. I was working with Tarik for some career-transition coaching when in one of our sessions, they told me about a very uncomfortable position they were in at work.

At an introduction meeting for a project, Tarik was misidentified as a cisgender man and one of the "guys on the team."

Tarik expressed their nonbinary status and preferred they/them pronouns to the group (which included some senior leaders), and there was an audible gasp and an uncomfortable giggle in the room. Later that day, by coincidence, a separate colleague called Tarik to a conference room by shouting, "Hey dude."

Tarik was unsettled by the change in their colleagues' demeanors. It made Tarik concerned for their safety and well-being at work, and feel a crisis of authenticity as the intersectional adversity of social belonging at work crossed with emotional and environmental adversities.

To address this crisis, Tarik started our next session by working through the values and core beliefs they held about themself (Authenticity). In that conversation they affirmed their core values of authenticity, truth, and respect for others. With that in mind, we worked on releasing negative thoughts and beliefs that popped up when they encountered the snickers, gasps, and comments made at work; Tarik needed to silence their inner critic, which dug up lingering doubt about their identity since coming out as nonbinary. In doing so, they were able to shift their emotional energy from negative to positive (Energy) by seeking out support in their community of fellow LGBTQ+ friends who had advice based on their own experiences of coming out at work (Love).

Tarik evaluated their choices and ultimately chose to take control of the situation (Reality) by creating an inclusion group for the company; they even acted as a panelist at events to help educate the rest of the organization on inclusion for marginalized gendered people.

Managing Expectations: Careless Mom Janice

Starting Point: Love

Pathway: Love → Authenticity → Energy → Reality

Janice contacted me during the height of the work-from-home surge of the COVID-19 pandemic. She sought my coaching because she felt like a horrible mother. By the third time she forgot to pick up her daughter from preschool, she was drowning herself in shame for neglecting the most important people in her life because of work.

It quickly became evident that Janice was suffering from Bad Mom Syndrome (that is, her inner critic constantly calling her one) because she was trying to do it all as a mom, a career woman, and a homemaker. She took care of her parents, her kids, her husband, and herself to the best of her ability—but the fact was she had taken on too much for her time-management abilities to handle.

We started by focusing on self-forgiveness (Love). In doing so, she was able to heal and show love and compassion for herself as a mother. This quickly revealed her core values of family, compassion, and respect for others, which she used as her north star to guide her plan for setting some boundaries and resorting her priorities going forward (Authenticity).

In the following sessions, Janice realized she had been putting her energies into the wrong places. She resented her boss for taking advantage of the fact that she no longer had to commute to the office; she felt like they expected her to spend the time she'd used to commute in the past working. The extra work was draining her physical and mental energies, but she still had to put in "full-time mom hours" after the extended workdays (Energy).

Realizing this, she understood the real adversity wasn't her parenting skills; it was time management and lack of boundaries at work (Reality). So, she took control back by talking with her boss about working hours. She committed to "turning off" outside of those hours and even found an advertunity in the situation—her boss actually respected her more for showing courage and setting firm boundaries!

PRACTICE MAKES PROGRESS

I hope these stories help you see that while there is no one-size-fits-all approach to it, the REAL model itself (in any arrangement of letters) is a universal fit. No matter what order you go in, the model leads you to answer the most important questions: *How can I get authentic? How can I be resilient? How can I make it count?*

Now you just have to go do it! Start practicing with a small adversity in your life. Go through the Pathway Framework in whatever order feels right. Building your resilience in this way can make all the difference in preparation for bigger adversities to come.

PROGRESS MAKES RESULTS

These ladies weren't clients, but I watched them work through this adversity all the same. When two of my friends, Elaine and Jennifer, were diagnosed with breast cancer within months of each other, I was blown away by how quickly they each worked their way through the Reality Curve. There was no denial or self-pity in their reactions. They both found a lump, went to the doctor, got their diagnoses, and immediately jumped into the mindset of forming an action plan and redirecting their energy into beating this disease. In the same breath that one of them told me that she had cancer, she also said she was going to kick cancer's butt.

Neither of these amazing women let cancer ruin their routine and steal their energy. They adjusted as needed (especially when starting chemotherapy), but they stayed true to their authenticity as they adjusted to this new aspect of their lives. They leaned on their community and led by example through love and purpose. They are truly ambassadors for authentic resilience if I've ever seen any.

I share the story because it continues to fuel and sustain my reason for becoming a coach. I want to help more people take charge of their adversities the way my friends Elaine and Jennifer did. That's the whole reason people hire a coach: to get insight, uncover things, and find evidence for that dormant inner nurturer to use in combat with your inner critic.

With or without a coach, you have the power to do that now, too. You can use the tools explained in this book to go through the REAL model and reveal those insights. Take that evidence and use it to live a more joyful and purposeful life. That evidence is your magic power to get to the life you want. This is how you make the REAL model count.

CONCLUSION

"EVEN THE BEST-LAID PLANS TURN TO HELL WHEN exposed to reality."

I always bristled at this quote by fantasy author Michael Anthony because the very foundation of the work I do (and the REAL model) is creating a plan and acting on it. Most of the time, those plans work great. On top of that, I *don't* consider adversity a hellish place.

But boy did I feel a poignant sense of irony while I was completing this book and confronted by the truth of his words.

My husband's and my best-laid plans went to hell when faced with the reality of living in a country that still considers same-sex marriage unlawful. We knew this when we moved there, of course, but we never imagined the discrimination would have as massive an impact as it did.

In February 2020, I moved to a small island nation to work for a company I believe in. It's a brand that advocates for equality, fairness, and sustainability, and I'm blessed to be part of a great team. My husband Ron is a well-traveled man with multiple passports and citizenship in more than one country.

But in spite of that—and the fact that we are married—he still needed a visa to join me in this country, so he enrolled in a school here and moved with me on a student visa.

   We had a plan that accounted for contingencies to ensure he could stay after his schooling was finished. By the time his student visa was set to expire, he would need either to find employment (to get a work visa) or to secure a long-term visit pass (LTVP), which can be attached to the work visa of a spouse. We even called the government and made sure we would be eligible to get an LTVP should we need it. We had a case number with a government officer on record telling us that two men could legally qualify for the LTVP.

   But when Plan A (the work visa) didn't work out and the time came to execute Plan B (the LTVP), the online system wouldn't even let us apply. We entered all my details for the visa that his pass would be linked to, and then, while we entered Ron's details, the system red flagged us. An error message said the gender of the applicant must be the opposite gender of the passholder.

   We'd been told that two married men could apply, so we thought there might have been a glitch in the system. We called the support hotline and explained the situation, but even after escalating to the supervisors in the office and calling them repeatedly for three days, we got the same answer. Same-gender spouses are not recognized by the government and therefore not eligible to apply for the LTVP. What made matters worse was the rude and pithy delivery of this information to us from the officer. It was hard not to take it personally despite the message being so matter-of-fact and impersonal. The tone was of condemnatory distaste for nontraditional families. It was so disheartening. The day after we got that final answer, Ron's school informed him they'd initiated the cancellation of his student visa and he had a month to get a new visa, leave, or face deportation.

A year of planning blew up in our faces, and we were left scrambling to figure out where he could go in the middle of a global pandemic with its various ensuing quarantine laws and travel restrictions. *Every time* we thought we had a solution, another bomb dropped.

We first tried to enroll him back in school for another program so he could renew his student visa. Three days after he applied, his visa was rejected. Boom. We were informed he could write an appeal letter to the government for the student visa extension. So we did, but the people in charge never got back to us. Boom. Each explosion created another adversity. We were running out of time for a solution. No work visa. No LTVP. No student visa answer.

This latter bomb in turn caused adversity between Ron and me. Ron wanted to wait for the answer to his appeal letter (we'd sent it in December, so a lot of places were closed for the holidays). But I wasn't going to just wait for the government to tell me what to do—especially with no guarantee the answer would be in our favor. I was writing a book on resiliency and how to take back control for goodness' ' sake! No way could I surrender control to some government that wouldn't even be giving me these problems if I was married to a woman. There were some arguments, but in the end Ron agreed to keep planning with me in case the appeal was rejected. We worked things out, but that didn't stop the bombs from dropping.

Our next plan was to fly to Los Angeles and spend some time in the United States. I was planning to take extended time off from work to join him. We booked his flight first but then mine wouldn't go through. After several attempts and two hours of holding on the phone with the airline, I learned that due to a change in the COVID-19 vaccination requirements, the government was no longer accepting flights into the country between December 22 and January 20. I didn't understand the problem because neither of us was planning to come back until February or March, but the representative said neither of our tickets was valid. Boom.

Another COVID bomb dropped when we tried to plan for Ron to stay with his parents in Macau. We were able to book a plane ticket, but there was no availability at any of the quarantine hotels accepting people from high-risk countries, such as ours. Boom.

Next, we considered Ireland because he has citizenship there. There were no quarantine or flight problems there, but he needed a specific health record that proved he had all the vaccinations required to travel to Europe. But with Ron's student visa expired, we had no way to access that information. We eventually figured out how to get it, but we had to apply to the government *again*, and the estimated date for delivery was in February—*after* Ron had to leave or face fines and deportation.

We looked at a few other countries but ran into similar challenges...one after another. We kept trying to look for advertunities and to engage a growth mindset, but we kept hitting walls. It was hard. It was unrelenting.

By this point, we were on our last nerves and not in a good place to be making hard decisions. Our relationship was strained and we as individuals were strained from dealing with all the stress and bitterness caused by the government tearing our family apart. This move was costing money, time, and energy, and we didn't know when we were going to see each other again or if I was going to have to give up my job to follow him.

Once we finally got on the same page about refusing to relinquish control to the government, we discussed the costs and benefits of each country and finally settled on Thailand. And it's a good thing we did—five days after he left, we got the appeal letter response explaining that the government would not extend his student visa. That one wasn't a bomb so much as a slap in the face.

In the span of thirty days, we endured adversity on every front. Being discriminated against for whom we love was incredibly painful. The toll was not only emotional and mental but physical too. Having to navigate a COVID-ridden environment because of a government that didn't want a gay couple in its country also destabilized our social and environmental well-being. And the money spent on different travel plans only to have them cancelled took a financial toll.

I can't speak for Ron's spiritual pain, but mine was most sharply felt every time I was reminded of my situation at work. As the top HR executive in the region and certainly the highest-ranking HR official in our regional office, I am the one who signs off on work visas and spouse/dependent applications for all of the company's foreign staff. Every time one of those applications comes across my desk, it's personal to me because I sign my name in full support of their families. And now I couldn't even do the same for my own.

At the time of this writing, Ron is living in Thailand and I'm still in our apartment in the small island nation. Our relationship is stronger for overcoming this adversity together and so are we as people. We faced our reality (even if it took a few arguments and a collective eight hours on the phone with airlines and government staff), reclaimed control, and with it got our energy back. We drew on our authenticity and love and worked through the REAL model in real time—and just as it always has for me, it saw us through to the other side. The REAL model is capable of lifting you above any adversity.

As for finding the advertunity in the situation, Ron has the chance to grow and further his education in another country. Together we have the chance to grow our resilience through being long-distance for now. And for me, well, at least this whole ordeal gave me a powerful anecdote for the conclusion of this book.

THE POWER OF LIVING AUTHENTICALLY

I'm not the first gay man to be bullied by a government for being myself, and sadly, I won't be the last. While enduring all that chaos, I took heart from the inspirational story of Frank Kameny, one of the grandfathers of the modern LGBTQ+ rights movement in the U.S. It was people like him who paved the way for people like me to live authentically in the United States, my home country.

Frank Kameny didn't start out as a gay rights activist. He was an astronomer with a doctorate from Harvard. In 1957, he scored a dream job at the United States Army Map Service. Five months later, he was fired for being gay. To add insult to injury, he was also barred from ever working for the federal government again.

Rather than let that adversity limit and define him, Frank decided to direct his energy into fighting back. He used his resilience to take control of his reality and advocate for his right to live authentically. He sued the U.S. government for wrongful termination, lobbied in court, and organized protests in front of the White House, Pentagon, United Nations, and U.S. Civil Service. In 1963, he launched a campaign to remove sodomy laws from Washington, D.C. He stuck with it for 30 years until they were finally overturned.

For ten years, Frank lobbied the American Psychiatric Association (APA) to remove homosexuality from its *Diagnostic and Statistical Manual of Mental Disorders*, which it published annually. In 1973, the APA complied. After the announcement, he stepped in front of a microphone and joked to the cheering crowd, "We're cured!"

He coined the phrase "gay is good" and used the power of love from the LGBTQ+ community to show the government that what it'd done to him and people like him was wrong. In 2009, when the U.S. government finally and officially apologized to Frank Kameny, he simply said, "Apology accepted."

I think of Frank's life often and like to share his story with my clients because it perfectly exemplifies the REAL model. Everything he did to face—then *change*—his reality through his energy, authenticity, and love can be seen in the steps I've laid out for you throughout this book. It goes to show that I'm not the creator of authentic resilience; I'm just the person who found the words to write it down for those who don't develop it as naturally as Frank did.

It makes me so happy to see the that REAL model is just as applicable in retrospect as it is today. It gives me hope that in the future, this message will help more people keep these tools at their disposal. And maybe that will help someone drive their resilience to create lasting change the way Frank did. You don't have to become an activist or some other kind of historical figure; even if it's on a small scale, we all do good in the world when we live authentically. Making your life count *does* create change.[80]

I'm not claiming to be the next Frank Kameny. After all, even despite my activist tendencies, I didn't make noise for gay rights when the government tried to erase my marriage. My husband's safety was my paramount concern, and my own visa—and the reputation of my employer—would be on the line if I tried to raise hell. But I *did* fight back in my own way. Most important, I got Ron safely out of the country. He is now investing his money and skills elsewhere.

THE PURPOSE OF THE REAL MODEL

The REAL model is helpful in times of adversity for several reasons.

First, it helps you check your impulses. It gets your thoughts moving from that faster fight/flight/freeze lower brain response to the upper brain, where you can insert some logic and feeling into your thought process before you act. When you work through the system, you won't make decisions you'll later regret.

The model also helps you bring self-awareness to the present moment. Our unique ability as humans to both ruminate on the past and visualize the future means we're generally not great at being present in the current moment. But focusing on the current moment is key to accepting your reality and formulating a plan to take control back (even if you start at a different point in the model), so it's important to have a function built into the process to do exactly that. You don't want to get stuck in the past or incorrectly predict the future (as is often our tendency). Bringing your awareness to the present through this method will help you bring your learning to the current moment and manage your expectations (both of others and yourself).

The REAL model is also a lens for analyzation; it's a tool for responding to stressors, obstacles, or other adverse events in the moment with more authentic decisions. You can use this process to discover, uncover, and explore your authentic resilience so that you're better prepared for adversity.

Earlier in the book, I wrote that during some of my own adverse experiences, I felt like I was in a movie, that my brain had left my body and was watching as if the adversities weren't happening to me. But your body and brain know better than that. There is no escaping adversity. The only way out is through. The goal of this work is to put your brain back in your body, so you can move through the adversity, process it, and take control of it, and use your energy, beliefs, and capacity for love to develop durable authentic resilience.

Your resilience draws from past learning, so when you are practiced at working through the model, you'll get clearer faster when future adversities hit. You will be more in control and better able to choose your own fate—and feel good about it even when the future is unclear.

TAKING THE REAL MODEL BEYOND THE PERSONAL

The point of the REAL model is to help people build their authentic resilience so that they can bounce beyond adversity and make life count. The magic of this process is that it doesn't only apply to individuals!

Think about the word "resilience" and how it's become a buzzword since COVID-19 turned the world upside down, particularly when talking about businesses. Businesses have had to be resilient just as much as the people who run them have. Some companies adapted quickly and are now thriving under the "new normal" of working from home and hybrid working. Others were slower, but eventually figured out how to make it work and are bouncing back.

And then there are the businesses that had to shut their doors forever. Some can blame a reliance on things that just weren't possible in the thick of the lockdowns (in-person services performed on the body like nails and massages come to mind). But in most cases, it's because those companies didn't have the resilience to acknowledge the adversity and work through the Reality Curve to adapt and move past it.

The companies that survived the pandemic are the ones that stuck to their brands' core values and treated their workers with love and authenticity. They focused their energies on learning this new environment and shifting their priorities to match; they made unprecedented changes so that people could take control back against the pandemic.

Beyond that, think about people like Frank Kameny. People who get REAL and take control back from adversity often go on to change the world for everyone around them too. I've changed several workplaces by applying the REAL model to company HR policies—especially after COVID hit.

The pandemic has been a once-in-a-lifetime global adversity that affects every single one of us. If we as people can collectively get through this adversity in a REAL way, we can change the world for the better. It starts with getting REAL for yourself first.

AUTHENTIC RESILIENCE IS A MAGIC POWER

I've shared a lot of key events of my life with you throughout this book. My hope is that in opening up to you, you'll see the power of authentic resilience and its ability to help you create a life beyond what you ever thought possible. I want to help you embrace your authentic resilience so that you can do things *your* way, with *your* tools, *your* core values, and *your* strengths and beliefs.

The REAL model is the process that will help you make that happen. I know it works because I've been doing it my whole life, and I've been helping others do it for a long time. I've had people listen to my story and say, "Oh my gosh, Nate, how do you deal with it all?" Before I developed this process, my response was usually along the lines of "I don't know, I think I'm just resilient." It's taken a lot of work to understand the sources of my ability to bounce beyond hardship and then find the language to turn that path into practical advice anyone can use. But it's my passion and my *purpose* to do so, and I want to share this message with as many people as possible while I'm on this earth (and if I'm lucky, even beyond then).

This isn't a book about well-being or happiness; it's about finding your authentic resilience and using this process to nurture it. Well-being and happiness are by-products of that. I created the REAL model because more than anything, I want to help people own their lives and make the absolute most of it all, even in the darkest of times. The REAL model is a formula that enables people to live, grow, and thrive in an ever-changing world. Change is one of the inevitabilities in life, so the greatest gift I can give to anyone who will listen is the gift of authentic resilience in the face of change.

I've given you everything you need to know to face your life and make it count. From this point on, it's up to you to bring all the tools together and foster your authentic resilience. Look how far you've come already:

You learned how to define and identify different types of adversity. There is power in naming the stressors that are challenging you—understanding what you're building resilience to is half the battle. You also learned where in the brain adversity is processed and the names of all the different areas that affect your responses. This is important to know because another special ability of human beings is to spend time on autopilot. Use the REAL model to hijack your brain and take control of the wheel again so that *you* can be in control of your journey.

You learned *why* authentic resilience makes you unstoppable, no matter what adversity you're facing. When you train yourself to react from a place of resilience that is based in your values, strengths, and lived experience, you'll react in a way that is aligned to your purpose—and people will notice. Living as your authentic self will give you the confidence you need to face anything, and your resilience will grow with your authenticity.

You learned how to work your way through the Reality Curve to accept the suffering in your life. You now know how to reframe your thinking to look for advertunities in the difficult situations you encounter, and how to use those advertunities to take back control. With the power to control your mindset, you can create a win for yourself out of any situation.

You learned how to identify and direct your energy so that you can make your life count. You got clear on what charges your batteries, what drains them, and how best to distribute that energy between all the things you need and want to do. Now you can welcome that power of choice with open arms and get authentic and resilient.

You learned the importance of putting yourself first so that you can own your resilience. Knowing yourself and living in your purpose is the path to releasing what doesn't serve you so that you can make room for what *does*—and in turn, show up as your best self for the world.

Finally, you learned about the power of speaking with love to affect your reality and that of the world around you. You need love—and the forgiveness, community building, communication, and humor that come with it—to make your life count. These are the flavors that augment life for everyone. Without love for yourself *and* others, ain't nobody going nowhere in the world!

You've gained so much knowledge and insight about your mind, body, and spirit from doing the work in this book. Now it's time to get REAL. Face the future *your way* and live the life you were meant to lead!

ACKNOWLEDGMENTS

A BOOK LIKE THIS ONE IS BUILT OFF THE SHOULDERS OF those scholars and scientists, coaches, teachers, and special people who set and laid down pathways of wisdom on which I have been privileged to walk and learn. I could not have written this book without the ingenuity, curiosity, and intellect of the scientific community and specifically, those in the vast depths of history, medicine, human development, neuroscience, psychology, and sociology. I would not be doing this work without the inspirations, teachings, and advancements of Martin Seligman, Mihaly Csikszentmihalyi, Carol Dweck, Nancy Segal, George Bonnano, Lucy Hone, Emmy Werner, Norman Garmezy, Viktor Frankl, Howard Gardner, Linda Graham, Rick Hanson, Sonja Lyubomirsky, Angela Duckworth, Daniel Kahneman, Jim Loehr, Tony Schwartz, Gail Gazelle, Adam Grant, Eric Cervini, Laurie Santos, Kristin Neff, and Brené Brown. I'd like to call attention to Paul Stoltz, who wrote about "advertunity" and to whom I credit the original phrase. For you and so many other researchers named and unnamed in this book, I am grateful for stirring up my own intellectual neural pathways and stimulating the concepts that came to become the anchors of the REAL model.

I'd be remiss if I didn't name some of my favorite writers who inspired my thinking—namely to Mike Robbins and his incredible vulnerability, fortitude, and drive to tell his own stories and inspire so many people with his many books. From his works I have found my own connections and application of authenticity, compassion, and love. It was, at first, a shock to find that Fatima Dorman published the book titled *Authentic Resilience* and when I found this gem halfway through my own research and writing, I was devastated the title had already been taken. But in the *advertunity* that followed, I found that Fatima helped validate some of the work of my anchors and that our work can sit together as complementary and supplementary to each other.

I discovered the Scribe Tribe and my publisher Lioncrest through the impressive output of first-time author and friend Shu Matsuo Post, who wrote a phenomenal book on authenticity, vulnerability, and feminism in *I Took Her Name*. Having met Shu and hired him many years ago, I felt the comfort of his advice when I asked whom I should trust with my ideas and manuscript outline. Without hesitation Shu led me to the team at Scribe. Fate plays an interesting hand when tethering career tracks and business relationships and for his "reverse-mentorship" and loving care, I am thankful to Shu for many things, not least of which was pushing me to "Just do it, Nate-san."

For my Scribe publishing team—it "jump-started" with Rikki Jump, who said to me honestly on day one, "Nate, you have a book or two in you, for sure." Thank you for that belief and getting me started in my publishing journey. Vi LaBianca was my first publishing manager and without their help, support, and REAL belief in me, and their fostering my own belief in writing for an LGBTQ+ audience, I may have only delayed and stalled. The reigns transferred to another amazing and brilliant Scribe member—my publishing squad captain and chief caregiver, Mikey Kershisnik. It would not have been possible to bring this whole project through start to finish without her care, numerous question-answer sessions, expertise, project management skills, and confidence in my output each time we had a deadline. My cover designer Anna Dorfman has the most unparalleled patience of any graphic designer I've ever met and a taste and aesthetic style that crushed the brief early in the cover design process. Although we had to go on a circular journey only to end up at the original with some tweaks, I am grateful to her insight and expertise in cover design. There were two Skylaers on the team—Skyler Gray (titles) and Skylar Griego (back cover copy writing). Thanks to each of you professional co-creators, the only words I can use to get close to describing the magic you bring to the tribe. Your ability to pull rabbits out of the hat with words and titles was ever so helpful. You all have helped leave an indelible mark on my book.

Without "The Gay Brigade" and my other trusted, eagle-eyed book cover jury, I might not have ever come to a decision on the cover. The insights, suggestions, and love from Luke Bradshaw, Mark Cosgrove, Eric Yung, Roy Chan, Giselle Bates, Niki Yuri Na, Karen Kwek, Amelia Vincent, Helen Ng, and Ross Campbell were helpful to land the final cover. Final thanks is given to the impeccable taste in hairstyling to Isk at Hair by Isk and the uncompromising aesthetic and magical eye of Singapore-based photographer Filan Pearson, both of whom helped with my "author photos." Gratitude is also given to my lifelong friend Bonnie Hawthorne for photo edit work.

Of the many and most important thanks I must give for

this book, I'm beholden to my chief-conspirator, collaborator, listener, advisor, humorist, scribe, and editor—the incomparable Jane Stogdill. There are no words left—they're all in this book, thanks to you. You've been the "person who holds the string to my balloon," the provocateur, the devil's advocate, the taskmaster, the Saturday morning manager, and person who helped me tell my story, in my own authentic way. You lived through some of my darker resilient days and advertunities (and helped me write about them!). You became a (writing) coach to the (resilience) coach. You've become my friend. The powers that be put us together for a reason and won't ever pull us apart. There might not be anyone quite like you in this universe and I'm so grateful to have you be part of my contribution to the world. For through it, we both live intentionally in our respective purposes.

I have to thank the coaches, scientists, and doctors I know personally who have influenced my life and my writing and those heartfelt gratitudes are extended to my friend Vivien Hau for her contributions on imposter syndrome, purpose, flow, and appreciative inquiry; to Dr. Kaili Chen, who saved my life and put 2019 in the reframe; "Dr. Sleep"—Dr. David Lee of Sleep Unlimited, UK, whose work continues to make impact in the world; Emma Bardwell for her inspiring connection and work on menopause; Philip Yue, my master's thesis advisor, friend, and intellectual cheerleader; Helen Barker, who was an inspiring coach and fostered my thinking; Dr. Paul Englert, who helped validate my framework; and to Rinkoo Ramchandani, a woman who impressively balances the art and science of everything, especially writing. Thank you for early reads of the manuscript and for your trust, honesty, notes, and comfort. You helped me get over that hump of fear. I wish to also thank alchemists Craig McKenzie and Tony Dickel of Transcend Academy, who trained me up as a coach many years ago and who continue to be coaching mentors to me and so many others doing good work in the world through the powerful two-way conversation that is coaching.

Along the way in writing a book there are stories that get collected, shared, and connected. So many storytellers, content inspirers, and contributors helped me along the way and I want to thank Sarah "Se-chan" Smith, Sue Bauer, Erica Rose, Lai Hing Chan, Amelia Morales, Grant Grabowski, Jennifer Gari and family, Janelle Aaker, Danielle and Evan Haner, Morgan Tan, Lesley Maness, Bonnie Hawthorne, Doug Bowen, Leina Lin, Natalie Brewster, Martin Mason, Christine Turner, Jodie Gear, Alison and Andy Massey, Helen and Andrew Ford, Diane Cuddy, Winnie Tse, Jeanne Webb, Donna Hoder, Lidia Argomaniz, Tracy Key, Teri Shambaugh, and so many at the Los Angeles Angels baseball organization. To Billy Bean, I am grateful for your bravery and courage in leading the way for baseball to be more inclusive and positively LGBTQ+-friendly.

My first baseball and HR boss, Ray Scott, ensured I got great projects, learned on the job, networked across the leagues, and sent me back to school for HR training. After certifying in HR, Ray and (now MLB Commissioner) Rob Manfred were directly responsible for my early HR experiences. Thanks to their guidance and trust, I built a massively successful career inside MLB, and America's pastime was very good to me. I am in a debt of gratitude for the chances and opportunities they gave me as a professional. To my many colleagues in baseball, I treasure you for the gift you gave me in forcing me to examine and define my authentic self; for it was after I left professional baseball that I never again returned to the closet.

Woven throughout my HR experiences, diversity pioneers and living legends Wendy Lewis, Todd Corley, Toya Alexander,

Ernest Adams, Ericka Jones, and Nykeba King taught me representation and equity matters and over many years not only helped foster my deeper understanding of diversity, equity, inclusion, and belonging but encouraged me to find my voice as an LGBTQ+ and well-being activist. Your teachings are not lost, rather, they are profoundly a part of my everyday life and spirit. Specifically, Nykeba has been such a champion and coach to me, impacting my understanding of intersectional queer life in the workplace in ways I never explored at work before. A valued collaborator in this REAL work, Nykeba aided in the workshopping of the title and the cover. I am grateful to you, my friend.

As a businessperson, I am grateful for those senior leaders who rolled the dice on me in my career as a passionate, ambitious, and determined HR professional. Deon Riley, Tony Park, and Eric Duerksen played a pivotal role in setting a course for my HR management career and are responsible for some of the learning stories in this book. Without Jennifer Woo, Andrew Keith, and the inimitable Ruth King, I might not have ever found my way to coaching. Maureen Vickers continues to be as strong a presence in my life as she was when she picked me up and helped sit me officially at "the boardroom table" for the first time. Without her direct feedback, honesty, and mentorship, I might not have realized my full potential as a leader. She helped me see my blind spots and pushed me to grow in ways I didn't think possible for myself. Louise Wilson, Katrina Wright, Paula Fallowfield, and the formidable leadership of David Boynton have proven to me that true leadership begins with love and that purposeful companies can heal the wounds of self-doubt and low self-confidence—in all of us. Thank you for trusting me to lead well-being and allowing me to be my authentic-resilient self every day.

The journey of Your REAL Life started many years ago as a child, growing up in the '70s and '80s. It was in *my* REAL life that some of the greatest examples of authentic resilience came in the form of my primary school teachers. Specifically, I want to thank Tammy Biandudi and Sandy Morgan for their guidance and safety as a young vulnerable student, their mentorship in my early "teaching" days and their lifelong love for me as a friend and family. Their own authentic resilience stories remain with me to this day. Without their commitment to excellence and teaching me to unlock my creativity all those years ago, I'd never have found my love of writing, sharing stories, or helping others. This book enables these three passions.

The chosen family plays a massive role in building resilience in our lives, mine especially; and it's worth calling special attention to key members of this unique pod of people. Thinking of this book for more than five years and bringing it to life during the COVID pandemic was spurred on by the love, generosity, encouragement, support, critiques, suggestions, and patience of so many—Daniel Stokes-McKeon, Oscar Fuchs, Denny Newell, all of whom contributed to the cover discussion, title, and content; Elaine Swanson and Jennifer Lawrence, who were generous with their own resilient stories and giving of support throughout my writing journey; Megan Cundari, who helped me tweak the title and reminded me that I "always chase my goals, don't give up now." I have also to thank all the teams of people (work-wives, work-husbands, and all) I have been a part of and have been privileged to lead in business, especially the many "squads" in Asia-Pacific who have championed me writing my book (and put up with me talking about it every day). Massive thanks to the Wellbeing Core team at TBS and especially Sophie Peaty, who helped co-create and reinvigorate the magic of the Lotus. Here it is, everyone.

Last but certainly not least in my menagerie of chosen family, perhaps my dear Stevie Frieder has been the one reminding me the longest that I "know how to work it, dish it, serve it, and keep it REAL," and that I needed to someday write a book. It is categorically wrong not to give credit to Steve for this record, but for also keeping the humor, content, the title ideations, the cover collaboration, and the stories (and secrets) all flowing and, namely, for being "all up in my bizniz" over the last three decades. I am indebted to your generosity and willingness to allow me to be right, much of the time.

Resilience runs deep and hardily in our Andres family veins. We're known to fight hard and long and always to the end. Writing a book was something that I often talked about with my Aunt, Jo Andres, who, while on her deathbed, made me promise to write and "tell my story." Her esoteric and mysterious mind never stopped inquiring or learning and served as a muse for my own intellectual creativity. She was the one who introduced me to the wisdom of Pema Chödrön before I was ready. And it was she, who over many a night discussing life philosophies with my Uncle, Steve Buscemi, helped comfort me during the bumpy ride of life from my 20s to my 30s. If it wasn't for Jo and Steve telling me to stop doing laundry at midnight, I might never have moved on with my (New York) life. I believe entirely that she was part of the making of this book—she is woven into the content both directly and indirectly. While she may not have an earthly chance to read my writing, I live with no doubt that she would be proud (and would likely have a few notes of improvement). Joyfully through the spirit channels and energy work of my Aunt Dayna Beth, I am thankful for the healing and chakra calibrations I received while writing over a year to help charge my own batteries in order to carry on. I continue to be inspired by your energy coaching and grateful for your gifts in communicating with the other side.

I want to thank my brother Corey Andres for his insights and content ideas, humor, and armor when I always needed it (then and now), despite being the younger brother. He and his family were cover design jury members and I "thank them for their service." Heaps of thanks to my sister Julie Caserta for her unwavering support of all of my writing endeavors over the years, especially when I was writing for her. Julie taught me early on what allyship and love looked like when packaged in courage and hope. Julie and her family were also cover design jury members and deserve thanks for their "votes." I aspire to be as strong a human as these two are as parents, teachers, and members of society who contribute at the highest levels of compassion, service, and excellence. As siblings you bring pride to my heart and joy to my life with the families you have each created.

A book doesn't get written without the express consent and support of a spouse or partner. I hit the jackpot with my husband Ronald Lau, who has been my rock. For so many years I talked about needing and wanting to write the book. Ronnie always reminded me in short, easy, and simple words (usually English, sometimes in Cantonese) to "just write it." When the time came during the COVID pandemic to make the decision to invest in "doing a book," without hesitation Ron said, "yes." Through months of separation and togetherness, the trials and tribulations of pandemic relocation, and later, immigration woes, Ron selflessly attended all my needs, those of our household, our dogs, and allowed me to write nearly every Saturday, even on vacations. Thank you, my prince. I love you.

I think authentic resilience and I were born on the same day. I get it from my parents Timothy and Carol Andres. Somehow before I knew the words or what they meant, I had it. As my mother's first-born child, I was an unexpected C-section. A breech baby of the '70s who had twirled into a last-minute position with our umbilical cord wrapped around my neck. From my early childhood days, I was able to navigate learning how to get back up again. It was little things at first, like falling off my bike, scraping a knee while on roller skates, or getting pushed and knocked around at school for being different than the other little boys. Later it was being a front-row witness to my father's lifelong battle with heart disease and being bullied for liking what I liked: art, theatre, music, writing, charity, and service. The point here is that it's most certain I was born with a little "extra" authenticity and resilience. Naturally, I'd have the same ounces of resilience and authenticity that we're all born with as humans; but actually, that little "extra" was a result of my parents' unwavering love and commitment to me. They chose my name Nathan because in Hebrew it means "gift from god" and yet I was the one who got the gifts—from them. It's from the two of them that I saw the conversations of the Reality Curve and developed this idea from a very early age; it's from the two of them that I came to respect energy management; it's in the two of them where purpose lives deeply and authenticity is unapologetic and direct; it's in the two of them where love—in all its forms—wraps my heart bountifully. For all of these gifts (and more), I may never be able to formulate the right words to convey my deep gratitude for all they have done for me, but for teaching me the ways of being REAL and inspiring confidence in me, as part of my appreciation, I have dedicated this book to them.

ADDITIONAL RESEARCH

BOOKS AND STUDIES

Ager, Alastair, Jeannie Annan, and Catherine Panter-Brick. "Resilience: From Conceptualization to Effective Intervention. Policy Brief for Humanitarian and Development Agencies." Policy brief presented at the IRC Strategic Planning meeting, May 6, 2013. https://crh.macmillan.yale.edu/sites/default/files/files/Resilience_Policy_Brief_Panter-Brick.pdf.

American Psychological Association. "The Road to Resilience." Washington, DC: American Psychological Association, 2014. https://advising.unc.edu/wp-content/uploads/sites/341/2020/07/The-Road-to-Resiliency.pdf.

Amthor, Frank. *Neuroscience for Dummies*. 2nd ed. Hoboken: John Wiley & Sons, 2016.

APA Dictionary of Psychology. Washington, DC: American Psychological Association, 2022. s.v. "reframing." Accessed November 27, 2022. https://dictionary.apa.org/reframing.

Arnold, Margaret, Robin Mearns, Kaori Oshima, and Vivek Prasad. "Climate and Disaster Resilience: The Role for Community-Driven Development." Washington, DC: World Bank Group, 2014. http://hdl.handle.net/10986/17553.

Becvar, Dorothy S., ed. *Handbook of Family Resilience*. New York: Springer, 2013.

Bonanno, George A. "Loss, Trauma, and Human Resilience: Have We Underestimated the Human Capacity to Thrive after Extremely Adverse Events?" *American Psychologist* 59, no. 1 (January 2004): 20–28. https://doi.org/10.1037/0003-066X.59.1.20.

Bonanno, George A. "Uses and Abuses of the Resilience Construct: Loss, Trauma, and Health-Related Adversities." *Social Science & Medicine* 74, no. 5 (March 2012): 753–756. https://doi.org/10.1016/j.socscimed.2011.11.022.

Bonanno, George A., Chris R. Brewin, Krzysztof Kaniasty, and Annette M. La Greca. "Weighing the Costs of Disaster: Consequences, Risks, and Resilience in Individuals, Families, and Communities." *Psychological Science in the Public Interest* 11, no. 1 (2010): 1–49. https://doi.org/10.1177/1529100610387086.

Bonanno, George A., and Charles L. Burton. "Regulatory Flexibility: An Individual Differences Perspective on Coping and Emotion Regulation." *Perspectives on Psychological Science* 8, no. 6 (2013): 591–612. https://doi.org/10.1177/1745691613504116.

Bonanno, George A., and Erica D. Diminich. "Annual Research Review: Positive Adjustment to Adversity—Trajectories of Minimal-Impact Resilience and Emergent Resilience." *Journal of Child Psychology and Psychiatry* 54, no. 4 (April 2013): 378–401. https://doi.org/10.1111/jcpp.12021.

Bonanno, George A., Anthony Papa, Kathleen Lalande, Maren Westphal, and Karin Coifman. "The Importance of Being Flexible: The Ability to Enhance and Suppress Emotional Expression Predicts Long-Term Adjustment." *Psychological Science* 15, no. 7 (2004): 482–487. https://doi.org/10.1111/j.0956-7976.2004.00705.x.

Bonanno, George A., Maren Westphal, and Anthony D. Mancini. "Resilience to Loss and Potential Trauma." *Annual Review of Clinical Psychology* 7, no. 1 (April 2011): 511–535. https://doi.org/10.1146/annurev-clinpsy-032210-104526.

Brown, Brené. *Dare to Lead: Brave Work. Tough Conversations. Whole Hearts.* New York: Random House, 2018.

Centers for Disease Control and Prevention. "Vital Signs: Adverse Childhood Experiences (ACEs)." Last modified August 23, 2021. https://www.cdc.gov/vitalsigns/aces/index.html.

Chödrön, Pema. "Free Yourself from the Story of You." Omega. Accessed November 27, 2022. https://www.eomega.org/article/free-yourself-from-the-story-of-you.

Cicchetti, Dante. "Annual Research Review: Resilient Functioning in Maltreated Children—Past, Present, and Future Perspectives." *Journal of Child Psychology and Psychiatry* 54, no. 4 (April 2013): 402–422. https://doi.org/10.1111/j.1469-7610.2012.02608.x.

Cicchetti, Dante. "Resilience under Conditions of Extreme Stress: A Multilevel Perspective." *World Psychiatry* 9, no. 3 (October 2010): 145–154. https://doi.org/10.1002/j.2051-5545.2010.tb00297.x.

Clance, Pauline Rose, and Suzanne Ament Imes. "The Imposter Phenomenon in High Achieving Women: Dynamics and Therapeutic Intervention." *Psychotherapy: Theory, Research & Practice* 15, no. 3 (Fall 1978): 241–247. https://doi.org/10.1037/h0086006.

Cuginotti, Augusto. "Multi-Stakeholder Engagement for Sustainable Development." The Learning Host. October 23, 2010. https://issuu.com/acuginotti/docs/multi_stakeholder_engagement.

deRoon-Cassini, Terri A., Anthony D. Mancini, Mark D. Rusch, and George A. Bonanno. "Psychopathology and Resilience following Traumatic Injury: A Latent Growth Mixture Model Analysis." *Rehabilitation Psychology* 55, no. 1 (2010): 1–11. https://doi.org/10.1037/a0018601.

Dunn, Elizabeth, and Michael Norton. *Happy Money: The Science of Happier Spending*. New York: Simon & Schuster, 2014.

Dweck, Carol S. *Mindset: The New Psychology of Success*. New York: Random House, 2006.

Eggerman, Mark, and Catherine Panter-Brick. "Suffering, Hope, and Entrapment: Resilience and Cultural Values in Afghanistan." *Social Science & Medicine* 71, no. 1 (July 2010): 71–83. https://doi.org/10.1016/j.socscimed.2010.03.023.

Felitti, Vincent J., Robert F. Anda, Dale Nordenberg, David F. Williamson, Alison M. Spitz, Valerie Edwards, Mary P. Koss, and James S. Marks. "Relationship of Childhood Abuse and Household Dysfunction to Many of the Leading Causes of Death in Adults: The Adverse Childhood Experiences (ACE) Study." *American Journal of Preventive Medicine* 14, no. 4 (May 1998): 245–258. https://doi.org/10.1016/S0749-3797(98)00017-8.

Furr, Jami M., Jonathan S. Comer, Julie M. Edmunds, and Philip C. Kendall. "Disasters and Youth: A Meta-Analytic Examination of Posttraumatic Stress." *Journal of Consulting and Clinical Psychology* 78, no. 6 (2010): 765–780. https://doi.org/10.1037/a0021482.

Graham, Linda. "Response Flexibility—Shifting Perspectives." LindaGraham-MFT.net. Accessed November 27, 2022. https://lindagraham-mft.net/tag/response-flexibility-shifting-perspectives/.

Graham, Linda. "Shit Happens...Shift Happens." LindaGraham-MFT.net. October 17, 2012. https://lindagraham-mft.net/shit-happens-shift-happens/.

Garmezy, Norman. "Children in Poverty: Resilience despite Risk." *Psychiatry* 56, no. 1 (1993): 127–136. https://doi.org/10.1080/00332747.1993.11024627.

Garmezy, Norman. "Resiliency and Vulnerability to Adverse Developmental Outcomes Associated with Poverty." *American Behavioral Scientist* 34, no. 4 (March/April 1991): 416–430. https://doi.org/10.1177/0002764291034004003.

Garmezy, Norman. "Stress-Resistant Children: The Search for Protective Factors." In *Recent Research in Developmental Psychopathology: Journal of Child Psychology and Psychiatry Book Supplement, No. 4*, edited by J. E. Stevenson, 213–233. Oxford: Pergamon, 1985.

Garmezy, Norman, Ann S. Masten, and Auke Tellegen. "The Study of Stress and Competence in Children: A Building Block for Developmental Psychopathology." *Child Development* 55, no. 1 (February 1984): 97–111. https://doi.org/10.2307/1129837.

Garmezy, Norman, and Michael Rutter, eds. *Stress, Coping, and Development in Children*. New York: McGraw-Hill, 1983.

Gazelle, Gail. *Everyday Resilience: A Practical Guide to Build Inner Strength and Weather Life's Challenges.* Emeryville: Rockridge Press, 2020.

Hampton Wright, Vinita. *Small Simple Ways: An Ignatian Daybook for Healthy Spiritual Living.* Chicago: Loyola Press, 2019.

Helmstetter, Shad. *Negative Self-Talk and How to Change It.* Gulf Breeze, FL: Park Avenue Press, 2019.

Helmstetter, Shad. *What to Say When You Talk to Your Self.* New York: Gallery Books, 2017.

Hobfoll, Steven E., Patricia Watson, Carl C. Bell, Richard A. Bryant, Melissa J. Brymer, Matthew J. Friedman, Merle Friedman, et al. "Five Essential Elements of Immediate and Mid-Term Mass Trauma Intervention: Empirical Evidence." *Psychiatry* 70, no. 4 (December 2007): 283–315. https://doi.org/10.1521/psyc.2007.70.4.283.

Karam, Elie G., Matthew J. Friedman, Eric D. Hill, Ronald C. Kessler, Katie A. McLaughlin, Maria Petukhova, Laura Sampson, et al. "Cumulative Traumas and Risk Thresholds: 12-Month PTSD in the World Mental Health (WMH) Surveys." *Depression and Anxiety* 31, no. 2 (February 2014): 130–142. https://doi.org/10.1002/da.22169.

Karatsoreos, Ilia N., and Bruce S. McEwen. "Annual Research Review: The Neurobiology and Physiology of Resilience and Adaptation across the Life Course." *Journal of Child Psychology and Psychiatry* 54, no. 4 (April 2013): 337–347. https://doi.org/10.1111/jcpp.12054.

Kim-Cohen, Julia, and Rebecca Turkewitz. "Resilience and Measured Gene-Environment Interactions." *Development and Psychopathology* 24, no. 4 (November 2012): 1297–1306. https://doi.org/10.1017/S0954579412000715.

Lundberg, Mattias, and Alice Wuermli, eds. *Children and Youth in Crisis: Protecting and Promoting Human Development in Times of Economic Shocks.* Washington, DC: The World Bank, 2012.

Luthar, Suniya S. "Resilience in Development: A Synthesis of Research across Five Decades." In *Developmental Psychopathology: Volume Three: Risk, Disorder, and Adaptation,* 2nd ed., edited by Dante Cicchetti and Donald J. Cohen, 739–795. Hoboken: John Wiley & Sons, 2015. https://doi.org/10.1002/9780470939406.ch20.

Luthar, Suniya S. "Vulnerability and Resilience: A Study of High-Risk Adolescents." *Child Development* 62, no. 3 (June 1991): 600–616. https://doi.org/10.2307/1131134.

Luthar, Suniya S., Dante Cicchetti, and Bronwyn Becker. "The Construct of Resilience: A Critical Evaluation and Guidelines for Future Work." *Child Development* 71, no. 3 (May/June 2000): 543–562. https://doi.org/10.1111/1467-8624.00164.

Maslow, Abraham H. *The Farther Reaches of Human Nature.* New York: The Viking Press, 1971.

Masten, Ann S. "Global Perspectives on Resilience in Children and Youth." *Child Development* 85, no. 1 (January/February 2014): 6–20. https://doi.org/10.1111/cdev.12205.

Masten, Ann S. *Ordinary Magic: Resilience in Development*. New York: The Guilford Press, 2014.

Masten, Ann S. "Ordinary Magic: Resilience Processes in Development." *American Psychologist* 56, no. 3 (2001): 227–238. https://doi.org/10.1037/0003-066X.56.3.227.

Masten, Ann S. "Resilience in Children Threatened by Extreme Adversity: Frameworks for Research, Practice, and Translational Synergy." *Development and Psychopathology* 23, no. 2 (May 2011): 493–506. https://doi.org/10.1017/S0954579411000198.

Masten, Ann S., and Dante Cicchetti. "Risk and Resilience in Development and Psychopathology: The Legacy of Norman Garmezy." *Development and Psychopathology* 24, no. 2 (May 2012): 333–334. https://doi.org/10.1017/S0954579412000016.

Masten, Ann S., and Joy D. Osofsky. "Disasters and Their Impact on Child Development: Introduction to the Special Section." *Child Development* 81, no. 4 (July/August 2010): 1029–1039. https://doi.org/10.1111/j.1467-8624.2010.01452.x.

Masten, Ann S., and Auke Tellegen. "Resilience in Developmental Psychopathology: Contributions of the Project Competence Longitudinal Study." *Development and Psychopathology* 24, no. 2 (May 2012): 345–361. https://doi.org/10.1017/S095457941200003X.

Neff, Kristin. *Self-Compassion: The Proven Power of Being Kind to Yourself*. New York: William Morrow, 2011.

Norris, Fran H., Susan P. Stevens, Betty Pfefferbaum, Karen F. Wyche, and Rose L. Pfefferbaum. "Community Resilience as a Metaphor, Theory, Set of Capacities, and Strategy for Disaster Readiness." *American Journal of Community Psychology* 41, no. 1–2 (March 2008): 127–150. https://doi.org/10.1007/s10464-007-9156-6.

Norris, Fran H., Melissa Tracy, and Sandro Galea. "Looking for Resilience: Understanding the Longitudinal Trajectories of Responses to Stress." *Social Science & Medicine* 68, no. 12 (June 2009): 2190–2198. https://doi.org/10.1016/j.socscimed.2009.03.043.

Orcutt, Holly K., George A. Bonanno, Susan M. Hannan, and Lynsey R. Miron. "Prospective Trajectories of Posttraumatic Stress in College Women following a Campus Mass Shooting." *Journal of Traumatic Stress* 27, no. 3 (June 2014): 249–256. https://doi.org/10.1002/jts.21914.

Osofsky, Joy D., and Howard J. Osofsky. "Hurricane Katrina and the Gulf Oil Spill: Lessons Learned about Short-Term and Long-Term Effects." *International Journal of Psychology* 56, no. 1 (February 2021): 56–63. https://doi.org/10.1002/ijop.12729.

Page, Ken. "An Interview with Marianne Williamson: Marianne Williamson's Insights for Everyone Seeking Intimacy." *Finding Love* (blog), Psychology Today, January 22, 2012. https://www.psychologytoday.com/sg/blog/finding-love/201201/interview-marianne-williamson.

Panter-Brick, Catherine. "Health, Risk, and Resilience: Interdisciplinary Concepts and Applications." *Annual Review of Anthropology* 43, no. 1 (October 2014): 431–448. https://doi.org/10.1146/annurev-anthro-102313-025944.

Panter-Brick, Catherine, and Mark Eggerman. "Understanding Culture, Resilience, and Mental Health: The Production of Hope." In *The Social Ecology of Resilience*, edited by Michael Ungar, 369–386. New York: Springer, 2012. https://doi.org/10.1007/978-1-4614-0586-3_29.

Panter-Brick, Catherine, Marie-Pascale Grimon, and Mark Eggerman. "Caregiver-Child Mental Health: A Prospective Study in Conflict and Refugee Settings." *Journal of Child Psychology and Psychiatry* 55, no. 4 (April 2014): 313–327. https://doi.org/10.1111/jcpp.12167.

Panter-Brick, Catherine, Marie-Pascale Grimon, Michael Kalin, and Mark Eggerman. "Trauma Memories, Mental Health, and Resilience: A Prospective Study of Afghan Youth." *Journal of Child Psychology and Psychiatry* 56, no. 7 (July 2015): 814–825. https://doi.org/10.1111/jcpp.12350.

Panter-Brick, Catherine, and James F. Leckman. "Editorial Commentary: Resilience in Child Development—Interconnected Pathways to Wellbeing." *Journal of Child Psychology and Psychiatry* 54, no. 4 (April 2013): 333–336. https://doi.org/10.1111/jcpp.12057.

Pietrzak, Robert H., and Steven M. Southwick. "Psychological Resilience in OEF-OIF Veterans: Application of a Novel Classification Approach and Examination of Demographic and Psychosocial Correlates." *Journal of Affective Disorders* 133, no. 3 (October 2011): 560–568. https://doi.org/10.1016/j.jad.2011.04.028.

Price, Richard H., Jin Nam Choi, and Amiram D. Vinokur. "Links in the Chain of Adversity following Job Loss: How Financial Strain and Loss of Personal Control Lead to Depression, Impaired Functioning, and Poor Health." *Journal of Occupational Health Psychology* 7, no. 4 (October 2002): 302–312. https://doi.org/10.1037/1076-8998.7.4.302.

Russo, Scott J., James W. Murrough, Ming-Hu Han, Dennis S. Charney, and Eric J. Nestler. "Neurobiology of Resilience." *Nature Neuroscience* 15, no. 11 (November 2012): 1475–1484. https://doi.org/10.1038/nn.3234.

Seligman, Martin E. P. *Authentic Happiness: Using the New Positive Psychology to Realize Your Potential for Lasting Fulfillment*. New York: Atria, 2002.

Sherrieb, Kathleen, Fran H. Norris, and Sandro Galea. "Measuring Capacities for Community Resilience." *Social Indicators Research* 99, no. 2 (2010): 227–247. https://doi.org/10.1007/s11205-010-9576-9.

Simeon, Daphne, Rachel Yehuda, Ruth Cunill, Margaret Knutelska, Frank W. Putnam, and Lisa M. Smith. "Factors Associated with Resilience in Healthy Adults." *Psychoneuroendocrinology* 32, no. 8–10 (September–November 2007): 1149–1152. https://doi.org/10.1016/j.psyneuen.2007.08.005.

Smith, Karen E., and Seth D. Pollak. "Rethinking Concepts and Categories for Understanding the Neurodevelopmental Effects of Childhood Adversity." *Perspectives on Psychological Science* 16, no. 1 (2021): 67–93. https://doi.org/10.1177/1745691620920725.

Southwick, Steven M., and Dennis S. Charney. *Resilience: The Science of Mastering Life's Greatest Challenges*. New York: Cambridge University Press, 2012.

Southwick, Steven M., and Dennis S. Charney. "The Science of Resilience: Implications for the Prevention and Treatment of Depression." *Science* 338, no. 6103 (October 5, 2012): 79–82. https://doi.org/10.1126/science.1222942.

Southwick, Steven M., Heather Douglas-Palumberi, and Robert H. Pietrzak. "Resilience." In *Handbook of PTSD: Science and Practice*, 2nd ed., edited by Matthew J. Friedman, Terence M. Keane, and Patricia A. Resick, 590–606. New York: The Guilford Press, 2014.

Southwick, Steven M., Brett T. Litz, Dennis Charney, and Matthew J. Friedman, eds. *Resilience and Mental Health: Challenges across the Lifespan*. New York: Cambridge University Press, 2011.

Southwick, Steven M., Meena Vythilingam, and Dennis S. Charney. "The Psychobiology of Depression and Resilience to Stress: Implications for Prevention and Treatment." *Annual Review of Clinical Psychology* 1 (2005): 255–291. https://doi.org/10.1146/annurev.clinpsy.1.102803.143948.

Ungar, Michael. "Resilience across Cultures." *The British Journal of Social Work* 38, no. 2 (February 2008): 218–235. https://doi.org/10.1093/bjsw/bcl343.

Ungar, Michael, ed. *The Social Ecology of Resilience: A Handbook of Theory and Practice*. New York: Springer, 2012.

Wallace, Stuart. *The Self-Talk Solution: The Proven Concept of Breaking Free from Intense Negative Thoughts to Never Feel Weak Again*. Austin: M & M Limitless Online, 2020.

Walsh, Froma. *Strengthening Family Resilience*. 2nd ed. New York: The Guilford Press, 2006.

Williamson, Marianne. *A Woman's Worth*. New York: Random House, 1993.

Yehuda, Rachel, Nikolaos P. Daskalakis, Frank Desarnaud, Iouri Makotkine, Amy L. Lehrner, Erin Koch, Janine D. Flory, Joseph D. Buxbaum, Michael J. Meaney, and Linda M. Bierer. "Epigenetic Biomarkers as Predictors and Correlates of Symptom Improvement Following Psychotherapy in Combat Veterans with PTSD." *Frontiers in Psychiatry* 4, no. 118 (2013). https://doi.org/10.3389/fpsyt.2013.00118.

Yehuda, Rachel, and Janine D. Flory. "Differentiating Biological Correlates of Risk, PTSD, and Resilience Following Trauma Exposure." *Journal of Traumatic Stress* 20, no. 4 (August 2007): 435–447. https://doi.org/10.1002/jts.20260.

Yehuda, Rachel, Janine D. Flory, Steven Southwick, and Dennis S. Charney. "Developing an Agenda for Translational Studies of Resilience and Vulnerability Following Trauma Exposure." *Annals of the New York Academy of Sciences* 1071, no. 1 (July 2006): 379–396. https://doi.org/10.1196/annals.1364.028.

Young, Valerie. *The Secret Thoughts of Successful Women: Why Capable People Suffer from the Imposter Syndrome and How to Thrive in Spite of It*. New York: Crown Business, 2011.

ONLINE PRESENTATIONS

Csikszentmihalyi, Mihaly. "Flow, the Secret to Happiness." Filmed February 2004 in Monterey, CA, at TED2004. TED video, 18:42. https://www.ted.com/talks/mihaly_csikszentmihalyi_flow_the_secret_to_happiness/.

Dweck, Carol. "The Power of Believing That You Can Improve." Filmed June 2012 in Norrköping, Sweden, at TEDxNorrköping. TED video, 10:11. https://www.ted.com/talks/carol_dweck_the_power_of_believing_that_you_can_improve.

Killingsworth, Matt. "Want to Be Happier? Stay in the Moment." Filmed at TEDxCambridge. TED video, 10:00. https://www.ted.com/talks/matt_killingsworth_want_to_be_happier_stay_in_the_moment.

Kober, Hedy. "How Can Mindfulness Help Us." Filmed October 2020 in Buenos Aires, Argentina, at TEDxRiodelaPlata. TED video, 17:47. https://www.youtube.com/watch?v=4hKfXyZGeJY.

Norton, Michael. "How to Buy Happiness." Filmed at TEDxCambridge. TED video, 10:42. https://www.ted.com/talks/michael_norton_how_to_buy_happiness.

NOTES

1 I've given ample credit to others wherever possible and worked tirelessly to build off their ideas to create my own.

2 While there may not be a definitive number of adversity types, I believe there is a link between kinds of experience and the seven themed dimensions I've noted here, which together encapsulate the more than ninety-nine traditionally studied dimensions of well-being. Therefore, for the purposes of this book, I have reduced the number to seven.

Jesus Alfonso D. Datu et al., "Is Grittiness Next to Happiness? Examining the Association of Triarchic Model of Grit Dimensions with Well-Being Outcomes," *Journal of Happiness Studies* 22, no. 2 (2021): 981–1009, https://doi.org/10.1007/s10902-020-00260-6; Myles-Jay Linton, Paul Dieppe, and Antonieta Medina-Lara, "Review of 99 Self-Report Measures for Assessing Well-Being in Adults: Exploring Dimensions of Well-Being and Developments over Time," *BMJ Open* 6, no. 7 (2016), e010641, https://doi.org/10.1136/bmjopen-2015-010641; Debbie L. Stoewen, "Dimensions of Wellness: Change Your Habits, Change Your Life," *The Canadian Veterinary Journal* 58, no. 8 (August 2017): 861–862, https://pubmed.ncbi.nlm.nih.gov/28761196/; Kelley Ann Strout and Elizabeth P. Howard, "The Six Dimensions of Wellness and Cognition in Aging Adults," *Journal of Holistic Nursing* 30, no. 3 (2012): 195–204, https://doi.org/10.1177/0898010112440883.

3 Sarju Sing Rai et al., "Intersectionality and Health-Related Stigma: Insights from Experiences of People Living with Stigmatized Health Conditions in Indonesia," *International Journal for Equity in Health* 19, no. 1 (2020): 206, https://doi.org/10.1186/s12939-020-01318-w.

4 Shahzadi Harper and Emma Bardwell, *The Perimenopause Solution: Take Control of Your Hormones before They Take Control of You* (London: Vermilion, 2021).

5 Linda Graham, *Bouncing Back: Rewiring Your Brain for Maximum Resilience and Wellbeing* (Novato, CA: New World Library, 2013), 15–24.

6   However, modern science is collecting evidence that some animals have memory and the ability to use that memory to create or predict the future. But none has the same complexity we have.

William A. Roberts, "Evidence for Future Cognition in Animals," *Learning and Motivation* 43, no. 4 (November 2012): 169–180, https://doi.org/10.1016/j.lmot.2012.05.005; Carl Zimmer, "Time in the Animal Mind," *New York Times*, April 3, 2007, https://www.nytimes.com/2007/04/03/science/03time.html.

7   Eyal Winter, "Why Is It Hard to Live for the Moment," *Feeling Smart* (blog), Psychology Today, September 19, 2016, https://www.psychologytoday.com/us/blog/feeling-smart/201609/why-is-it-hard-live-the-moment.

8   Graham, *Bouncing Back*, xxviii.

9   George A. Bonanno et al., "Psychological Resilience after Disaster: New York City in the Aftermath of the September 11th Terrorist Attack," *Psychological Science* 17, no. 3 (March 2006): 181–186, https://doi.org/10.1111/j.1467-9280.2006.01682.x.

10 Sometimes, hardiness is used as a component in the definition of resilience: Paul G. Stoltz, *Adversity Quotient: Turning Obstacles into Opportunities* (New York: John Wiley & Sons, 1997), 62–63.

For more on hardiness, see research by Suzanne Ouellette (nee Kobasa), which indicates people who have hardiness suffer fewer negative side effects following adversity:

Suzanne C. Kobasa, Salvatore R. Maddi, and Stephen Kahn, "Hardiness and Health: A Prospective Study," *Journal of Personality and Social Psychology* 42, no. 1 (January 1982): 168–177, https://doi.org/10.1037/0022-3514.42.1.168; Suzanne C. Kobasa, Salvatore R. Maddi, and Marc A. Zola, "Type A and Hardiness," *Journal of Behavioral Medicine* 6, no. 1 (1983): 41–51, https://doi.org/10.1007/BF00845275; Salvatore R. Maddi and Suzanne C. Kobasa, *The Hardy Executive: Health under Stress* (Burr Ridge, IL: Irwin Professional Publishing, 1984); Suzanne C. Kobasa et al., "Effectiveness of Hardiness, Exercise and Social Support as Resources against Illness," *Journal of Psychosomatic Research* 29, no. 5 (1985): 525–533, https://doi.org/10.1016/0022-3999(85)90086-8; Salvatore R. Maddi and Suzanne C. Kobasa, "The Development of Hardiness," in *Stress and Coping: An Anthology*, 3rd ed., ed. A. Monat and R. S. Lazarus (New York: Columbia University Press, 1991), 245–257; Suzanne C. Ouellette, "Inquiries in Hardiness," in *Handbook of Stress: Theoretical and Clinical Aspects*, ed. L. Goldberger and S. Breznitz (New York: Free Press, 1993), 77–100.

11 Mike Robbins, *Be Yourself, Everyone Else Is Taken: Transform Your Life with the Power of Authenticity* (San Francisco: Jossey-Bass, 2009), 5.

12 Robbins, *Be Yourself*, 2.

13 Ananda B. Amstadter, John M. Myers, and Kenneth S. Kendler, "Psychiatric Resilience: Longitudinal Twin Study," *The British Journal of Psychiatry* 205, no. 4 (October 2014): 275–280, https://doi.org/10.1192/bjp.bp.113.130906.

Building off of Amstadter's work, the University of Oslo in Norway also conducted twin research in 2021 that indicates genes or environmental effects on genes contribute about 30 percent of psychological resilience and various other environmental factors account for as much as 70 percent of psychological resilience. Twins are not necessarily equally psychologically resilient [Live Skow Hofgaard, Ragnhild Bang Nes, and Espen Røysamb, "Introducing Two Types of Psychological Resilience with Partly Unique Genetic and Environmental Sources," *Scientific Reports* 11, no. 1 (2021): 8624, https://doi.org/10.1038/s41598-021-87581-5].

Another study found 40 percent of resiliency in twins was due to genetic factors [Trine Waaktaar and Svenn Torgersen, "Genetic and Environmental Causes of Variation in Trait Resilience in Young People," *Behavior Genetics* 42, no. 3 (2012): 366–377, https://doi.org/10.1007/s10519-011-9519-5].

14 For background on how these ideas developed, see Robbins, *Be Yourself*, 8–9.

15 Cyrus Farivar, "Japan Shifted," DW, March 14, 2011, https://www.dw.com/en/quake-shifted-japan-by-over-two-meters/a-14909967; Kenneth Change, "Quake Moves Japan Closer to U.S. and Alters Earth's Spin," *New York Times*, March 13, 2011, https://www.nytimes.com/2011/03/14/world/asia/14seismic.html; Andrew Moseman, "How the Japan Earthquake Made the Day Shorter," *Popular Mechanics*, March 15, 2011, https://www.popularmechanics.com/science/environment/a6543/how-the-japan-earthquake-made-the-day-shorter/.

16 My Reality Curve was inspired by Elisabeth Kübler-Ross's grief model and the Change Curve.

Elisabeth Kübler-Ross, *On Death and Dying* (New York: Macmillan Publishing, 1969), 38–137; "The Change Curve," University of Exeter, accessed November 27, 2022, https://www.exeter.ac.uk/media/universityofexeter/humanresources/documents/learningdevelopment/the_change_curve.pdf.

17 Stoltz, *Adversity Quotient*, 63.

18 Graham, *Bouncing Back*, 326.

19 Graham, *Bouncing Back*, 323–335.

Further research on this concept can be found at the following sources:

Linda Graham, *Resilience: Powerful Practices for Bouncing Back from Disappointment, Difficulty, and Even Disaster* (Novato, CA: New World Library, 2018), 8; Jenny E. Moffett and David J Bartram, "Veterinary Students' Perspectives on Resilience and Resilience-Building Strategies," *Journal of Veterinary Medical Education* 44, no. 1 (Spring 2017): 116–124, https://doi.org/10.3138/jvme.0216-046R1.

20 Seligman literally wrote the book(s) on this. For a good place to start, see Martin E. P. Seligman, *Helplessness: On Depression, Development, and Death* (New York: W. H. Freeman and Company, 1975).

21 Carl R. Anderson, "Locus of Control, Coping Behaviors, and Performance in a Stress Setting: A Longitudinal Study," *Journal of Applied Psychology* 62, no. 4 (1977): 446–451, https://doi.org/10.1037/0021-9010.62.4.446.

22 Daniel Kahneman, *Thinking, Fast and Slow* (London: Allen Lane, 2011), 20–24.

23 Kahneman, *Thinking*, 378–385.

24 Sheryl Sandberg and Adam Grant, *Option B: Facing Adversity, Building Resilience, and Finding Joy* (New York: Alfred A. Knopf, 2017), 16.

25 Emmy E. Werner has published multiple books and works on this longitudinal study. For more information, see the following:

Emmy E. Werner, "Protective Factors and Individual Resilience," in *Handbook of Early Childhood Intervention*, ed. Jack P. Shonkoff and Samuel J. Meisels (New York: Cambridge University Press, 2000), 115–132, https://doi.org/10.1017/CBO9780511529320.008; Emmy E. Werner and Ruth S. Smith, *Kauai's Children Come of Age* (Honolulu: University of Hawaii Press, 1977); Emmy E. Werner and Ruth S. Smith, *Vulnerable but Invincible: A Longitudinal Study of Resilient Children and Youth* (New York: McGraw-Hill, 1982); Emmy E. Werner and Ruth S. Smith, *Overcoming the Odds: High Risk Children from Birth to Adulthood* (Ithaca: Cornell University Press, 1992); Emmy E. Werner and Ruth S. Smith, *Journeys from Childhood to Midlife: Risk, Resilience, and Recovery* (Ithaca: Cornell University Press, 2001).

For more on resiliency, read Maria Konnikova, "How People Learn to Become Resilient," *The New Yorker*, February 11, 2016, https://www.newyorker.com/science/maria-konnikova/the-secret-formula-for-resilience.

26 Martin E. P. Seligman, *Learned Optimism: How to Change Your Mind and Your Life* (New York: Alfred A. Knopf, 1991), 175.

27 Victor E. Frankl, *Man's Search for Meaning: An Introduction to Logotherapy*, trans. Ilse Lasch (Boston: Beacon Press, 1962), 65.

28 This is a phrase I adapted from fascinating research by Dr. Laurie Santos, cognitive scientist and professor of psychology at Yale University famous for her research on the science of well-being, as well as from research by University of Pennsylvania professor Dr. Karen Reivich and University of Arizona professor Dr. Andrew Shatté, who discuss similar brain distortions in their book *The Resilience Factor*.

Laurie Santos, "The Science of Well-Being," Coursera, accessed November 27, 2022, https://www.coursera.org/learn/the-science-of-well-being; Karen Reivich and Andrew Shatté, *The Resilience Factor: Seven Keys to Finding Your Inner Strength and Overcoming Life's Hurdles* (New York: Broadway Books, 2002).

29 Santos, "Science of Well-Being"; Reivich and Shatté, *Resilience Factor*, 55.

30 Psychologist J. P. Guilford first coined the term "divergent thinking" (and "convergent thinking") as part of his groundbreaking Structure of Intellect (SI) theory. Joy Paul Guilford, *The Nature of Human Intelligence* (New York: McGraw-Hill, 1967).

31 David L. Cooperrider and Diana Whitney, *Appreciative Inquiry: A Positive Revolution in Change* (San Francisco: Berrett-Koehler Publishers, 2005); David L. Cooperrider and Suresh Srivastva, "Appreciative Inquiry in Organizational Life," *Research in Organizational Change and Development* 1, no. 1 (January 1987): 129–169, https://www.oio.nl/wp-content/uploads/APPRECIATIVE_INQUIRY_IN_Orgnizational_life.pdf; David L. Cooperrider and Suresh Srivastva, *Appreciative Management and Leadership: The Power of Positive Thought and Action in Organization* (Brunswick, OH: Crown Custom Publishing, 1999); David L. Cooperrider and Suresh Srivastva, eds., *Organizational Wisdom and Executive Courage* (San Francisco: The New Lexington Press, 1998).

32 Stoltz, *Adversity Quotient*, 51–52.

33 Stoltz, *Adversity Quotient*, 52.

34 Jim Loehr and Tony Schwartz, *The Power of Full Engagement: Managing Energy, Not Time, Is the Key to High Performance and Personal Renewal* (New York: Free Press, 2003), 11–12.

35 Angela Duckworth, *Grit: The Power of Passion and Perseverance* (Toronto: Collins, 2016), 74.

36 Duckworth, *Grit*, 143.

37 Loehr and Schwartz, *Full Engagement*, 10.

38 Loehr and Schwartz, *Full Engagement*, 13.

39 Charlotte Leedy, "The Effects of Tournament Chess Playing on Selected Physiological Responses in Players of Varying Aspirations and Abilities," (EdD diss., Temple University, 1975), https://www.proquest.com/openview/0a376cdaa9e3d56975c06b6d658ccc03/1?pq-origsite=gscholar&cbl=18750&diss=y; Charlotte Leedy and Leroy Dubeck, "Physiological Changes during Tournament Chess," *Chess Life and Review* 26, no. 12 (December 1971): 708, http://uscf1-nyc1.aodhosting.com/CL-AND-CR-ALL/CL-ALL/1971/1971_12.pdf.

40 Robert M. Sapolsky, *Why Zebras Don't Get Ulcers* (New York: Henry Holt and Company, 1994).

41 Pema Chödrön, *When Things Fall Apart: Heart Advice for Difficult Times* (Boston: Shambhala Publications, 1997), 33.

42 Sonja Lyubomirsky, *The How of Happiness: A Scientific Approach to Getting the Life You Want* (New York: Penguin Press, 2008), 250.

43 David R. Lee, *Teaching the World to Sleep: Psychological and Behavioural Assessment and Treatment Strategies for People with Sleeping Problems and Insomnia* (New York: Karnac Books, 2017).

44 Lyubomirsky, *How of Happiness*, 89–100, 125–135; Santos, "Science of Wellbeing."

45 Lyubomirsky, *How of Happiness*, 190–204.

46 Marcus E. Raichle and Debra A. Gusnard, "Appraising the Brain's Energy Budget," *Proceedings of the National Academy of Sciences* 99, no. 16 (2002): 10237, https://doi.org/10.1073/pnas.172399499.

47 John Fleming and Robert J. Ledogar, "Resilience, an Evolving Concept: A Review of Literature Relevant to Aboriginal Research," *Pimatisiwin* 6, no. 2 (Summer 2008): 7–23, https://pubmed.ncbi.nlm.nih.gov/20963184/; Steven M. Southwick et al., "Resilience Definitions, Theory, and Challenges: Interdisciplinary Perspectives," *European Journal of Psychotraumatology* 5, no. 1 (2014), https://doi.org/10.3402/ejpt.v5.25338.

48 Glenn Lawrence Burke is the other. He played for the Los Angeles Dodgers and Oakland Athletics. As of this book's publication, they are the only two players who've ever disclosed. (Sean Conroy was first to come out while playing in the independent league for the Sonoma Stompers and, later, David Denson was the first active player within a Major League Baseball organization to come out to the public.)

49 Donald O. Clifton's grandson Tom Rath wrote the often-referenced book *StrengthsFinder 2.0*, which I also recommend.

50 Mihaly Csikszentmihalyi, *Flow: The Psychology of Optimal Experience* (New York: Harper & Row Publishers, 1990), 4.

51 Rick Hanson, *Resilient: How to Grow an Unshakable Core of Calm, Strength, and Happiness* (New York: Harmony Books, 2018), 43; Graham, Bouncing Back, 42–43, 161.

52 Pema Chödrön, *Welcoming the Unwelcome: Wholehearted Living in a Brokenhearted World* (Boulder: Shambhala Publications, 2019), 161–164; Chödrön, "Free Yourself."

53 Sandberg and Grant, *Option B*, 23–24.

54 Rick Hanson, *Resilient*, 121.

55 The phrase "imposter syndrome" was coined by Pauline Clance and Suzanne Imes in 1978 ("The Imposter Phenomenon," 241–247).

56 Jaruwan Sakulku and James Alexander, "The Impostor Phenomenon," *International Journal of Behavioral Science* 6, no. 1 (2011): 73, https://doi.org/10.14456/ijbs.2011.6.

57 Brené Brown, *Rising Strong: How the Ability to Reset Transforms the Way We Live, Love, Parent, and Lead* (New York: Random House, 2017), 4.

58 Brené Brown, *Daring Greatly: How the Courage to Be Vulnerable Transforms the Way We Live, Love, Parent, and Lead* (New York: Avery, 2012), 33.

59 Ingrid Handlovsky et al., "Developing Resilience: Gay Men's Response to Systemic Discrimination," *American Journal of Men's Health* 12, no. 5 (September 2018): 1473–1485, https://doi.org/10.1177/1557988318768607.

60 Huey Lewis and the News, "The Power of Love," track 1 on *Back to the Future: Music from the Motion Picture Soundtrack*, Geffen, 1985.

61 Graham, *Bouncing Back*, 184; Graham, *Resilience*, 161; Hanson, *Resilient*, 244–249; Lyubomirsky, *How of Happiness*, 170; Michael E. McCullough and Charlotte V. Witvliet, "The Psychology of Forgiveness," in *Handbook of Positive Psychology*, ed. C. R. Snyder and S. J. Lopez (Oxford: Oxford University Press, 2002), 446–447.

62 Lyubomirsky, *How of Happiness*, 172.

63 Lyubomirsky, *How of Happiness*, 173.

64 Lyubomirsky, *How of Happiness*, 171.

65 Michael E. McCullough, "Forgiveness: Who Does It and How Do They Do It?" *Current Directions in Psychological Science* 10, no. 6 (December 2001): 194–197, https://doi.org/10.1111/1467-8721.00147; McCullough and Witvliet, "Psychology of Forgiveness," 450–453.

66 Lyubomirsky, *How of Happiness*, 172; McCullough, "Forgiveness: Who Does It," 196.

67 Johan C. Karremans, Paul A. M. Van Lange, and Rob W. Holland, "Forgiveness and Its Associations with Prosocial Thinking, Feeling, and Doing beyond the Relationship with the Offender," *Personality and Social Psychology Bulletin* 31, no. 10 (October 2005): 1315–1326, https://doi.org/10.1177/0146167205274892.

68 C. Kitzinger, "Lesbians and Gay Men in the Workplace: Psychosocial Issues," in *Vulnerable Workers: Psychosocial and Legal Issues*, ed. M. J. Davidson and J. Earnshaw (London: John Wiley & Sons, 1991), 223–240; Celia Kitzinger et al., "Towards Lesbian and Gay Psychology," *The Psychologist* 11, no. 11 (1998): 529–533, https://psycnet.apa.org/record/1999-00710-001; Jeffrey P. Aguinaldo, "The Social Construction of Gay Oppression as a Determinant of Gay Men's Health: 'Homophobia Is Killing Us,'" *Critical Public Health* 18, no. 1 (2008): 87–96, https://doi.org/10.1080/09581590801958255; Kyung-Hee Choi et al., "Experiences of Discrimination and Their Impact on the Mental Health among African American, Asian and Pacific Islander, and Latino Men Who Have Sex with Men," *American Journal of Public Health* 103, no. 5 (May 2013): 868–874, https://doi.org/10.2105/AJPH.2012.301052; Anthony Lyons, "Mindfulness Attenuates the Impact of Discrimination on the Mental Health of Middle-Aged and Older Gay Men," *Psychology of Sexual Orientation and Gender Diversity* 3, no. 2 (February 2016): 227–235, https://doi.org/10.1037/sgd0000164.

69 Lyubomirsky, *How of Happiness*, 138–139.

70 Nicholas Epley and Juliana Schroeder, "Mistakenly Seeking Solitude," *Journal of Experimental Psychology* 143, no. 5 (2014): 1980–1999, https://doi.org/10.1037/a0037323; David G. Myers, "The Funds, Friends, and Faith of Happy People," *American Psychologist* 55, no. 1 (2000): 56–67, https://doi.org/10.1037/0003-066X.55.1.56; Nicholas Epley, *Mindwise: How We Misunderstand What Others Think, Believe, Feel, and Want* (New York, Alfred A. Knopf, 2014), 57–58.

71 Ed Diener and Martin E. P. Seligman, "Very Happy People," *Psychological Science* 13, no. 1 (January 2002): 81–84, https://doi.org/10.1111/1467-9280.00415.

72 Chalmers Brothers, *Language and the Pursuit of Happiness* (Naples, FL: New Possibilities Press, 2005), 19–23.

73 Brothers, *Language*, 20.

74 Matthew Budd and Larry Rothstein, *You Are What You Say: A Harvard Doctor's Six-Step Program for Transforming Stress through the Power of Language* (New York: Crown, 2000).

75 Kim Scott, *Radical Candor: Be a Kickass Boss without Losing Your Humanity* (New York: St. Martin's Press, 2017), 21.

76 Gabe's own authentic resilience saved his life. He told me that once he realized staying in bed for two months like a sick person was not who he was or wanted to be, he snapped right into a drug therapy that has enabled him to live a happy, healthy life for thirty years and counting.

77 Mike Robbins, *Nothing Changes until You Do: A Guide to Self-Compassion and Getting Out of Your Own Way* (Carlsbad, CA: Hay House, 2014), 114.

78 To learn more about the incredible power of gratitude, check out the writings of Lyubomirsky, Hanson, and Graham, as well as Jeremy Adam Smith et al., eds., *The Gratitude Project: How the Science of Thankfulness Can Rewire Our Brains for Resilience, Optimism, and the Greater Good* (Oakland: New Harbinger Publications, 2020).

79 Lyubomirsky, *How of Happiness*, 253–254; Sonja Lyubomirsky, Laura King, and Ed Diener, "The Benefits of Frequent Positive Effect: Does Happiness Lead to Success?" *Psychological Bulletin* 131, no. 6 (November 2005): 803–855, https://doi.org/10.1037/0033-2909.131.6.803; Dacher Keltner and George A. Bonnano, "A Study of Laughter and Dissociation: Distinct Correlates of Laughter and Smiling during Bereavement," *Journal of Personality and Social Psychology* 73, no. 4 (1997): 687–702, https://doi.org/10.1037/0022-3514.73.4.687.

80 For a comprehensive profile on Frank Kameny, read the book *The Deviant's War* [Eric Cervini, *The Deviant's War: The Homosexual vs. the United States of America* (New York: Farrar, Straus, and Giroux, 2020)].

INDEX

Page references in italics indicate illustrations.

Aaker, Janelle, 138
adversity, 29–41. *See also* suffering, coping with
   the brain's processing of, 35, *36*, 37–38
   cancer, 220–21
   case studies in, 212–20
   change through conditioning, 39–40
   COVID-19 epidemic, 225–27, 231–32
   deaths/near-deaths of loved ones, 89–90
   embracing, 25–26
   emotional, 31–32
   environmental, 33
   and feeling stuck, 15
   financial, 33
   importance of addressing, 14
   intersectionality of, 31, 34–35, 213
   mental, 32
   natural disasters, 59–63, 84–86
   physical, 31
   political conflict, 89–91
   reframing, 81–82
   and resilience, 38–39
   social, 32–33
   spiritual, 32
   types of, 14, 31–33, 212, 255n2
   unfulfilling work, 90–92
advertunity (growth + optimism)
   benefits of, 66
   definition/characterization of, 66, 76–77
   and energy, 109–11
   and growth mindset, 74
AIDS, 55, 177, 179
American Psychiatric Association (APA), 229
Amstadter, Ananda B., 257n13
Andres, Jo, 29–30, 89
Anthony, Michael, 223
apologizing, 190
appreciative inquiry, 83–84
authenticity, 121–61
   beliefs, identifying, 129, 133
   of coming out of the closet, 122–24, 127–28, 135–36, 158–60, 188, 260n48
   core values, identifying, 125–29, *127*, *130*, 151–52
   definition of, 48–51, *49*
   knowing yourself, 19, 124–36, *130*, *210*
   loving yourself, 19–20
   and negative self-talk (your inner critic), 142–47, 152–53
   negative thoughts, combating, 137–40
   obstacles to, 50

overview of, 19–20
power of, 228–30
price of living inauthentically, 135–36
purpose, identifying, 131–32, 134–35, 137
releasing yourself, overview of, 19, 136–37, *210*
resistance to, 50
and self-advocacy, 156–57, *157*, 177
and self-care, 153–54, *155*
self-coaching on, 217–18
and self-love, 150–57, *155*, *157*, *210* (*see also* self-compassion)
and self-sabotage, 140–42, 145
strengths, identifying, 129, 131
and the uniqueness of your resilience, 123–25
vulnerability, embracing, 147–50
authentic resilience, 43–57
adversity overcome through, 15–16
during a blackout, 43–47
definition/characterization of, 16, 48–52, *49*, 256n10
of New Yorkers, 47, 50–51
power of, 56–57, 77, 159, 232–35

Bauer, Sue, 164
Bean, Billy, 122–23
behavioral dependency, 146–47
beliefs, identifying, 129, 133
binary (all-or-nothing) thinking, 79
blackout (2003), 43–47
brain
adversity as residing in, 35, 37–38
amygdala, 37, 67–68, 140, 201
distortions of, 78–84, 258n28
frontal lobe, 31–32, 37
hippocampus, 37
and learning, 114
left hemisphere, 37
and memory, 38, 256n6
parts of, *36*, 37
prefrontal cortex, 37–38, 67–68, 132
rewiring of (*see* neuroplasticity)
right hemisphere, 37
Brothers, Chalmers, 184
Brown, Brené, 147–48
Budd, Matthew, 185–86
Buddhism, 68–69, 75, 79
bullying, 149, 163–66
Burke, Glenn Lawrence, 260n48
Buscemi, Steve, 29–30

Cavallo, Josh, 136
change, 67–69
Chen, Kaili, 102–3
child psychology, 54–55
Chödrön, Pema, 102, 139
choices, ritual of, 112–14
choices, systems for making, 73–74
circadian rhythms, 106, 111
circular reference, 56–57
Clance, Pauline, 260n55
coaches, role of, 24. *See also* self-coaching
communicating with love, 20, 181–92
community, 55, 177–81, *211*. *See also* LGBTQ+ community
compassion, 170, 176–77
conditioning, 39–40, 67, 69, 73, 114
connection, power of, 180–81
Conroy, Sean, 260n48
convergent thinking, 83
Cooperrider, David, 83
COVID-19 epidemic, 225–27, 231–32
Csikszentmihalyi, Mihaly, 132
Cura Personalis ("care for the whole person"), 22

Davidson, Richard, 40
Denson, David, 260n48
depression, 71, 92, 97, 186
Diagnostic and Statistical Manual of Mental Disorders, 229
diet, 106
divergent thinking, 82–83, 259n30
dopamine, 95
Downs, Alan: *The Velvet Rage*, 146
Duckworth, Angela: *Grit*, 96, 115
Dweck, Carol, 72

ego, 70, 81–82
empathy, 33, 95, 148–50, 170, 176–77, 181, 191, 215
endorphins, 95
endurance, 48, 51. *See also* resilience
energy, 89–119
and the advertunity mindset, 109–11
auditing, 102–4
charging your batteries, 98–99, 104–9
choices, ritual of, 112–14
core tenets, overview of, 93
domains of, 18
emotional, 95, 97, *98*, 107
as interconnected, 97–99, *98*, *100*

learning, ritual of, 114–15
making it count, ritual of, 115–17
mental, 95–96, 108
oscillation of energies, 94
overview of, 18–19
physical, 94–95, 97, *98*, 105–7
purpose, aligning with, 117–18
recovering, 19, 100–111, *209*
regulating, 18, 94–100, *98*, 109–10, *209*
self-coaching on, 197–99, 214–17
spiritual, 96, 108–9
using, 19, 111–17, *209*
exercise, 106

faith in yourself, 32
family, support from, 179
fight/flight/freeze response, 37, 39, 67, 137, 201, 230
flow, 132, 134
Ford, Henry, 185
forgiveness
    closure through, 167
    exercises, 174
    learning through, 172
    power of, 167, 171–73, 175–77
    reconciliation through, 169–72
    toward others, 166–67, 191, *211*
    toward yourself, 152, *211*, 219
    vs. vengeance, 170
fortune-telling distortion, 79
Frankl, Viktor: *Man's Search for Meaning*, 77
Fukushima Daiichi Nuclear Power Plant explosion (Japan, 2011), 62–63, 84–86, 194

Gallup, 131
Ginza (Japan), 59–60
Graham, Linda, 68
gratitude, 107, 192
Grit (Duckworth), 96, 115
growth, stress as key to, 99
growth mindset, 72–74, 80, 85
Guilford, J. P., 259n30

Handlovsky, Ingrid, 156, 177, 179
Hanson, Rick, 156
happiness, 180, 192
hardiness, 256n10. *See also* resilience
Hebb, Donald, 172
helplessness. *See* learned helplessness

High5 Strengths Finder, 131
HIV, 55, 156, 177–78, 189–90, 262n76
Holocaust survivors, 77
homosexuality. *See* LGBTQ+ community
Hong Kong, 89–91
hopelessness, 91–92, 97, 141
humility, 190–91
humor, 149, 168, 193–94

Ignatius Loyola, St., 22
Imes, Suzanne, 260n55
imperfection, 79, 152
impermanence, 69
imposter syndrome, 144–45, 147, 260n55
individualism, 16
internalized oppression, 138, 142
isolation, 181

Jesuits, 22

Kahneman, Daniel, 73–74
Kameny, Frank, 228–29
kindness, 107, 152

Lady Gaga, 106
language. *See* communicating with love; positive thinking/language; words
laughing at yourself, 192–94
learned helplessness, 75
    from adversities piling up, 91
    as a brain distortion, 78
    breaking from (*see* energy)
    and finding hope, 87, 93
    and hopelessness, 91–92, 141–42
    immunizing against, 71–72, 78
    and the spiral of despair, 71, 91, 118, 141–42
learned optimism, 66, 74–76, *76*
learning
    the brain as built for, 114
    energy spent on, 114–15
    through forgiveness, 172
    of resilience, 52–55, 115
    ritual of, 114–15
LGBTQ+ community, 175–76
    accepting one's sexuality, 163–64
    activism by, 177–78, 228–29
    bullying of, 163–66
    coming out, 122–24, 127–28, 135–36, 158–60, 188, 260n48

"gay is good," 229
gay-radar of, 158
handling the "banter," 158–59
and homophobia/discrimination, 123, 156, 178, 223–28
homosexuality as a mental disorder, 229
nonbinary status/pronouns, 217–18
in professional sports, 136
same-sex marriage, 223–26
self-advocacy by, 55, 157, 177
sodomy laws, 228–29
Loehr, Jim, 97, 99
The Power of Full Engagement, 94, *98*
love, 163–96
and apologizing, 190
authentic community, developing, 177–81, *211*
communicating with, 20, 181–92, *211*
forgiveness, 20, 166–67, 169–77
and fun, 20, 192–94, *211*
and gratitude, 192
overview of, 20, 163–66
power of, 166–67
role in the REAL model, 167–69
self-coaching on, 219–20
support system, 20
Lyubomirsky, Sonja, 171

magnification distortion, 80
Major League Baseball. *See* MLB
Manfred, Rob, 159
Man's Search for Meaning (Frankl), 77
Marquette University, 22. *See also* Midwestern Catholic university
Maslow, Abraham, 99, *100*
McKenzie, Craig, 148–49
meditation, 108, 154
memory, 38, 256n6
menopause, 34–35
mental health, speaking out about, 186
Midwestern Catholic university, 189
mindfulness, 107–8, 154
MLB (Major League Baseball), 121–24, 158–59, 260n48

Nazi concentration camps, 77
needs, hierarchy of, 99, *100*
Neff, Kristin, 151–52
negativity. *See also* positive energy/feelings; positive thinking/language; positive values
bias toward, 137–38, 143–44
combating, 137–40
delivering bad news, 183
and energy, 103
imposter syndrome, 144–45, 147, 260n55
as internalized oppression, 138, 142
negative self-talk (your inner critic), 142–47, 152–53, 192, 217–18
"never," 185
shame, 146–47, 153
neuroplasticity (rewiring)
and adversity types, 64
through an advertunity mindset, 76
and conditioning/learning, 39–40, 114–15, 172
energy/control needed for, 66–67
through a growth mindset, 72–73
through perspective change, 68
resilience built through, 186
through self-coaching, 199–200
New York City, 47, 50–51
numbness, 51–52

objectivity, 80
oppression, internalized, 138, 142
optimism, learned, 66, 74–76, *76*
oxytocin, 95

perfectionism, 79
permanence, 74–75
perseverance, 48, 51, 96, 115, 117. *See also* resilience
personalization ("It's my fault"), 74
personalization distortion ("Why me?"), 79–80
pervasiveness, 74
pessimism, 74–75, *76*
positive energy/feelings, 95, 97, 102, 104–8, 128, 134, 139–40, 154, 178
positive thinking/language, 79, 81, 83–84, 137–38, 143, 145, 153, 181–83
positive values, 128–29, *130*, 131–32
positivity, toxic, 138–40, 147
The Power of Full Engagement (Loehr and Schwartz), 94, *98*
process addiction, 146–47
promises, 154
purpose
and core values, 126, 128
energy aligned with, 111, 115, 117–18
and faith in yourself, 32

identifying, 131-32, 134-35, 137
self-coaching on, 198
and spiritual energy, 96
statement of, 134-35

reality, 59-88. *See also* suffering, coping with
acceptance of, 66, 68, 70-71
acting on your solutions to adversity, 84
brain distortions, 78-84, 258n28
Control It, 18, 63, 65, 66, 72-76, *208*
and coping with suffering, 71-72
core tenets, overview of, 63-67
Face It, 18, 63-65, 65, 67-72, *208*
facing reality in action, 84-87
ideating solutions to adversity, 82-84
of natural disasters, 59-63, 84-86
Plan It and Take Action, 18, 65, 66, 77-84, *208*
Reality Curve, 64-66, 65, 184-85
reframing false beliefs/adversity, 78-82 (*see also* positive thinking/language)
Three Marks of Existence, 68-71, 75, 79

REAL model. *See also* authenticity; energy; love; reality; self-coaching
creation of, 24, 233
goal of, 15, 57
overview/summary of, 15, 17, *17*, 233-35
purpose/benefits of, 230-31
where to start, 206-7

reconciliation, 169-72, 190-91
Reivich, Karen, 258n28
resilience. *See also* authentic resilience
building, 39-40, 73, 104-5
of businesses, 231-32
in children, 54-55
and community, 55
definition of, 51-52, 256n10
vs. endurance, 48, 51
learning, 52-55, 115
neuroplasticity used to build, 40
vs. numbness, 51-52
vs. perseverance, 48, 51
research on, 52, 55, 257n13
role models of, 53-55
and stress, 47, 51, 56
uniqueness of your resilience, 123-25

Robbins, Mike, 50, 125, 191
Rothstein, Larry, 186
Rough, Chevy, 115-16
RuPaul, 192-93

Sandberg, Sheryl, 74, 141
Santos, Laurie, 258n28
Sapolsky, Robert, 101
Schwartz, Tony, 97, 99
The Power of Full Engagement, 94, *98*
Scott, .Kim, 187-88
Scott, Ray, 122, 159
second derivative feelings, 141
self, 74
self-advocacy, 55, 156-57, *157*, 177
self-awareness, 199, 230
self-care, 153-54, *155*
self-coaching, 197-221
action, 204-5
on adversity, case studies in, 212-20
analyzing, 202-4
on authenticity, 217-18
on core values, 214-15
on energy, 197-99, 214-17
on love, 219-20
on managing expectations/time, 219-20
on negative self-talk, 217-18
neuroplasticity (rewiring) through, 199-200
Pathway Framework to resilience, 206-7, *208-11*
practicing and making progress, 220-21
process, overview of, 199-200
on protecting your needs, 216-17
on purpose, 198
recording yourself, 201-2, 205
reflecting, 200-201
self-awareness as key to, 199
self-compassion, 129, 143-44, 151-53
selfishness, 150
self-love, 19-20, 150-57, *155, 157*, 210
self-love, trifecta of
self-advocacy, 55, 156-57, *157*, 177
self-care, 153-54, *155*
self-compassion, 129, 143-44, 151-53
self-sabotage, 140-42, 145
Seligman, Martin, 71, 75
September 11 terrorist attack (2001), 30-31, 46, 50
serotonin, 95
shame, 34, 146-47, 153
Shatté, Andrew, 258n28
silence, weight of, 187-91
sleep, 106, 111
Smalley, Stuart, 152

social media relationships, 180
soul, 69–70
spiral of despair, 71, 91, 118
Srivastva, Suresh, 83
Stoltz, Paul, 66, 91
story, controlling/owning, 184
strengths, identifying, 129, 131
stress
    as key to growth, 99
    mental, physiological responses to, 101
    and resilience, 47, 51, 56
Structure of Intellect (SI) theory, 259n30
suffering, coping with
    through an advertunity mindset (*see* advertunity)
    by avoiding learned helplessness, 71–72
    through a growth mindset, 72–74, 80, 85
    through learned optimism, 74–76, *76*
    seeing suffering as inevitable, 69
support system, 177–81

Three Marks of Existence, 68–71
Tōhoku earthquake and tsunami (Japan, 2011), 60–63, 84–86, 194
toxic positivity, 138–40, 147
transgender people. *See* LGBTQ+ community

values
    conflicts among, 214–15
    identifying, 125–29, *127*, *130*, 151–52
The Velvet Rage (Downs), 146
VIA Character Strength, 131
vulnerability, 147–50

well-being
    seven dimensions of, 31–33, 38–39, 255n2 (*see also* adversity)
    speaking out about, 186
William, Prince of Wales, 116–17
words
    power of, 184–87
    reconciliation, finding the words for, 190–91
    saying hard things, 188–91
Wright, Vinita Hampton, 170